REASON AND SELF-ENACTMENT
IN HISTORY AND POLITICS

McGill-Queen's Studies in the History of Ideas
Series Editor: Philip J. Cercone

REASON AND SELF-ENACTMENT IN HISTORY AND POLITICS

Themes and Voices of Modernity

F.M. Barnard

McGill-Queen's University Press
Montreal & Kingston · London · Ithaca

© McGill-Queen's University Press 2006
ISBN-13: 978-0-7735-2965-6   ISBN-10: 0-7735-2965-9

Legal deposit first quarter 2006
Bibliothèque nationale du Québec

Printed in Canada on acid-free paper that is 100% ancient forest free
(100% post-consumer recycled), processed chlorine free.

This book has been published with the help of a grant from the
Canadian Federation for the Humanities and Social Sciences, through
the Aid to Scholarly Publications Programme, using funds provided
by the Social Sciences and Humanities Research Council of Canada.
Funding has also been received from the J.B. Smallman Publication Fund,
Faculty of Social Science, The University of Western Ontario.

McGill-Queen's University Press acknowledges the support of
the Canada Council for the Arts for our publishing program.
We also acknowledge the financial support of the Government
of Canada through the Book Publishing Industry Development
Program (BPIDP) for our publishing activities.

Library and Archives Canada Cataloguing in Publication

Barnard, F. M. (Frederick M.)
Reason and self-enactment in history and politics :
themes and voices of modernity / F.M. Barnard.

(McGill-Queen's studies in the history of ideas; 40)
Includes bibliographical references and index.
ISBN-13: 978-0-7735-2965-6   ISBN-10: 0-7735-2965-9

1. History–Philosophy. 2. Political science–Philosophy. I. Title. II. Series.

D16.8.B28 2006   901   C2005-903400-9

This book was typeset by Interscript in 10/12 Baskerville.

To Yvonne, Joshua, and Nicholas, and
in Memory of
Rachel Zeisler and Martha Mann

Contents

Preface

AS THIS BOOK'S TITLE INDICATES, "modernity" is here viewed in a de-limited way, its areas of concern being confined to self-enacting reasons in history and politics. In tracing and characterizing these reasons as causalities, I see "self-enactment" in modernity essentially as a search for new answers to old questions such as: Who am I? What are others to me and I to them? And, perhaps most crucially, where do I fit in? What is the space in which I am placed, its scope and its boundaries? These are, therefore, questions of identity, mutuality, self-location, and range of agency, which confront the self in the changing modern world. Both parts of the book variously point to new understandings or directions that modernity's answers to these questions arguably yield.

While no attempt is made to elicit features of modernity as a whole – as a cultural epoch or a cosmology – and, likewise, neither part of the book claims comprehensiveness in the themes and voices chosen, I do believe that both parts offer core insights into prevalent trends of historical and political thinking during the period. Perhaps I might add that, although the chapters are internally connected and, in places, overlapping, they can be read for the most part as self-contained.

Two occurrences, separate in time, gave the earliest incentives to the book's overall thrust. The first consisted of having my attention drawn in the early sixties to R.G. Collingwood (by Isaiah Berlin, in connection with my interest in Herder's philosophy of history), particularly to his paper on political action.* The second came chiefly in the form of a conference, given in honour of Hannah Arendt, in Toronto in 1972, in

---

* R.G. Collingwood (1889–1943), "Political Action," *Proceedings of the Aristotelian Society*, New Series, XXIX (London: Harrison and Sons, 1929), 155–76.

which I was invited to participate.** In their predominant temper of thinking, both Collingwood and Arendt display an unusual grasp of the fractured sense of self-mastery that, I feel, typifies modernity. And, while recognizing "self-enactment" as its central aspiration, they nevertheless see its effective expression paramountly in actions of joint endeavour, as modes of purposive striving within a context of others, and of others as equals. Hence, to them, engaging in political action, and public life in general, consists neither of issuing orders, nor of submitting to commands, but of acting on impersonal principles of associational mutuality. And it is above all this *quasi*-Montesquieuian mode of thinking that colours their brand of political ethic.

In pursuing this vision of public co-authorship throughout the themes and the voices, I am therefore much indebted to both thinkers; in neither case, however, does my indebtedness signify uncritical acceptance. I have a hunch that Collingwood, as much as Arendt, would not have wished it otherwise. For, from what I have been able to learn about them, neither ever had the slightest desire to inaugurate systems or "schools" and collect faithful disciples. Hannah Arendt, in particular, was profoundly dismayed by the very suggestion. Indeed, few things triggered a more angry response in her than bigoted sectarianism or the faddish following of whatever academic fashion was in vogue.

There is, however, another feature that Arendt shared with Collingwood, a feature implicit in their joint insistence upon viewing particularity within universality, namely, the intriguing belief that philosophy, as reflective thinking, could help to enlarge our understanding of causality in the human world. Indeed, they went one step further, in suggesting that some such reflecting upon, and imaginative re-enacting of, history might also uncover hitherto hidden possibilities of practical reasoning and purposive striving.

Cherishing this suggestion, I should like to believe that the themes and the voices discussed in the following pages afford glimpses of such hidden possibilities.

In writing this book, I had chiefly students interested in the history of ideas and the philosophy of history and politics in mind. Two readers of the manuscript have, however, expressed the view that, by so closely

** Hannah Arendt (1906–1975) who, without giving a formal lecture, actively participated in the conference. A symposium of it, edited by Melvyn A. Hill and entitled *The Recovery of the Public World* was published in 1979 (New York: St Martin's Press).

associating political thought with the ambient texture of broadly cultural categories, the book may appeal also to a broader audience.

Perhaps, this is as good a place as any to thank Margot again for her patient and critical support, to Philip Cercone, the editor of McGill-Queen's University Press's series on the history of ideas, for his encouragement when it was most needed, and to the press's readers for their highly perceptive comments. I was fortunate, too, in having once again Jane McWhinney edit the script and who, with her customary energy, has taken great care to make me "watch my language." Finally, I want to thank the editors of *History and Theory*, *Review of Politics*, and *Deutsche Vierteljahrsschrift für Lieraturwissenschaft und Geistesgeschichte*, for allowing me to use material they originally published in parts for chapters 1, 5, and 8.

REASON AND SELF-ENACTMENT
IN HISTORY AND POLITICS

Introduction

Faced by so vast a subject, I feel my vision hazy and my judgment hesitant.

Alexis de Tocqueville

FEW WHO HAVE INVESTED TIME AND EFFORT in exploring the precise meaning of "rationality" will deny that it is an overwhelming, if not altogether frustrating, task – as subsequent chapters also in their turn disclose. Mercifully, in what follows in these introductory remarks, I am principally concerned with reason or reasons in a causal sense. And, although there is also an undeniable ambiguity in speaking of reasons as causes, the ambiguity may be potentially fruitful in calling attention to causal meanings radically different from those associated with mechanical or organic processes. To wit, that linking reasons with intentions, goals, convictions, or commitments – as both parts of the book typically do – implies a causality other than that identifiable with psycho-physical *conditions*. In so doing, "rational causality" (in the indicated sense) invites the distinction between "*giving* cause" in an indirect way, and "*being* cause" in a direct way, as well as the distinction between purposive reasons *for* and dispositional reasons *from*.

The concept of "reason" itself has, moreover, if used as a practical causality, a meaning different from its meaning as a theoretical category. This transformation of meaning has in fact lent force to "historical consciousness" as a rational causality, even though "practical reason" as a concept is not itself entirely free from ambiguity. Thus, while Kant as much as Thomasius thought of reason as a creative power, Kant put major emphasis on understanding it in terms of its intrinsic objectivity or impartiality, whereas Thomasius rather stressed its external usefulness.[1] Regardless of preferred usage or particular emphasis, however, they both equally recognized that, in the absence of its creative propensity, reason would have no causal power whatsoever. In that event, it would

1 On the transformation of reason, see ch. 5 below, sect. 1.

therefore make no sense to offer it as explanation or justification of human action. And no amount of persuasion or extent of painstaking formulation would render it intelligible as the source of bringing anything about. Its causality would simply be a total enigma.

RATIONAL CAUSALITY: INTRINSITY AND INSTRUMENTALITY

It follows that inferring causal intelligibility is not simply a matter of being familiar with a given language; rather, it rests on familiarity with modes of explaining or justifying human conduct and on experience with the interrelation of things. To be communicable as intelligibly causal, means-to-ends reasons must, accordingly, draw their relational meaning from people's having discovered what commonly goes with what in order to achieve certain outcomes or results. And the more familiar they are with such instrumental reasons, the less likely it is that they will inquire into their causal relationship; for example, people rarely ask why one puts on gloves in winter.

Much the same is true of intrinsic reasons, although the basis for not asking further questions is not the same. If we are told that x plays the piano, not in order to give public performances or to prevent arthritis in the fingers but for its own sake, we may believe it or not; but we are unlikely to get any further by asking more questions, since additional reasons in this case would probably be mere restatements – amounting virtually to an immanent circularity of reasons. And while we may find intrinsic reasons to be less communicable than instrumental reasons, we do not necessarily doubt their causal authenticity or their substantive veracity.

Veracity apart, however, intrinsic reasons may prove problematic in politics, especially as regards authentic governmental accounting, since they may invite abuses by being presented as self-evident truths that defy discursive challenge or the striking of bargains. To be sure, such a stance need not necessarily imply deception. Intrinsic reasons, unlike instrumental reasoning, almost definitionally possess elements of "consecration," that is, sanctioning grounds involving values or ends that transcend everyday mundane reasoning – the "extra-ordinary" in Arendt's political vision. "Hallowed authority" could admittedly be taken for a pleonasm, but something of this consecrating quality may be held to enter into reasons as ends in themselves, which *does* render the striking of deals difficult, if not impossible, the stakes being too high.

Understandably, democracies of modernity, professing to rest on *conditional* authority as their validating sanction, commonly opt for less consecrated sources of commitment. And, whatever party-political *practices* suggest to the contrary, democratic public philosophy shuns unconditional dedication, commitments that demand categorical allegiance. Indeed, unconditional commitment, as much as unchallengeable authority, is viewed as inimical to an open society, as an illicit transfer of sentiments appropriate in personal relations to a sphere in which coercive power can neither be ignored nor whisked away.[2]

Supposing we accept such distaste for or fear of unconditional dedication in democratic politics, should we therefore envision political relations, actions, and attitudes as no different from other spheres, in which trade-offs and pay-offs are thought perfectly apposite? Posing this question raises, I believe, one of the most fundamental issues in deciding whether deeds and values in politics are *sui generis*. I have no ready or irrefutable answer to this question, but it seems to me that Christian Thomasius was right in looking upon it as a central concern of any political philosophy that is more than, in his own words, "useless pedantry.[3] Presumably, a wholly intrinsic or consecrational mode of thinking, implying indisputable truths, ends, or values is totally at odds with any politics that sees in contestability the defining quality of its operational ethos. For such an intrinsic understanding of causal reasons clearly makes challenges to, and regular accounting of, governments problematic, as it may invite the kind of abuses Rousseau warns against.[4] Sharing Rousseau's fears, most mainstream democrats therefore favour conditional authority, whose acceptance is a matter of intelligibly communicable reasoning. At the same time, there are those, including myself, who do not want to abandon a line of thought that stresses the honouring of

2 This is the usual consideration raised against all forms of political romanticism. See also my *Herder on Nationality, Humanity, and History* (Montreal: McGill-Queen's University Press, 2003), ch. 2.

3 See ch. 5 below, sect. 2, and notes 16–20. Few writers to my knowledge have raised the question I pose more forcefully than Edmund Burke who, while accepting the idea of society as a "contract," nevertheless refused to go along with the view that the state was "nothing better than a partnership agreement in a trade of pepper and coffee, callico or tobacco." *Reflections on the Revolution in France* (1790), ed., W.B. Todd (New York: Holt, Rinehard and Winston, 1962), 117.

4 See ch. 6 below, sect. 2, notes 25, 26, and 30–2.

causal reasons for their own sake, notably as procedural standards, which, sanctioned by time-hallowed use, have acquired a certain abiding, if not *quasi*-universal, property. Thus, while I agree that institutional principles in politics ought to be distinguished from strictly universal principles that are unbounded and unconditional in their validity, I nevertheless wish to maintain that the former, as *principles*, must resist wilful or all-too-frequent alteration.

UNIVERSALITY WITHIN PARTICULARITY

In adopting this position, I take the central drift of Collingwood's plea in support of principled argument in politics to be the proposition that, without any institutional "sticking points," there can be no rule-governed safeguards of constitutional integrity. For these demand fairly constant principles in the ongoing exercise of political power. Therefore, while fully accepting Thomasius's and Kant's distinction between the contingent nature of political norms and the categorical nature of moral norms, I nevertheless agree with Collingwood that there can be no societal order without (directional) normative safeguards. And these, to serve as *standards*, must not be too freely exposed to the winds of change.[5] Clearly, principles that are entirely flexible cease to be principles.

In effect this means that in any political system other than that of despotic rule, procedural standards call for a certain (protected) continuity. And, if they are to promote an overall climate of lawfulness, standards must contain ingredients of universality in terms of fundamental constitutional principles that are generally accepted to validate the operation of a given political system. Hence, while not identical with the universality of moral standards, as *political* standards they must nevertheless enjoy unquestioned consecration in order to be seen as indispensable to a system's continued identity. For example, it is commonly regarded as an unchallenged norm of liberal democracies that elections be held at regular intervals, so as to open up alternative choices of party governances. Democracies reared within the fabric of these kinds of norms are expected to ensure their preservation, as evidence of their constitutionality. Otherwise, in failing to observe them

---

5 The Constitution of the United States, for example, has had a virtually unbroken continuity since its adoption in 1788; whatever changes it has undergone were validated by principles it had itself prescribed for itself. This endurance of principle is surely remarkable.

and thereby to honour them as unquestionably valid, they risk, sooner or later, their own demise on what Max Weber described as the slippery slope of "plebiscitary democracy," whether they do so deliberately or simply by default.

What kindled my interest in Collingwood's conception of action in politics, therefore, was his emphasis on the requirement that such action embody a *general* principle as its crucially distinctive validation. On this view, whenever we say it is the "principle of the thing" that we insist upon, there is "an element of universality in the particular and essential to it." Without it, he adds, "the *political* value of the act would disappear." It is precisely this linking of universality of principle with the particularity of implementational action that establishes a strikingly close parallel between Collingwood's political philosophy and Hannah Arendt's overall vision of politics.[6]

Collingwood's conception of principled political action reverberates in his philosophy of history through its insistence on *purpose* – or, more precisely, the thought of it – as the hallmark of human history; an insistence that echoes Vico's and Herder's distinction between causal teleology in human agency and causal teleology in processes outside it. This distinction (as I argue in chapter 1) forms the central theme of subsequent theorizing on historical consciousness and historical understanding, as it also informs Collingwood's thesis of "re-enactment," and crucially underlies the doctrine of *Verstehen*.

In both principled actions and purposive actions, reasons as answers *can* be expected, unlike in deeds wholly rooted in reverence for unchallengeable traditions or carried out in compliance with commands backed by force. No one, to my knowledge, made this clearer within the context of politics than David Hume.[7] And, like Hume, Collingwood argued that what makes explanations or justifications intelligibly credible in politics or history is the interlacing of causal reasons with universal principles, notably those derived from philosophical systems of belief. For the latter provide clues to whatever generally valid point there is in proposed or completed courses of action.[8]

6 R.G. Collingwood, "Political Action," 163. Seyla Benhabib, in *The Reluctant Modernism of Hannah Arendt* (Thousand Oaks, California: Sage, 1996) lends considerable support to this fusion of universality and particularity in Arendt's prevailing political and historical thinking.

7 *David Hume's Political Essays*, ed., Charles W. Hendel (New York: Liberal Arts Press, 1953), 43–61, "Of the Original Contract."

8 Collingwood, "Political Action," 163.

CAUSAL INTELLIGIBILITY AND RATIONAL VERACITY

Inasmuch as any reason is therefore emphatically designed to be a *causal* reason, it has to be, to meet purely formal requirements, communicably intelligible. And, to be *politically* valid, it must also possess a rightness and objectivity, by virtue of which it can, as *public* reason, demand general acceptability. It should be noted, therefore, all four of the following voices insist, that what makes reasons quintessentially public is no less than what (for Rousseau) makes will *general*, namely, an intrinsic, self-sustaining quality, and not simply extrinsically apparent plausibility. Operationally, with Collingwood, as with Hume and Tocqueville before, this kind of intrinsically validating publicness must reside as general principles within whatever specific (or "positional") claims are made politically.

Admittedly, while reasons may thus qualify as publicly valid causalities, it is not self-evident why they should also *necessarily* imply veracity, although presumably this is definitionally assumed. Still, whether they are true or not, they can hardly be of practical use as *causal* reasons unless they are related to actions in a consequential manner. Regarding this consequential force, I am therefore arguing that as grounds *from* which actions ensue, or as those *for* which they are undertaken, reasons must yield causal meanings as origins or purposes. And while veracity does not in itself establish their causal intelligibility, such intelligibility is implicitly associated with a content of recognizable factual or doctrinal truths. Usually this is so not merely with respect to the *things* being said but also to the *persons* saying them. This presupposes, however, that people have sufficient experience of how things are related as well as of how persons commonly behave – the latter of which we generally call their *character*. Clearly, if they have not the slightest idea of what goes with what and are unable to judge human conduct, they can neither understand nor not understand, because they cannot at all make out what is going on, what it is all about, or what normally can or should happen.

Usually, however, understanding by believing, let alone approving of, what has been said or done calls for more than experience of what goes with what, or of certain conduct as appropriate behaviour. And this "more" is as complex, we shall note, as the leap from accepting something as true, or appropriate, to acting upon it. "Understanding," therefore, as much as "rationality," "meaning," and "commitment," demands closer elaboration, although, as the next two chapters disclose, attempts in this direction may not free us from puzzling unclarities. Still, it does not require undue semantic sophistication to recognize that these concepts derive a good deal of their intelligibility from the context in which they are used or from the particular appeal they have, in the manner that beauty has in the eye of the beholder. In other words, what "makes sense" or seems of interest, causally, is for the most part a matter of contextual comprehension or perception, and not of analytical knowledge. For example, to understand that turning the key starts the car does not require us to know anything about internal combustion or automotive electronics.

We may, of course, make up reasons that are not the reasons for which we acted; not necessarily because we want to conceal the real reasons, but rather because we think that the real reasons may not be plausible enough, in terms of what general experience commonly associates with rational action or appropriate conduct in a given context. Alternatively, we may in fact have had no particular reasons in mind as purposes, and simply acted because we just happened to feel like it but were unwilling to admit it. All we no doubt *should* have done in this event is to acknowledge authorship by owning up, and by confessing that we were taken by a merely passing mood we cannot explain, or that what happened was an involuntary activity like breathing or swallowing, a deed committed under the influence of drugs or in response to physical threat. As a rule, we ask for no reasons when we know of circumstances such as these, which require no exercise of will or which prevent its exercise. Intrinsic reasons, we found earlier, often appear in the same light; in truth, however, they present a different situation from that which ensues from involuntary behaviour. For in *choosing* an activity, and doing so for its own sake, we telescope, as it were, reasons and goals, but we still consciously engage in a purposive act. Admittedly, we can give no reasons beyond the end itself, because the end *is* the reason. To account for an act would therefore get us no further than a restatement, or redescription, of itself – which would make it seem comparable to the earlier situation, in which we do something simply because we want to.

In fact, however, the resemblance is more apparent than real. For, besides not acting on a mere impulse or in a state of sheer wilfulness, there is, in relationships of intrinsic causality, another feature of profound relevance. And this feature stems from a distinct and highly incommensurable quality whose value would be negated as an intrinsic value if it were redescribable in terms of instrumentality or randomness. Clearly, love or friendship would cease to be what either intrinsically means, if we accounted for it by citing reasons of material advantage or those consisting in one passing mood or another. What principally differentiates intrinsic reasons from instrumental reasons, accordingly, is that, whereas in instrumental reasons means and ends are separate, intrinsic reasons telescope means and ends within a unique *telos* of their own; that is, within a purpose beyond which there is no other purpose. As for reasons as dispositions *from* which we act, they generally *impel* us to act, with little or no reflection of the kind that purposive reasons *for* normally entail.[9] Indeed, at times we may be at a loss to understand them ourselves, since they confront us as totally inexplicable, even quite distressingly so.[10] In such predicaments, in thinking about our "deeds," we are usually thrown back on particular antecedent conditions or states of mind that "made us do" whatever we happened to have brought about, or which induce us to invent reasons to disguise our alarm.

There are occasions, however, when we do vaguely remember our purposive reasons *for* but cannot recall them exactly, and hence make up reasons after the event, not necessarily in order to deceive but because we know that reasons are *expected* from us in cultures of modernity. Such situations, we shall note, are not uncommon in cases of political accounting, in which the proffering of phoney reasons is not infrequently the result of embarrassment at having forgotten the genuine reasons – and of an understandable reluctance to admit it.[11] All in all, therefore, causal intelligibility and rational veracity need not coincide.

PURPOSE, HISTORY, AND COMMITMENT

Collingwood's argument in support of a general principle in politics and a compelling purpose in history strikes indirectly at the root of modern Existentialist thinking and its cultivation of the absurd (as a generalizable phenomenon) in and through the notion of purposelessness. And, although his argument does not rule out the possibility that this notion (invoked by Schopenhauer, Kierkegaard, some Nietzsche, and Sartre) may have validity in art and religion, it questions its applicability to history and politics, because the typifying agency in these domains is that of conscious purpose, of deliberately pursuing set goals. Thus, like Thomasius, Vico, and Herder before him, Collingwood bases

9 The difference matches that between "causing" and "giving cause," as also the distinction between antecedent and directional reasons.

10 Rousseau recounts such a situation in Jean-Jacques Rousseau, *Confessions*, trans. J.M. Cohen (Harmondsworth: Penguin Books, 1953), 297.

11 Precisely because, as Hume observed, reasons are *expected*, they are at times calculatingly designed to *conceal* the real reasons; so that, whatever reasons are offered are merely meant to *ring* true.

his philosophy of history on emphasizing the purposive thought behind choice in the focused way of *minding* what is to be achieved. And it is this internal (conscious) "minding" in human agency which demands a causal approach different from that applicable to the uncovering of causality in other occurrences.

Hence, methods proving perfectly adequate in the study of processes in which intentions and goals have no place may be entirely inadequate to yield meaningful results in the study of purposive actions. It is fortunate, therefore, Vico and Herder argued, that in the latter we *can* penetrate into additional layers of causality, notably into the relation between thought and action, as Collingwood pointed out. However, as it involves considerations of *value*, as much as of purpose, its causal understanding calls for evaluative weighing in addition to cognitive perception. And it is by virtue of this added process of evaluative (inner) judging that the kind of historical understanding that Vico and Herder pioneered can bring forth a pattern of causality not to be found in the non-human world; that is, a mode of causal understanding that subsequently has become known as *Verstehen*.

Were we unable to penetrate thus into the inner causality of human occurrences, we would most likely find ourselves adrift to a degree of "purposelessness" that would render us incapable of speaking of reasons as causes in any intelligible way. In these circumstances neither Weber's "value rationality" – distinguishing intrinsic reasons from instrumental reasons – nor Kant's limitation of reason to a mere postulate in the causality of ethical conduct would carry any communicable meaning.[12]

It was therefore precisely the assumption that humans *were* able to draw meaning from the inner working of causal reasons which not only underpinned *Verstehen* but also, by linking outward action with an inner (conceptual) source, encouraged Rousseau (and Kant) to advance the possibility of *moral* freedom in civil society, as opposed to the *natural* freedom found under pre-political conditions. And while I am not happy with the phrase, lest it be taken for an extension of Hobbes's "positive freedom" (the inner power to do as one would), I fully acknowledge that the distinction aptly characterizes the difference between self-*enactment* and self-*determination*, as it also rightly suggests that no authentic action, including moral action, is at all conceivable without freedom as a performative causality, the central point in Hobbes's

12 Regarding Kant's critical approach to reason, see below, ch. 7, sect. 3, and notes 20–3.

formulation.[13] Only there *is* a danger (I argue) in conflating freedom as such with some moral quality, as though it were a higher or "processed" form of freedom. Instead, it seems to me desirable to distinguish freedom as a *condition* of morality – in terms of *giving* cause – from freedom as *implying* morality – in terms of *being* its cause.

On similar lines, I question the potential conflation of conviction and commitment, whenever their interrelation is viewed as a necessary continuum, so that, once again, the latter is considered to be a mere extension from the former. At least such a conflation appears to be involved in the so-called unity of theory and practice. For the phrase conveys the impression that the shift from reasons as convictions to reasons as commitments entails a kind of automatic causality. If so, it conveys the wrong impression, since, as in the transformation of freedom into morality, the shift is far less direct, or far more tenuous, than the "unity" thesis leads one to believe. Chapter 2, below, in struggling to unravel the complexity (if not the mystery) of the shift, admittedly sooner clarifies what its causality is *not* than what it is. Yet, despite the negativeness of the outcome, the chapter discloses that the shift is no mere change of degree – such as gaining a more sharpened focus of seeing by using a magnifying lens – but a more fundamental change in *kind*. Two central affirmations are therefore made throughout the argument: one, that commitments, by reflectively minding the what, why, and when, of acting, entail a conceptual form of causality; and, two, that such commitments, by virtue of it, inescapably involve contingency in their binding force. Taken together, therefore, conceptuality and contingency fundamentally differentiate the causality of *enactment* from that of *determination*.

A conceptual form of causality does not therefore ensure a binding commitment by way of individual or collective self-enactments; yet it is hard to envision how any commitment could come about in its absence. Even if it were conceded that the meaning of "commitment" itself is not unproblematic, this would not undermine the essential role of reflective conceptuality within *self*-enacting commitments, whether as dispositional reasons *from* or as purposive reasons *for*.

Interestingly, the rise of modern nationalism yields a striking illustration of dispositional and purposive reasons coalescing, in reinforcingly fuelling self-enacting commitments. Indeed, from now on, nationalities aspiring to political recognition could make little headway, unless they could stake conceptual claims that pressed into service the combination

13 Thomas Hobbes, *Leviathan* (New York: Dutton, 1950), Part I, ch. 14; see also Part II, ch. 21, esp. 106, 177.

of a dispositional historical memory and a self-imposed purposive duty to preserve their distinctive cultural heritage.[14] Therefore, those in search of identifying signposts within demands for separate statehood could no longer neglect to take into account these conceptual causalities as justifying rationales for such individually and collectively perceived self-obligations. But, whether reasons *from* and *for* coincide, as in cultural nationalism, or not, the most important thing to note is that, as *conceptual* causalities, they are contingent, and only indirectly give cause for occurrences, in contrast to causalities which directly and necessarily cause given outcomes to occur.

HISTORICAL UNDERSTANDING: ENACTMENT *VERSUS* DETERMINATION

No less interestingly, attempts to understand the conceptual ways in which nationalists aspire to justify their demands for the transformation of their existing ethnicity into future nation-states – in terms of a virtual fusion of cultural origins and political projections – illustrate the frequent conflation of enactment and determination. Especially in the propagation of the concept of *Verstehen* by Wilhelm Dilthey and Max Weber, such nationalist demands have increasingly been interpreted as instancing national self-*determination*. This is most unfortunate, because it suggests a form of causality radically different from that which governs both individual and collective variants of self-enactment. For, whereas "enactment," we noted, is indirect and mediated, "determination" is the work of a direct and immediate causal force, paralleling the causality of physical processes such as the freezing of water in sub-zero temperatures. Hence, to speak of self-determination as a causal category in the human world is worrisome, not least in an age ridden with misleading analogies. For, what it amounts to is the total assimilation of deliberative and evaluative processes, and their attending contingency, to the inexorable necessity of literally mindless occurrences.

If Thomasius, Rousseau, and Kant were already painfully aware of tendencies to confuse "minding" with mere "happening," it was Arendt who must acutely espied the incongruity of "self-determination." Notably, in her Existentialist moods, she almost echoes traditional Christian

14 On this point, see my *Herder on Nationality*, ch. 2, esp. 41–50. See also, for a contemporary treatment of the question of pre-political foundations of nationhood, Bernard Yack, "Popular Sovereignty and Nationalism," *Political Theory*, 29 (2001), 519–21.

doctrines in which this incongruity starkly comes to light – a line of thinking that Vico, despite his alleged secularism, never questioned.[15] But, regardless of what humans can know in striving toward self-enactment, why
and how should the study of history, or an understanding of past strivings,
make any difference?

Addressing this twofold question, Thomasius strikes a hopeful note. We
may not know what makes us strive, nor can we be certain of the outcome
of our efforts, but we do know that others feel and think like us; hence we
can understand them and they can understand us.[16] And it is on the basis
of this assumption that Thomasius put his faith in making sense of past
human strivings, arguing that such understanding was possible in a way
no understanding of nature was.[17] This confidence in the intelligibility of
causal reasons in human action contrasts, however, rather sharply with
that of Rousseau and, subsequently, with that of Hannah Arendt. For, although Thomasius conceded that things could be misinterpreted, if not
falsified, he was not obsessed with the incidence of self-deception to the
extent that both Rousseau and Arendt were.

For Rousseau the source of self-deception was principally wishful
thinking, whereas for Arendt it was, even more alarmingly, attributable
to "lying to oneself." And both feared that the combination of deception and *self*-deception could assume proportions liable to negate not
only historical understanding but the study of history itself. For, as a result, one may never be able to free what actually has happened from the
disguise of words.[18] Thus, unlike Collingwood who, echoing Thomasius's optimism, held that historians *could* discover authentic purposive
reasons behind actions,[19] Rousseau doubted that they could truly rid
themselves of bias. All one could therefore realistically expect, he felt,
were, at best, "reasonable conjectures."[20]

15 I am at variance here with Michelet's interpretation of Vico's philosophy
of history. For an insightful discussion of Michelet's interpretation, see Patrick H.
Hutton, "Vico's Theory of History and the French Revolutionary Tradition,"
Journal of the History of Ideas, 37 (1976), 241–56.

16 See below, ch. 5, notes 28, 39.

17 Ibid., note 39.

18 Jean-Jacques Rousseau, *Emile*, ed. A. Bloom (New York: Basic Books, 1979),
237. (*Oeuvres Complètes*, ed. Pléiade, Paris, 1959–69), IV, 525–6.

19 Collingwood, *The Idea of History* (Oxford: Oxford University Press, 1946,
1961), 304.

20 Rousseau, *Emile*, 239–40 (*Oeuvres*, IV, 529–30).

Despite his scepticism regarding the attainable degree of true understanding, Rousseau nonetheless believed that, in order to recognize reasons as *causes*, such causes must be searched for within the human mind itself. Here too, however, he impresses upon historians the need for extreme care in analysing motives as purposes. He instructs them, in particular, to be aware of the fact that humans acting purely as individuals are often motivated by purposes strikingly different from those that stir them as members of a multitude. All the same, he agrees that in both instances people, in committing themselves to pursue a course of action, do so by engaging reasons and will *jointly*, in mental processes that Habermas was to call "will-formation."[21]

In point of fact, it is precisely by assuming that such processes of reflective deliberation precede humans' acting in public that Thomasius, Vico, and Herder felt confident that historical understanding might be attained by imaginatively focusing on such hypothetical processes. For, at heart, they envisaged such focusing as a form of qualitative "taking-in" which, unlike logical deduction, demanded the enlisting of creative empathy, identified by Collingwood (after Herder) with conceptual re-enactment. In it, historians are to appropriate whatever they come to know about past actions, as though they had themselves brought them about or experienced their effects. Yet, this vibrant reliving of the past, he made clear, is not akin to intuition, let alone to mystical divination. Rather, it appears closer to re-rendering a piece of music the way it was intended by its composer or to recalling what it was like to go through occurrences of a comparable kind. In the main, perhaps, this manner of re-conceptualizing the past calls, therefore, for a certain *intratextual* sensitivity, for a capacity to understand given situations from the inside, so to speak.

Hobbes's image of two faces of freedom seems to me of possible relevance here by shedding light on structural components of such intratextual understanding. Emphasizing the contingent nature of the will as the prime motor of choice, he discloses the problematically complex implications of Collingwood's notion of historical re-enactment. Human choices being *reasoned* choices, the operation of will involves additional, indirect, and highly tenuous options between choosable ends that, for the most part, are not of our own making. Whatever we choose to do for reasons of our own, accordingly, cannot be detached from

---

21 Rousseau, ibid., 240 (*Oeuvres*, IV, 530). J. Habermas, "Popular Sovereignty as Procedure," in J. Bohman and W. Rehg, eds., *Deliberative Democracy* (Cambridge: MIT Press, 1997), 35–65, esp. 57–60.

contextual factors over which we have little or no control. *In* choosing, therefore, we do so within boundaries *of* choosing. Consequently, unlike processes of *determination*, which operate as directly compelling forces, those of *enactment* inject elements of contingency and indeterminacy.

From Hobbes's account it is evident, therefore, that there is no necessary or direct continuum between action-*promoting* reasons and action-*compelling* reasons, in that one does not determine the other within a dynamic of inevitable causality. Having reasons for acting does not *make* us act, nor do such reasons *entail* a commitment to do so. Knowledge of questionable practices on the part of leading members of a party need not induce other members to leave the party; they may find the practices utterly abhorrent, and yet fail to act, because circumstances as well as conflictual considerations militate against an automatic switch from reasons as beliefs to reasons as commitments – a predicament that the notion of self-*determination* tends to blur or altogether obscure.

IDEOLOGICAL PRINCIPLES AND REVOLUTIONARY RHETORIC

Not rarely, conflictual predicaments of this nature are attributed to the intrusion of *ideologically* based commitments in politics. And such commitments are seen as inseparably linked with one-party regimes and their use of terror. Hannah Arendt, indeed, goes further by associating ideologies with systematic deception. Almost going beyond Marx – one of the best-known exponents of ideology as a pejorative concept – she maintains that those who succumb to ideologies not only deceive themselves but simultaneously also deceive others.[22]

In the projected reappraisal of political ideology, I question the conflation of believing and deceiving, as also the identification of ideological politics with one-party despotism. Apart from leaning on Hume's, Tocqueville's and Collingwood's political thinking, the proposed alternative heavily draws on two principal sources. One is Hobbes's portrayal of inner causality in human thought and action – forcefully echoed in Thomasius's, Vico's, and Herder's approaches to history –, according to which humans, unlike meteors, act on motives, and, in view of it, can understand causes from *within*. Ideological thinking, analogously, is made possible by virtue of this capacity, and so is its sharing with others. On this view, therefore, it is a sort of parallel to historical thinking. The other source is Thomasius's pioneering philosophy of competing truths.

22 See below, ch. 3, notes 1, 14, 15.

Its central thesis – eloquently restated by J.S. Mill – asserts that the public domain is a space in which several truths jostle for recognition – a thesis that has obvious bearing upon the suggested reappraisal. For, in it, proponents of an ideology must win support amidst contending claims. Moreover, since they have to do so publicly, such proponents, as party leaders, are more bindingly committed to honouring avowed ideological claims than leaders functioning within contexts of "pragmatic" politics. Why? Because, within these contexts, party leaders as a rule prefer "elite accommodation," since it avoids open debate, whose limelight is evidently counter-productive to their scheme of things.

This line of argument is elaborated in chapter 3 below. Contestable or not, in emphasizing publicity and discursiveness as hallmarks of an ideological style of politics, it builds upon the legacy of Enlightenment thinkers, to whom these characteristics typified legitimate statehood. Additionally, while they did recognize and emphasize the difference between (political) society and (religious) community, they nevertheless insisted on civic interdependence, governmental accountability, and modes of associational mediation, in contrast to Ferdinand Tönnies's celebrated distinction (over a century later) between the wholly integrated community and the wholly atomistic society. Not surprisingly, because of its unduly polarized character, Tönnies's approach is of dubious relevance to my suggested reappraisal of ideology.

Similarly, although I envision the suggested reapparaisal to be perfectly in tune with *discursive* expressions of democracy, I do not consider it germane to its *revolutionary* expressions. Karl Marx's vision of revolutionary-political change, it is true, does allow for the use of parliamentary means – as distinct from non-parliamentary means – but this does not alter the fact that the choice between these two routes is liable to confuse the method of travelling with the nature of the destination, as I argue in chapter 4. An entirely smooth regime change, that is to say, is no warrant for the absence of a subsequent onslaught of violent measures in the direction of a radical transformation of social and political life, just as, conversely, a violent seizure of governmental power need give no birth to a turn around of things. Regardless of revolutionary strategy, however, *any* revolutionary consciousness – or, for that matter, any ideological consciousness – is hardly thinkable at all without the prior existence of a historical consciousness, since no one could then even begin to envisage alternatives to the status quo.

Given, then, that no revolutionary consciousness can dispense with a historical consciousness, to what extent can the rationally-purposive rhetoric in support of revolutionary claims be taken seriously? There has, to be sure, been no shortage of doubters. Edmund Burke, perhaps the best-known of them, in fact roundly rejected the claimed rationality of French revolutionary purposes as nothing but unadulterated marketing talk. Thomasius, although he favoured highly revolutionary reforms, was exceedingly pessimistic about the realizability of overly redemptive claims, suspecting that they involved almost inexorably authoritarian pressures of an unprecedented intensity – strikingly anticipating Friedrich Engels's thesis that revolutions were the most authoritarian things that ever were. Rousseau, while he profoundly wished to believe that transformed institutions could vastly improve the lot of humanity, at the same time fiercely distrusted the rhetoric typifying revolutionary agitation, since he doubted that it could be taken for truly binding commitments. Not unlike Kant, after him, he felt most uncertain that humans, as they are, really could be expected to match words with deeds, notably in the public realm. For his own part, Kant went further still, firmly denying that even the most radical changes would yield reforms in ways of thinking among the majority of humankind, although (in contrast to Burke) he did not question the authenticity of the moral claims professed by French revolutionaries without, admittedly, lavishing on them the kind of accolades Arendt bestowed on the American Revolution.[23]

REASON, WILL, AND SELF-ENACTMENT

Although "reason" figured prominently in revolutionary claims, this did not abate apprehensions about its effective causality *vis-à-vis* "will." As we observed, even one of the boldest founders of the *Aufklärung*, Christian Thomasius, agonizingly doubted that reason, however liberated from error and prejudice, could succeed in controlling will in the pursuit of the right and the good, unless will itself underwent a most drastic transformation.

Rousseau, perhaps more than anyone, stressed the autonomy of will; but this did not stop him from qualifying its operation by tempering force with restraint. Will, since it is required to enact the laws the public

23 On Thomasius's thoughts regarding authoritarian "guidance," see below, ch. 5, notes 41–47; on revolution, see below ch. 4, note 6 regarding Arendt, and regarding Kant, ch. 7, notes 87, 89. On Engels, see F. Engels, "Über das Autoritätsprinzip," *Die Neue Zeit*, 32, 1 (1914). Virtually echoing both Rousseau and Kant, Tocqueville sharply points to the almost invariable discrepancy between consistency in speech and inconsistency in action. In *Democracy in America*, ed. J.P. Mayer (New York: Doubleday, 1969), 20.

domain demands, must, in turn, submit to the laws enacted. For only then can laws serve as instruments of civic freedom and self-mastery.

Kant, although he attributed to reason the power to drive humans beyond the knowable and impart to law its (postulated) objectivity – as a *rational* legal system – nevertheless shared Thomasius's uncertainty about creating an ethical community by engaging the mediation of reason and will alone without simultaneously enlisting divine intervention. His (critical) faith in reason has little in common, therefore, with Condorcet's confidence in the "march of reason."

Finally, Arendt, who, following Kant, combined the meaning of reason with the creative force of reflective thinking as well as with the impartiality of "representative thinking," had to concede that, even if unopposed by will, reason had to contend with *time.* Transcending modernity in and through "new beginnings" cannot come about with a clean slate. Hence she had to agree with Marx that, like the most drastic revolutions, new beginnings had to start from somewhere; plunging into history is not achievable by ignoring history.

None of the four voices denied that modernity had invigorated people's consciousness of self-empowerment; yet the voices, as the themes, disclose a growing and chastening recognition that emancipated reason, even if it is aligned with a transformed will, may not be enough in the absence of one's *freedom* to act. Increasingly, therefore, it became evident that in society freedom itself needed to be redefined. Thus Kant, no less than Thomasius and Rousseau before him, knew and emphasized that liberty, left unbounded, could entail and entrain unbridled egoisms and thereby override any system of rights. A constitution, if it is to bring forth *justice,* and not merely *legality,* can therefore not afford to leave freedom wholly unchecked.[24]

Similarly, modernity's alleged faith in "progress" was not an unmixed faith. Assuredly, the idea of progress, together with the idea of liberty, was pre-eminent during the rise of political liberalism; but this does not mean that attempts to interpret or implement either were tarred with the same brush. Kant's liberalism, for example, or that of his closest political follower, Wilhelm v. Humboldt, fails to fit neatly

24 While stressing freedom and self-enactment as individual values, Kant at the same time made clear (as ch. 7 below discloses) that if reciprocity was to govern rights in society and gross inequalities before the law were to be eschewed, freedom needed to be protected by laws and standards which, in order to be generally observed, would call for a system of universal (coercive) constraints.

into the mould of the founders of liberal rationalism or of proponents of an individualism of unencumbered selves.

If common threads run through the themes and the voices, therefore, notably in going beyond seventeenth-century understandings of the social contract by resting the foundational ethos of states on "public reason" as the supreme arbiter, there are also significant variations among them. Similarities and divergences aside, however, none of the four voices is free of the tensions that beset ages in which "self-enactment" did not assume centrality. Michael Polanyi, commenting on these tensions, and expressly on the odd combination of burgeoning progressivism (if not millennialism), with the mounting erosion of faith in the human spirit and the power of reason, uses the image of a "chisel of scepticism driven by the hammer of social passion."[25] And yet, despite admittedly dealing sharp blows to the modern world, the sceptical chisel has not, as I see it, been entirely destructive in its effect on the modern mind.

For, with all the doubts and uncertainties, there also surfaced a new critical stance, from which modernity came to appraise old verities and anything else that had been taken for granted or left unchallenged. If, therefore, what is true about cumulative attainments in science and technology is markedly less true about the enactment of political ends, this may not be unconnected with the newly emerging perspective of critical seeing, from which successive generations were seeking to discover anew what is what amidst being, becoming, and overcoming.

However, this is not the place to pontificate on such asymmetries or, for that matter, on whatever vistas subsequent chapters may offer. The added Epilogue attempts this kind of assessment in the course of emphasizing major overlaps between the themes and the voices. Here and there, and especially toward the end, it admittedly also hazards a number of observations, for whose elaboration another book might well be called for, if not necessarily justified.

As for introducing the present book, I have sought to indicate its concern with the broader implications of reason and self-enactment as dominant concepts in modernity's historical and political thinking. In particular, I have focused on the qualified way in which both concepts came to be understood, with reason serving as a causal category in the indirect sense of giving cause, and self-enactment understood in the circumscribed sense of occurring within a relation of reciprocity with others. Among the broader implications, I have singled out the opposition

25 Michael Polanyi, *The Logic of Liberty* (Chicago: University of Chicago Press, 1958), 4.

of enactment and determination, purpose and function, and historical consciousness and historical inevitability. At the same time, I have also stressed the need for *blending*, notably between particularity and universality, instrumentality and intrinsity, as well as between political action and public reason.

In essence, both the blending and the contrasting are but part and parcel of an attempt to redefine basic political constructs such as liberty, mutuality, commitment, ideology, and revolution, in which the themes and the voices variously engage. And, as Hannah Arendt most expressly discloses, these preoccupations ultimately seek to drive home the conviction that the public realm is a space in which the cultivation of a sense of appropriateness, decorum, or good taste matters just as much as the acquisition of cognitive strategies in the pursuit of power.

PART I

From Historical
to Revolutionary Consciousness:
Four Themes

1

Reasons in History:
Causality of Ends

MUCH OF WHAT FOLLOWS IN THIS CHAPTER may be viewed, albeit in
a qualified sense, as a vindication of R.G. Collingwood's philosophy of
action-in-history. I say in a qualified sense, because although I do en-
dorse Collingwood's principal thesis that actions are the essential stuff
of history and that it is therefore through actions that the historian can
seek to penetrate into what people are doing and for what reasons or
ends, I do not altogether share his faith in the historian's intuitive capacity to discern meanings to a degree of authenticity that falls little
short of an action's re-enactment.

But, even to accept Collingwood's principal thesis, we must be able to
assume that events can be traced to recognizable agents who make things
happen for reasons pointing in an intended direction. Two interrelated
considerations, therefore, seem central: (i) the identity and circumscribed
context of human agency; and (ii) the efficacy of reasons as purposive
causalities. Although these considerations are analytically distinct, they are
clearly in reality so intimately connected as to be virtually inseparable.

REASONS AS PURPOSES

In order to establish in what sense reasons as purposes can be said to
have causal power in history, it seems desirable to set apart purposes *in*
history from purposes *of* history, that is, to separate *human* teleology
from what has been aptly referred to as "cosmic" teleology.[1] For, in light

---

1 Isaiah Berlin, "Historical Inevitability," in *Four Essays on Liberty* (Oxford: Oxford University Press, 1969), 51–5. Nevertheless, implicit in *any* conception of teleological reasoning, it seems to me, is an element of consequentialism, insofar
as "purpose" entails the thought of a particular end. Unfortunately, the idea of

of this distinction, human action may qualify as purposively rational, whether or not we believe in supra-human ends or some form of histori- cally immanent reasons as purposive ends. And, although I grant that te- leological reasoning – thinking and choosing in terms of purposes – occurs not *in vacuo* but within specific contexts, I am reluctant to con- cede that human ends are the "products" of contexts, and thus are re- ducible to them for their meaning or significance. For, even if purposes may not claim a self-sustaining status in an absolute sense, neither they nor acts arising from them are mere reactions to temporal and spatial circumstances, divorced from modes of personal engagement involving reasoned intentions. Some measure of underived (autonomous) exist- ence of reasons as purposes must therefore be presupposed in whatever is intended and not fortuitous.

Thus, whether or not reasoned purposes are the sole grounds for human agency, or invariably the most decisive, we commonly envision them as Collingwood does, that is, as forming an integral part of *action* in its coming about, be it in the past or the present. Whatever has been done on purpose, accordingly, involves *reasoned* choice and, with it, an act of will or, more precisely, a process of will-*formation*. And this process is generally considered as conceptually distinct and logically prior to the actual overt deed, unless the intervention of willing is denied as a sepa- rate process. Also, except in certain variants of Existentialism, we usually link an action's *meaning* with such a process of conscious choosing.

Acting meaningfully is therefore closely associated on the whole with the existence of reasoned purposes. In view of it, the question arises how closely purposes have to relate to actual outcomes to enable the historian to speak of purposive *continuity*. I have elsewhere inquired, accordingly, into the extent to which such proximity sheds light on the way meaning or meanings are interpreted within the stream of historical causation. In particular, I explored the weight that can be attached to intentions and accomplishments respectively.[2] This issue inevitably surfaces in any discussion of human agency in history. Indeed, it seems particularly

---

"consequentialism" is not infrequently associated with a highly pejorative under- standing of Utilitarianism, perhaps especially since Kant's emphasis on acting *for the sake* of duty or other moral precepts.

2 F.M. Barnard, "Natural Growth and Purposive Development: Vico and Herder," *History and Theory*, 18 (1979), 16–36. This is not to deny that a good deal of what happens in human history is the "work" (as we tend to say) of *un*intended outcomes. On this point, see Richard Vernon, "Unintended Consequences," *Political Theory* 7 (1979), 57–73.

germane to the matter at hand, and is therefore far from peripheral to any attempt that focuses on explaining such agency, on the *point*, that is, of its very occurrence.

Insofar as desired outcomes form an entailment of the idea of "intention," they could be said to constitute the purposive link that *joins* what the dimension of time, in distancing intentions from outcomes, *separates*. Accounting for actions retrospectively therefore involves a two-directional switch from outcomes to intentions and from intentions to outcomes. And this holds true for first-person accounting as much as for third-person accounting by the historian, albeit in ways that "internally" diverge. For, whereas the actor scarcely knows, when acting, what the historian knows in viewing outcomes, the historian scarcely knows, in the way the actor knows, what made the action happen. Despite the practical question of the weight that can reliably be accorded to an actor's own explanations – a question equally significant to law-enforcing agencies and to historians – there seems little or no sense in speaking of *action* in the first place (as occurrences in history) unless there is a way of relating in some such manner what has been said or done to particular intentions.

Accordingly, I propose to dwell on five central points in this discussion. First, I want to consider the relation between knowing and doing by exploring the causal mediation of "minding" as its conceptual component. Next, I wish to look more closely at the link between this focused way of "taking-in" and the nature of historical understanding. Third, I shall inquire into the bearing of such understanding (in terms of purposiveness, rationality, and autonomy of choice-making) on "historical consciousness," as the anchorage for retrospective studies of human action. Fourth, I seek to appraise the extent to which contexts, roles, rules, or "forms of life" impinge upon *purposive* meanings, as distinct from *functional* practices. And, finally, I return to, and comment on, the thesis that a conception of purposive human history hinges on the stipulation of an overall cosmic teleology.

By way of conclusion, I am contending that principal (let alone exclusive) emphasis on historical causality in terms of impersonal "interactions" not only seriously calls into question Collingwood's theory of historical understanding but also most problematically undermines the idea of rational purpose, if not of human action itself.

REASONS AS "KNOWLEDGE"

It is not uncommon that, when prompted by self-reflection or external challenges, we are at times embarrassed or puzzled at having to account for what we allegedly have brought about. Did we know what we were doing? Whenever we are thus uncertain or wholly in the dark over what made us do what we did, our uncertainty or failure to understand derives from, or is indeed identical with, our inability to recognize a deed or conduct ascribed to us as our own. We cannot "own up to it" because we cannot intelligibly appropriate the occurrence as the outcome of our aim or intention. And whether or not we may justly be called upon to accept responsibility for what we evidently brought into being, we can scarcely be expected to explain what caused us to do what we did if we have no knowledge of having intended it. Not having *minded* what we undeniably "did" forces us to the conclusion that what we did was done inadvertently, or out of blind impulse, under extreme stress, in self-defence, or under the influence of drugs. We may still be blamable for the harm we occasioned, for we could conceivably have exercised greater care, controlled our rages and impulses, refrained from overreacting in the face of danger, or abstained from indulging in drugs. Wholly unintentional behaviour still has consequences, and we are commonly held responsible for such consequences and not merely for our intentions and motives. While only those consequences which actors wish to bring about are attributable to them as *purposes*, those which form no part of their design may in fact contribute as much toward shaping the course of events as any they did have in mind.

Generally, though, a distinction is made between behaviour that is not intended and behaviour pursued with a particular end in mind. And it is the deliberate striving in a purposive direction, when we know the goal we wish to attain, that we (and others) think of *action*. It is then that we not only recognize *what* we are doing but also know the reasons *why* we are doing it, and thus are able subsequently to recall what entered our will in choosing our goal. Accordingly, it is this merging of will and reasoned purpose which, notably since the Enlightenment, has rightly received emphasis; so that it is not so much will-*power* as it is will-*formation*, the process I essentially identify with "minding," that principally matters.[3]

By means of such focused minding we therefore retrospectively distinguish not only purpose from accident but also self-*enactment* from self-*determination*, that is, we differentiate between mediated and

---

3 Echoing Thomasius, Rousseau, and Kant, Jürgen Habermas speaks of "will-formation" not merely *within* individuals but also *among* individuals. See his "Popular Sovereignty as Procedure," in J. Bohman and W. Rehg, eds., *Deliberative Democracy* (Cambridge: MIT press, 1997), 35–65, esp. 57–60.

direct causality. By the same token, it is the process of will-formation that in essence forms the basis of rational accounting.[4]

Complications arise, however, when, though conscious of our purposive reasons, we later discover that we did not *fully* know what we were about. Usually, this may mean either or both of the following possibilities. Since action necessarily has a spatial and temporal context, we may have inadequately understood or incorrectly interpreted the facts of a situation. "Facts" here embrace the given circumstances, rules, hopes, or fears in which a situation is embedded. Put simply, our knowledge can be faulty; we may overlook facts or underrate obstacles because we act in haste, lack experience, judgment or intelligence, or, because we are biased, indulge in wishful thinking or overrate our own abilities in one way or another. On the other hand, we may have taken every possible care, applied utmost prudence, tact, and circumspection, and still fail to accomplish what we set out to do, because there are situations so complex, so opaque, or so rapidly changing that we indeed *could* not know what in fact we did not know. Alternatively, we may have misjudged the probable consequences for a variety of reasons, not least because we may have underrated the likelihood of the unexpected. In a sense we knew *what* we wanted, yet we did not accurately evaluate all that it implied. And by saying that we both did know and did not know, we may think ourselves paradoxical, but in truth we are involved in an experience that, perplexingly vexing though it may be, is so familiar that it needs little elaboration.

More problematic still, if not also more disturbing, are situations in which people, despite having full knowledge of the relevant facts, act (or fail to act) as if they had no such knowledge. Do they know or do they not know? They *do* know, whether they mind what they know or not. Smokers generally know now that cigarettes are injurious to their health; speedsters on the road know the hazards to themselves and others. Rousseau recounts (in his *Confessions*) that he well knew the risks of visiting a Venetian courtesan, that he was wholly cognizant that no one

---

4 The significance accorded to an agent's own account of this process is a central issue in the philosophy of jurisprudence. See on this, notably, H.L.A. Hart and A.M. Honoré, *Causation in the Law* (Oxford: Clarendon Press, 1959) and J.L. Austin, "A Plea for Excuses," in Alan R. White, ed., *The Philosophy of Action* (London, 1968) or Joel Feinberg, "Action and Responsibility," in his *Doing and Deserving: Essays in the Theory of Responsibility* (Princeton: Princeton University Press, 1970), 95–119. For an historical account, see John Dunn, *Interpreting Political Responsibility* (Princeton: Princeton University Press, 1990).

"could leave the embraces of a padoana unscathed." And yet, his inclinations, feelings, reason, and will to the contrary, he allowed himself,
much to his own puzzlement, to be "dragged off." It was, as he admits,
"one of those inconsistencies that I find difficult myself to understand."[5]
Paloczi-Horvath, a dedicated Hungarian Communist who took an active
part in the Hungarian Revolution, admitted knowing all along of the
lying and corruption in the Party, of its methods of extracting confessions, of the terror and the camps. "Of course I knew how history was
falsified. Of course I had heard about the mass purges in the Soviet
Union. Of course among thousands of other facts my memory stored
the facts about eliminating whole peoples and nations by the Kremlin
leaders. Of course I knew everything."[6] Horvath was not moved to act by
new information; there was nothing further to be known. He did not
see what he had not seen before, in the way we discover distant objects
through the telescope. Nothing new is discovered, but a new frame of
mind emerges. The same knowledge that had hitherto failed to induce
Horvath to act became the compelling ground for action.

Once again we are seemingly faced with a conundrum in having to
admit that the same knowledge could be wholly ineffective to move us to
act at one point in time, and be powerfully effective at another. Reality,
however, confirms that what on the face of it is highly exasperating
should only truly startle those who have an inordinate faith in knowledge to move mountains, especially if "knowledge" is viewed as identical
with "rationality," and moral agency is viewed as a virtual entailment of
rationality. Kant, for example, may be quite correct in speaking of moral
duties, strictly interpreted, as rationally binding principles, that is, as imperatives of categorical validity, insofar as being rational implies acting
independently of our likes or dislikes, advantages or disadvantages. Yet,
in practice, whatever we decide to do against or in spite of our feelings,
or contrary to personal gain, involves more, I believe, than rationality
(however defined), for us to translate known (objective) precepts into
operative (subjective) maxims. And this "more" includes above all what
I earlier described as "minding"; we have to reflect and care enough in
order to want to act. But both the minding and the choosing are activities characterized, we found, by contingency; there is therefore nothing
"categorical" about either. Choice, moreover, may mean having to opt

5 Jean-Jacques Rousseau, *Confessions*, transl. J.M. Cohen (Harmondsworth:
Penguin classics, 1953), 297.

6 George Paloczi-Horvath, *The Undefeated* (London: Secker and Warburg,
1959), 191. I am indebted to Professor J.M. Porter for this reference.

between opposing reasons or competing rules, such as telling the truth and helping people in distress. And under these circumstances knowledge of the precept of truth-telling as a universal (rational) principle is of little avail.

Precisely when we most need guiding precepts to tell us what to do, we may find ourselves adrift. It seems that in human conduct, as distinct from technical operations, there often are no maxims or rules without exceptions, no once-for-all guidelines that relieve us of the burden of choice. To postulate an *inherently* rational-moral will is therefore uncomfortably close to rendering moral action trivially unproblematic.[7] This is not to deny the need for standards or noms as the matrix of a social order. What it does mean, though, is that they may not prove sufficient in themselves to generate binding commitments. It evidently requires the mediation of personal minding to bring about the conversion of objective standards into subjective maxims, although even personal minding may, in itself, be no guarantee of action.

Thus, while we need benchmarks to guide us, they do not constitute what Hannah Arendt calls "banisters," that is, moral *causalities*. We cannot, it seems, take for granted that knowledge of maxims will instruct us what to do in particular circumstances or, even if they do – and there are no conflicting options among principles – that they will induce us to heed them. Nor can we blandly assume that our perception of reality has in itself direct causal power. To perceive injustice, for example, does not necessarily make us seek redress, advocate reforms, or engage in revolutionary resistance. To be sure, to find something unjust *does* imply taking a stand on justice; in itself it does not, however, indicate the intensity of our perception, of *how* unjust we feel it to be or how *much* we really *mind* it. It follows that there simply is no necessary or causal continuity between perception and response, between knowledge and action.

All this is not new. People generally have been aware for a long time that to know is not the same as to act upon one's knowledge. *Minding*, I suggest, potentially provides a mediating link between knowledge

7 If an *inherently* moral will renders moral action ontologically necessary, or if autonomous action is made a matter of rational necessity, what is left of *choice*? I originally came across the distinction between technical operations and practical conduct in Herder's writings, particularly in his pioneering essay on the origin of language. (J.G. Herder, *Sämtliche Werke*, ed. B. Suphan, 33 vols., Berlin: Weidmann, 1877–1913, v, 531–2.) Although the distinction can be traced to Aristotelian origins, it has attained more recent prominence chiefly through the writings of Hannah Arendt and Jürgen Habermas.

and wanting to act upon it. But I believe that, to have action-promoting, if not action-compelling, power, minding involves more than a cognitive change, say, a sharpened form of perception or a clearer vision. In the next section I want to have a closer look at the kind of change that seems to me essential to create in any historical context a situation in which agents do not suddenly know more by minding, but know *differently*.

REASONS IN "MINDING"

In essence, I want to argue that "minding" (as used here) involves a distinctly qualitative change, a change in kind and not merely in degree. And, to do so, minding, I suggest, should be viewed as a form of *reminding*, as a process of directing attention to what one already knows. One *sees for oneself* in a new way what one has known all along, in that one recovers a meaning that was there for the grasping once it was properly taken in. Thus viewed, minding recalls Plato's theory of learning in the *Meno*, according to which the teacher does not so much impart new information as he merely helps the students discover what they already know. For the most part, this is what students can learn and teachers teach.

The Platonic idea of "seeing for oneself" is undoubtedly an important component of minding, but it is not all there is to it, since cognition is not enough. For a smoker to give up cigarettes, for a speedster to slow down, for a Rousseau to resist his seducers, or for a Horvath to repudiate Stalinism, minding requires more than cognitive recollection. Just as doing one's dudy demands more than one's bare knowledge of it, minding demands more than the mere rehearsing of facts. This "more" I see in the enlisting of one's imagination, of one's capacity to assimilate what one already knows in its utmost concreteness – what Collingwood, after Herder, means by re-enactment. It is to feel oneself into what one knows and to appropriate it in its most vivid reality for oneself. Such "taking in" is, accordingly, an act of personal discovery which, unlike logical inference, cannot simply be deduced; it has to be *erlebt*, lived through.[8]

The capacity for reflective and imaginative minding is for Collingwood, as it was for Vico and Herder, the essential prerequisite for *understanding* what we already "know" about actions of the past. While I am very much in sympathy with this line of thinking, I sense a danger that

8 For a rejection of Collingwood's thesis by Michael Oakeshott, see W.H. Dray. "Michael Oakeshott's Theory of History," in Preston King and B.C. Parekh, eds., *Politics and Experience* (Cambridge: Cambridge University Press, 1968).

this capacity for uncovering the inner meaning of occurrences might be viewed as an exclusively intuitive affair – a danger that Collingwood at times underrates. To understand "what it is like" to act in a particular historical context does indeed require imaginative minding, but for such minding to achieve a measure of penetration into how anything "actually did happen" demands not just intuition but a sense of realism born of experience of or familiarity with a variety of situational components – including consequences – that make up a given historical context. Above all, it should comprise a perceptive understanding of openings, limits, hazards, expectations, and trepidations as they appear to people at a particular juncture of time and space, and such understanding can hardly be had solely by enlisting one's "natural" powers of intuition. One can scarcely understand, for example, how a Rousseau could succumb, against his better judgment, to the temptations of a brothel if one has not the slightest experience of sexual deprivation or sheer loneliness; or the torments of a Horvath in keeping silent over Communist malpractices if one has no idea of the dedication, if not submission, that is expected from members of a Communist party.

Of course, Collingwood well knew that no practising student of history, let alone renowned writer of history, would rely entirely on his or her powers of intuition. Yet, not unlike Herder, he occasionally went rather far in debunking the collection of data, in favour of enlisting "imaginative construction" as he called it.[9] At such times he was at pains to press the point that there was no basic difference between the work of the historian and that of the novelist. And while, again like Herder, he was not insensitive to the need for evidence, he seemed to overlook that the novelist, in constructing a "coherent picture," did not have to share the historian's concern over the veracity of the picture. Still, all Collingwood sought to state was that collecting data was not the crux of the matter; that what transformed the tracing of the past into *history* was the historian's ability "to re-enact the past in his own mind."[10] And such re-enacting rested for Collingwood on the assumption that what was done had been done on purpose. Whatever was not so done he therefore categorically dismissed as forming no part of the subject-matter of history.[11] It was the thought behind the deed, and only the thought, that was within the ken of historical recovery. Hence Collingwood's

9 R.G. Collingwood, *The Idea of History* (Oxford: Oxford University Press, 1961, 1946), 244.

10 Ibid., 246, 282.

11 Ibid., 310.

celebrated statement: "Of everything other than thought, there can be no history."[12] Purposive actions alone, in this view, can be the concern of history precisely because it is purposes only, as expressions of what I call minding, that are susceptible of human understanding.

But does "imaginative construction" unfailingly recover past minding in the form of purposes? Here again, Collingwood, like Herder, was quite optimistic about the chances of authentic recovery, as he was about the historian's ability to "feel himself into" actions of times other than his own or to "enter sympathetically" into thoughts or purposes very different from his own. Yet, despite this professed faith, Collingwood was too honest a scholar to wholly conceal his doubts. He conceded that there are purposes that the historian "cannot fathom" and hence cannot historically reconstruct.[13] It would appear, therefore, that we are forced to judge the historicity of an action by the historian's capacity to understand the purposes that brought it about. The trouble, clearly, with such a delimitation of the cognizance of history is its potential arbitrariness.

However, to me the real problem lies elsewhere. It lies in the ambiguity of the word "understand" or "fathom." We may know very well – and in this sense "understand" – the reasons that prompted a Hitler or a Stalin to send people to extermination camps and, at the same time, be totally unable to understand or fathom how anyone could think of constructing camps for the wholesale killing of innocent and helpless people. Can we, or should we even want to "enter sympathetically" into their thoughts or purposes? How are we to "mind" something that is utterly beyond the grasp of our sensibilities? But does this mean that "history" or historians should ignore or forget such actions, let alone bend over backward to find excuses, if not justifications, for them? Collingwood would possibly reply that we should most certainly record them and, in this sense, mind them, but that such recording and minding would only furnish *evidence* for history; it would not *constitute* history, since the meaning of the actions recorded is outside the capacity of our understanding to penetrate, and hence wholly resists historical conceptualization.

Leaving aside the validity of this view as a basis of establishing the historicity of human actions, it is clear enough from it that we may know and yet not know, mind and still be unable to understand or "take in," what makes or made humans do what they do or did. Whether or not

12 Ibid., 304.
13 Ibid., 310.

this view calls for a lowering of expectations with regard to historical understanding, or to the grasping of reality itself, it has made evident a most problematic hiatus between what we "know" and what we "understand" or see meaning in. Moreover, as Rousseau has observed, people acting in the multitude do so for reasons other than those for which they act individually, apart from frequently hiding their real designs. Hence, to assess motives or intentions correctly may prove a tall order indeed. Add to this difficulty the selectiveness and bias of historians, or their tendency to fall victim to the danger of misplaced concreteness (by focusing on palpable facts rather than on occurrences whose causes are invariably hidden), and the chance of penetrating events to their sources and purposes appears slim indeed.[14]

Perhaps it was precisely the realization of the contingency of understanding the motives and purposes in history which has led philosophers of history such as Vico, Herder, and Collingwood to press into service the idea of empathetic "feeling-into" as the ultimate – and almost poetic – attempt to re-enact in one's mind what otherwise escapes comprehension. Although this move was to distinguish most markedly historical understanding from understanding in the natural and physical sciences, it has, albeit unwittingly, also called attention to problems in the study of history that we are spared in the study of hormones.

HISTORICAL CONSCIOUSNESS
AND RATIONAL CAUSALITY

The core of these problems seems to lie in the *rational* causality claimed for purposive human action. Encouraged by the transformation of theoretical reason into a category of practical action, humans came to view themselves not only as possessors of this practical causality and, therefore, as actors who could *make* things happen, but also as agents who could *choose* what is to happen for reasons of their own. Cumulatively, these "discoveries" have given birth to the "new science" of history and the notion of "historical consciousness," although, simultaneously, they have helped to disclose also the *contingency* within human causality and, with it, the chasm dividing it from the causality of the non-human world.

14 Rousseau, *Emile*, ed. A. Bloom (New York: Basic Books, 1979), 237–40. (*Oeuvres Complètes*, ed. Pléiade, Paris, 1959–69, 525–30). For a discussion of Rousseau's fascinating observations on history and historiography (in conjunction with those by Herder) see my *Herder on Nationality. Humanity, and History* (Montreal: McGill-Queen's University Press, 2003), ch. 7.

For the most part, language itself drove home this lesson by demonstrating that words like "can" or "could" (typifying contingency) would be almost entirely vacuous in the vocabulary used to characterize the functional determinism of nature and machines.

To be sure, putting utmost emphasis on "rationality" as a causality in human history, *via* purposive meanings, has not made the notion any the less problematic – a point to which I return below. What it *has* done, however, is to lend added force to the postulates of intentionality, of choosing between alternatives, and of the idea of a rational structuring of human agency.[15] In so doing, it has given significant impetus to the *prospective* application of historical consciousness within both revolutionary and non-revolutionary strategies of political action, and conferred further prominence upon Hegel's pioneering conception of "rational necessity."

Unfortunately, if not paradoxically, what was intended as a *distinction* turned into a *conflation*. For, instead of invigorating Vico's and Herder's stress on radically distinguishing causality in history from causality within non-human concerns, these developments beclouded it, notably within attempts to *fuse* rational necessity with natural necessity – a central complaint of chapter 4 (below).

Understandable though the conflation possibly is in view of the endemic ambiguity of "rationality," as also of its undeniable usefulness rhetorically, it rather worryingly suggests that the process of reasoned choosing implies choosing the right reasons in a logically causal, physically causal, or morally causal sense. Worse still, perhaps, it may sweepingly be assumed that whatever is found to be rationally causal is thus simultaneously moral *and* natural. Hegel, of course, can neither be blamed for, nor credited with, these linkages, since he expressly *opposed* rational necessity to natural necessity. And, in contrast to Kant before him and John Rawls after him, for whom rationality was respectively a predicate in the definition of the ethical and the good, rationality had no inexorably moral implications for Hegel.[16]

I have more to say on merging the rational and the moral in the next chapter and in Part II. However, invoking "rationality" here, by way of reasoned choosing, I had better make clear in what sense it is invoked within the context under discussion. Essentially, I seek to distance myself from loading rationality with any absolute values, be they morally or

15 I am thinking here primarily of the revival of philosophical jurisprudence, associated chiefly with H.L.A. Hart.

16 John Rawls, *A Theory of Justice* (Cambridge: Harvard University Press, 1971), 399–400. Regarding Kant, see ch. 7 below.

religiously grounded. Thus delimited, it serves as a medium to express the manner in which positions are formulated or purposes projected. Either way, rationality is applied as a *modality*, enabling explanations or justifications of what has been said or done to be made conceptually intelligible. At the same time, resting actions on such a modal-rational basis is not to claim indisputable validity or to demand categorical acceptance. Yet, precisely because of its challengeability, modal rationality yields a discursive openness that substantive rationality, by virtue of its indisputable truth content, precludes.

Although (as I maintain in the next chapter) such openness is eminently suitable for political systems of contestable governance, it does not save modal rationality from objections to it as a historical causality. In particular, it does not escape strictures expressed by various shades of Marxian, Freudian, or Existentialist approaches to causality. But justified or not, do such strictures invalidate purposive reasons as causes in history, simply because we cannot unearth the reasons that "at bottom" move people to act, under whatever circumstances, anywhere and at any time, or because we cannot always be certain of their truth content?

Clearly, from what has been said so far, this is not necessarily so. While chapter 2 (below) argues this point further, I merely want to add here that, throughout this chapter, I have so far (in conformity with Collingwood) been principally concerned with "rationality" as a *purposive* causality; that is, in terms of directional reasons, rather than in terms of antecedent conditions. My grounds for having done so are inherent in the overall thrust of this chapter, but also because usually people, acting in a particular situation can do little about the matrix in which they find themselves, about what is *there*, and in whose creation they had no say whatsoever. Even those sharing modernity's faith in self-direction have to accept that for these givens, and *their* causes, known or unknown, people can hardly be held accountable, since they obviously could have had no control over them.

However, the problem does not end here. Evidently, what is at issue is not only the *type* of causal reasons properly ascribable to human agency, whether as antecedent reasons *from* or as purposive reasons *for*, but also their validating *source*. Indirectly, this poses the question of the extent to which "historical consciousness" can be taken to serve as a *human* rationale, if we bear in mind the distinction I made at the outset between rational causality *in* history and the rational causality *of* history. Kant, we shall note, was torn between drawing this line and transcending it, faced as he was with the problem of increasing people's confidence in self-enactment. For he keenly sensed the danger of what I elsewhere have called (following Goethe's *Faust*) the frenzy of "titanism," insofar as the same science that feeds our pride in mounting abilities to master nature simultaneously undermines it, by treating us, the "masters," as mere products of non-rational nature, that is, of processes in which the causality of reason plays little or no part.[17]

Rational validation, in short, problematic enough as regards the operation of causal reasons *in* history, seems even more perplexing in terms of the rational causality *of* history. Vico, Herder, and Collingwood, evidently recognizing these difficulties (notably in strictly empirical modes of verification), argued therefore that causality in its application to historical understanding rests on forms of verification different from those that prevail in the natural sciences.

Supposing we granted the cogency of this argument with respect to the rational causality operative *in* history, conceived as the area of *human* strivings; would it dispose of the question concerning the assumption of rational causality *of* history itself? Clearly, as I have indicated, *this* question is not only far more perplexing, it is also potentially alarming. For how can humans appropriate as their purposive reasons a causality of outcomes whose coming about is attributable to natural or providential or cosmic teleology, or to a "rational necessity" inherent in history, that is, to occurrences that had to happen anyhow within the stream of time? By the same token, how can praise or blame be ascribed to human action in the case of such occurrences?

These are questions that I found impossible to resolve when discussing Herder's philosophy of history. Apparently, however, several thinkers of modernity, from Voltaire, Kant, Herder, and Hegel to Marx and Arnold Toynbee, have had no problem reconciling rational causality within time itself with the idea of historical consciousness. And, far from viewing the perception of rational immanence in history as a constraint upon human self-enactment, they looked upon it as a *spur,* a stimulus to people's shaping their own future. In effect, the purposiveness they associated with rational causality in history was transferred in its inner

17 In my *Herder on Nationality, Humanity, and History,* ch. 4. On this point, see also Charles Taylor, *Philosophy and the Human Sciences* (Cambridge: Cambridge University Press, 1985), II, 187, 210. Ernest Gellner has captured Kant's anguish rather well. He sees Kant's greatness in not concealing two conflicting fears: the first, "that the mechanical vision does *not* hold; the second, that it *does.*" The first fear was for science, the second for morality. Gellner describes him therefore as "a philosopher of both the ghost and the machine." In *Legitimation of Belief* (Cambridge: Cambridge University press, 1974), 185.

dynamic to *human* striving, emboldening it to pursue the attainment of aspired ends with heightened confidence.[18] This line of thought, and the self-creativity it promoted, possibly helped to shift emphasis from non-choosable antecedents to choosable objectives. And, in so doing, it may have broadened the perimeters of purposive thinking and conceptually mediated causation in the study of human history and human action, as opposed to forms of causation that involve processes of law-like regularity, independently of human intentions, such as those of physics and biology. Likewise, the idea of rational causality in history may also be said to have strengthened, however obliquely, Collingwood's thesis that purposive reasons are the fulcrum of history. Even so, the questions I raised remain unresolved.

DIRECTIONAL REASONS: PURPOSE AND FUNCTION

In whatever ways purposive reasons operate, however, they clearly do so differently from mechanical causation or the workings of organic processes. But this, I contend, hardly amounts to viewing their causality in a purely "metaphorical way," even if the reasons given by people are at times spurious.[19] For, to view reasons in this way misleadingly suggests that the relation between reasons and actions is either non-existent or too loose to count as a causality. Misleadingly, because, as I argued earlier, to concede that reasons operate in a non-mechanical form or are not always authentic does not disqualify them as causes.

There could be situations, though, in which we do see causal meaning in what is done, but cannot quite comprehend the reasons for it because we cannot understand their purposive drift.[20] Thus, we may accurately interpret the signals given by a motorist, yet be unable to take in why the driver wants to make a left turn, since there is no road branching off to the left. Hence, in order to comprehend actions of others, in

18 Although Herder repeatedly emphasized a purely empirical basis grounding his philosophy of history, the influence of G.E. Lessing's Enlightenment interpretation of the traditional Christian doctrine of *Heilsgeschehen* seems unmistakably greater than that of Voltaire. For a more detailed discussion, see my *Herder on Nationality, Humanity, and History*, in its attempt to grapple with this problem (ch. 5).

19 I am quoting here Kurt Baier's influential *The Moral Point of View* (Ithaca: Cornell University Press, 1958), 142.

20 Roger Trigg, *Reason and Commitment* (Cambridge: Cambridge University Press, 1973), 82.

history or in the here and now – to explain or to justify them – we evidently need to grasp the meaning of *what* they were or are doing in terms of general practices, on the one hand, and in terms of particular intentions or purposes, disclosing *why* they are doing what they are doing, on the other.

Either way, however, as soon as we deny any causal relation between actions and reasons, it is a matter of indifference whether reasons are phoney or authentic, for neither would then carry any intelligible meaning as causes. Unlike such a state of utter meaninglessness, however, the "motorist" example cited discloses a situation in which we do see meaning by way of understanding directional signs, yet nonetheless fail to grasp their *purpose*.

Partial understandings of this nature may occur also when the locus of meaning is too narrowly restricted by being confined to characteristics of certain collective forms of life (*Lebensformen*) or, alternatively, to features associated with unique types of context.[21] For then we use a net either too coarse or too arbitrary to capture causal levels of meaning in terms of which people most frequently account for their actions. I return to this theme in the next section. Here I merely mention such practices in order to draw attention to the kind of ambivalence that we may encounter in searching for the locus of meaning. For, clearly, they reveal the possibility of our simultaneously understanding and *not* understanding what is what or why.

Thus, observing a driver's signals with any degree of comprehension implies that we understand the practice of signalling. As a rule we know what the signals are intended to mean; hence we do not speculate upon the reasons for the signals' being what they are by reflecting on the driver's state of mental or physical health, subconscious desires, or marital life. In our example, we simply interpret the signalling as indicating the intention to make a left turn. In other words, we seek meaning in teleological terms in the form of "in order to" explanations, as distinct from dispositional explanations in terms of "because of" reasons. At the same time, it may happen that reasons in teleological terms may fail to account for the driver's behaviour and impel us therefore to turn to reasons in terms of "because of" causality. If, for instance, people not only mistakenly signal because they are unfamiliar with the locality, but

---

21 Unfortunately, the concepts of "context" and "*Lebensform*" are at times pressed into service as almost unproblematical. I think it is important to distinguish between context as external cause *determining* roles and duties and context as an inherent cultural *Lebensform – influence.*

constantly change signals, we begin to wonder if they suffer from some physical or mental defect. We do so because we fail to relate their practices to purposive reasons, that is, to what we identify as action. In effect, we cease to associate any rationality or meaning with it; we understand the practice, but cannot see its point.

Teleological causality, by way of directional reasons, could at times be ambiguous in a different sense, however, in that it could imply a *telos* in terms of *functions* as much as in terms of *purposes*.[22] Although both words are frequently used interchangeably, the source of most confusions lies in the concept of "purpose" because "function" is usually understood as an instrumentality, deriving its meaning from the purposes it serves or from the system of which it is a part, whereas "purpose" can be validly applied to both instrumental and intrinsic ends. And, to complicate things further, purposes, while viewed as non-derivative or self-sustaining in meaning, are not, for all that, invariably made of whole cloth. To be sure, in pursuing purposes of their own choice, humans make their own history, as Vico, Herder, and Marx insisted. Even so, their purposive thinking can nevertheless not be entirely divorced from conceptual categories of the past. As Marx put it, in purposively transforming the present in order to create something new, humans cannot do without "borrowed language" without a matrix of traditional meanings.[23]

The *telos*, therefore, underived and self-sustaining though it may be, is not chosen within a contextual emptiness. Contrary to Arendt's perception, purposive human actions are *not* like miracles; they do not drop out of nowhere.[24] They occur within institutional structures and systems of rules, conventions, and mutual understandings. People choose between alternatives, they do not just choose, and even if they act in order to reject existing alternatives, they do so *because* of these alternatives, and not in their absence. In short, there are boundaries to human self-direction, notably in the form of institutional structures. However, I

22 I have discussed the distinction in some detail in F.M. Barnard and R.A. Vernon, "Pluralism, Participation, and Politics: Reflections on the Intermediate Group," *Political Theory* 3 (1975), 180–97. See also Robert K. Merton, *Social Theory and Social Structure* (Glencoe, Illinois: Free Press, 1957), 19–84, and Dorothy Emmet, *Function, Purpose, and Powers* (London: Macmillan, 1958), 46–51 and 106–11.

23 Karl Marx, "The Eighteenth Brumaire of Louis Bonaparte," *Selected Works*, transl. Foreign Languages Publishing House, (Moscow, 1968), 96.

24 Hannah Arendt, "What is Freedom?" *Between Past and Future* (New York: Doubleday, 1968), 169.

emphasize throughout the book that structures do not *determine* purposes, just as purposes, in turn, are not derivative from particular systems or social orders in the way *functions* are. Vico, Herder, and Marx were undoubtedly right in stating that structures are what they are because humans have made them. In view of that, they argued, humans can also change them, since structures are only functional if and when they serve ends that people view to be in accordance with their overall purposes. Which is perhaps just another way of saying that, although purposive choice occurs within the boundary of existential givens, the latter form no causally determining source in the way soil, seeds, or the weather determine the life of plants. This does not rule out, however, that functional explanations add meaning to historical accounts, even though they in essence give empirical descriptions.

Linking teleological explanations with empirical descriptions may, moreover, indirectly or unwittingly help to sharpen the contrast between causality in history and causality in biological growth, or, by the same token, between *rational* causality and *natural* causality – a contrast that characteristics associated with natural causality are liable to blur. For these undoubtedly comprise such typifying features as self-regulation and self-direction, insofar as their activities involve development directed toward the future. Furthermore, they possess structures of their own which interact to maintain the organism as a whole. All this suggests a plausible analogy between functions and purposes and, by the same token, between teleology in organic processes in nature and teleology in purposive action in history. Unfortunately, both analogies are seriously misleading, especially as regards action in history and politics.[25] Although biological processes consist of functional-structural interactions, organisms do not choose what they do; they do what they do because they are what they are. Human actions differ from organic biological processes in that they involve choice and purpose *in addition* to functions and structures. Humans are not merely what it is *in them* to become, they are also what they *want* to become. And it is by virtue of the existence of chosen purposes that one seeks a level of meaning in human structures and human functions that one does not look for in the structures and functions of biological organisms.

It follows that purposive actions, as distinct from functional processes, presuppose an agent capable of understanding and choosing whatever goal is to be attained. And the goal in this case is not something that is latently there already, merely awaiting development. Rather, it is a *creation*, the outcome of active will-formation, involving not simply

25 Barnard, "Natural Growth and Purposive Development," 34–6.

functional ends, as in nature, but ends as purposive reasons that we consciously *mind* to bring about. And such ends are neither predetermined nor inevitable.

CONTEXTS AND MEANINGS

The pursuit of purposive reasons containing meaning in their own *telos* is not incompatible, however, I maintained, with the position that what gives meaning to purposive action is not wholly detachable from a matrix of common understandings. What we do as drivers, cooks, physicians, teachers, or soldiers is done within recognized roles and rules; the roles we thus assume each entail specified rule-governed actions that form an essential part of the meaning we assign to what is done, or expect to be done. In an important sense, therefore, the "meaning" of a role lies in the tasks we ally with it; their being carried out is the essence of a role's rightful existence. Kant gives the example of an executor of a will, whose task is to do what he is directed to do by the will, whatever he may think about the wisdom of the legacy.[26] It is not the agents themselves, therefore, who decide what is to be done; it is the roles they assume; and the roles, in turn, are what they are in accordance with common understandings regarding their meaning. But while a role is thus fixed at any particular time, common understandings are not necessarily determined once and for all.

Acting within role- and rule-governed contexts is therefore not tantamount to the perpetuity of established norms or their permanent observance. Norms change because they rarely remain uncontested. Even when they are not openly challenged – or indeed challenged at all – norms may fail to be adhered to, and hence be profoundly at odds with actual practices.[27] Accordingly, we cannot simply *deduce* meaning from normative structures alone on the model of logical

26 Immanuel Kant, "On the Common Saying: 'This May be True in Theory, but it does not Apply in Practice'" (1784), in Hans Reiss, ed., *Kant's Political Writings* (Cambridge: Cambridge University Press, 1970, 1991), 70–1. Kant's intention is to demonstrate the futility of Utilitarian premises as a basis for moral duty – a view that has variously been challenged since, and, most recently by J.W. Bailey, *Utilitarianism, Institutions, and Justice* (New York: Oxford University Press, 1998). My concern here, however, is to demonstrate the derivation of a duty from an agreed ethos about the meaning of a given role.

27 The discrepancy between institutional norms and actual practices is illustrated in A. MacIntyre, *Against the Self-Images of the Age* (London: Duckworth, 1971), 255; see also 207–8, and 215–17.

inferences or empirical generalizations, and attribute to them determinate causal properties. If I am correct in this, the notion of pervasive patterns, structures, ideas, and beliefs, whether understood in terms of *Lebensformen* or expressions of *Zeitgeist* determining actual conduct and perceived meanings, should be treated with care, despite the fact that the contextual force of prevailing currents of thought is not called into question. Even if values and meanings undergo change, we may imperceptibly be affected by earlier ways of thinking and acting which are so deeply ingrained in our traditional texture of life that we are no longer distinctly aware of them. On the other hand, we may be strongly influenced by manners and ideas of our own time, although they represent views that are not necessarily widely diffused – causal indeterminacy once again.

Indeed, it is precisely the possibility of *diverse* generative sources of meaning which lends point to Max Weber's insistence that "subjective" meanings are indispensable aids to the recognition of occurrences as *actions.*[28] It is one thing, therefore, to recognize the significance of contexts and common practices in their bearing upon meanings *vis-à-vis* the causality of individual purposive reasons and subjectively cherished meanings. Yet it is quite a different thing to expect subjective purposes and meanings to be disclosed by simply studying "objective" (or impersonal) statistical surveys, contextual roles and rules, or forms of life. For, to do so may turn out to be as misguided as using wholly personal inclinations as sources to distinguish between *deeds* and *events* in history, or between *action* and *behaviour* in daily life.

In essence, this is to reiterate that there is no lack of contingency in uncovering bases of meaning, functionally or purposively, in the past or the present. My reference to practices, roles, and rules is principally intended, therefore, to call attention to the vast and manifold plurality of possible contexts and levels of understanding, in view of which interpreting, accounting for, or justifying human actions may involve an exceedingly complex and conceivably also more baffling understanding of human purposes than the idea of some overarching *Lebensform* might suggest. Indeed, the latter could easily *withdraw* attention from what in fact crucially confers meaning on actions by foreclosing the comprehension of a person's *intentions,* insofar as it might conflate a directional "because" (in terms of purposes) with a conditional "because" (situational antecedents, psychological states, and so on) in a manner comparable to

28 See Max Weber, *Gesammelte Aufsätze zur Wissenschaftslehre* (Tübingen: J.C.B. Mohr, 1922; 2nd ed., 1951), 93.

the assimilation of "reasons for" with "reasons from." In short, it could explain away meaning rather than illuminate it. Grasping the point of an action in terms of roles and rules or common understandings clearly is not all there is to capturing meaning.[29] For example, if we blandly assumed that Abraham's offer to sacrifice his only son, Isaac, was merely symptomatic of a common practice of child sacrifice, we would wholly fail to understand the point of the biblical story. For the significance of Abraham's offer manifestly lies in its *extraordinariness.*

By now it should be obvious that efforts to account for actions in history bring into play a considerable variety of explanatory approaches that have no analogue in inquiries into the non-human world. Reliance, let alone exclusive reliance, on antecedent contexts is liable to distract from, if not altogether cloud, whatever meaning human action had for its author. Conventional practices, likewise, such as doffing one's hat or kissing the hands of ladies in Vienna make perfectly good social sense, without carrying particular meaning as actions. Or, to revert to the biblical example, making sacrifices to God was indeed a common practice; yet this in no way diminishes the uncommon and highly personal sacrifice offered by Abraham. It is precisely *in contrast to* the conventional form of sacrifice that Abraham's offer stands out by its extraordinariness. Evidently, not all purposive behaviour that makes social sense or conforms to common practices constitutes purposive *action.*[30] All the same, this does not alter the validity of a point made earlier that reasons, given as grounds for actions, must contain some shared elements of meaning if they are to be intelligible as explanations or justifications. Otherwise "accounting for actions" would prove impossible. In other words, grounds given for an action must make sense to others, and not only to myself. Wholly private idiosyncracies, therefore, are no candidates for rational accounting.

HUMAN PURPOSES AND COSMIC FORCES

Perhaps I should state once more that a conception of purposive action, as advanced here, does not presuppose a theory of cosmic or divine

29 What I question is the notion that common usage is the only source of meaning, or that norms are unproblematically causal agents.

30 While it is true that *social* behaviour, to be meaningful, presupposes roles, rules, and a given setting linked to given traditions and practices, the reverse is not necessarily true; namely, that what is meaningful *must* be derivative from a particular social context.

purposes. The validity of "purpose" as an explanation or project of action is not contingent, that is, on the demonstrable existence of an overall cosmic design or providential order. Spinoza, by conceiving of purpose as a purely human category, helps to guard against the tendency to think of human goals as disguised "functions," as merely pseudo-purposes within a cosmic or divine scheme of things. Conversely, accepting a providential design still does not commit one to accepting the idea of "derivative" purposes, since the existence of a providential design by no means implies that humans therefore possess infallible or compelling purposive guides for action. Even if people did know what they ought to do in order to act in congruence with "Providence," "objective necessity," or the "laws of history," it does not follow that they would do so, that they would "mind" this knowledge. Therefore, to concede the possibility of an all-encompassing or supra-personal cosmic order does not necessarily involve the denial of human self-direction as the mainstay of human history. Faith in the existence of a cosmic or divine order presumably need not rule out that people wittingly or unwittingly act independently of, or altogether in opposition to, such an order.

Yet, while we may accept a "cosmic" theory of history without it impairing our belief in self-chosen ends, and, by the same token, go along with Kant's interpretation of it as a spur to self-enactment, we may nevertheless feel profoundly uneasy about its possible implications, as I indicated earlier. Here, however, I am chiefly concerned with two issues: the status of "minding" and the status of civic self-understandings. To the first issue I variously return in subsequent chapters, although my earlier references should make it evident that I do not exclude "reckoning with consequences" from its full connotation – that is to say, caring about outcomes – since, unlike Kant, I do not identify consequentialist thinking, *per se*, with "utilitarian" approaches in terms of calculating gains and losses.

On the second issue, I sense a risk of rampant discontinuity between cosmic and human agency, and its possible impact on people's self-identification as autonomous members of a particular political order. Kant was not unaware of the dangers of paternalism or despotism under conditions of civic passivity, but that these could result from the kind of discontinuity I am referring to, does not appear to have bothered him as, for example, it bothered both Tocqueville and Collingwood. Indeed, Collingwood found these dangers even more disquieting; for, although he fully shared Tocqueville's dread of a loss of identifiable and accountable agency in history and politics, as an upshot of which either might defy comprehension, he could not bring himself to agree with Tocqueville's proposals to view groups as analogues to individual agents as a possible remedy, since he doubted that intentions and purposes could be ascribed to them – despite the fact that Tocqueville made his proposals contingent on there being *multiple* units of acting entities.[31]

Another way out, though less comforting, would be to conceive of human history as the workings of unintended consequences, as the realm of myriad interactions, resembling vast market operations in which outcomes are "produced" that have little or nothing to do with what individual people intended, and in which, therefore, the locus of agency is obscured beyond recognition. Less comforting, because it is hard to see how, under conditions such as these, a theory of action-in-history on the lines of Collingwood's thinking could find *any* application. But if this alternative seems dismal, viewed from the perspective of Collingwood's thesis, it seems no less dismal viewed from any other angle from which one could try to discover the nature of purposive ends or the reasons that prompt people to pursue them. For, while there are undoubtedly processes and events which happen independently of human intentions, to envisage human history solely as the work of unintended outcomes might prove acutely deceptive and, in the final analysis, trivial.

A theory of history in terms of unintended consequences courts the danger of being deceptive, because to put so great an emphasis on everything being the result of impersonal forces could well blur historical vision to a degree that could blind it to the fact that the intentions of some people carry so much more weight than the intentions of others.[32]

31 Alexis de Tocqueville, *Democracy in America* ed. J.P. Mayer (New York: Doubleday, 1969), 189–95. Although sharing Tocqueville's fears, Collingwood was highly suspicious of "groups" serving as analogues for purposive agency by individuals (see also ch. 2, note 23). Too much, he felt, was at stake.

32 While we generally expect actions to be congruent with what is intended, they are not, admittedly, necessary entailments of intentions. And although failing to carry out one's intention may be thought morally reprehensible, unintentional neglect is commonly viewed as merely a mistake. (See, for example, G.E.M. Anscombe, *Intention* (Oxford: Clarendon Press, 1959.) Concerning the unequal incidence of intentionality, see Stuart Hampshire, *Justice in Conflict* (London: Duckworth, 1999). Heinich Heine, on the other hand, adamantly supported Herder's emphasis on purposive ideas as a historical force (*Drang*) of the highest order, and opted for intentionality in place of the "fatalism" of cyclical theories of history. For an evocative interpretation of Heine's (little known) philosophy of history, see Hanna Spencer, "Heine's 'Various Concepts of History,'" in J.M. Porter and Richard Vernon, eds., *Unity, Plurality and Politics: Essays in Honour of F.M. Barnard* (London: Croom Helm, 1986), 1–11.

And it would be ultimately trivial if not meaningless, since to speak of unintended consequences in this totalistic manner is to strain language and meaning to their utmost limits. For, when all history is perceived as devoid of intended ends, the real purport of "consequence" is lost – it ceases to be a causal category of any kind. If nothing is *meant*, history is indeed literally meaningless.

REASONS AND ACTION IN HISTORY: CONCLUDING THOUGHTS

Collingwood's philosophy of history, as that of Herder, was an attempt to mediate a link between action in daily life and action occurring in the realm of history. As in his conception of political action, the unique and the universal were to form a convergence comparable to an integral whole. The degree of conceptual fusion that either linkage calls for is no doubt daunting as well as controversial. However, any alternative that entails a total denial of the continuity between identifiable agency and purposive intentionality, or between the particular and the general, might defy the intelligibility of authentic action in history as much as in politics.

Clearly, a defiance of this extent could raise a spectre of humanity that not only flouts Collingwood's ideas of enacting purpose in history and enacting principle in politics but also renders any notion of "purpose" or "principle" itself almost absurdly arcane. By the same token, a revision of historical thinking that implied, the complete severing of happenings from identifiable doers would mean the total collapse of directional reasons into antecedent (conditional) reasons, and thereby remove any basis for their distinction. Under such circumstances, the quality of "action" that differentiates it from the workings of pistons or hormones would simply be eclipsed.

A postulate of *autonomous* human agency would then seem manifestly non-sustainable, both individually and collectively; likewise, self-enactment directed toward the advancement of the lot of humankind by way of social reforms would, in effect, be virtually inconceivable. Also, once this option were removed from the orbit of *choosable* alternatives and replaced by "inner purposes of history" or the "hidden plans of nature," *human* efforts, as far as I can judge, would become painfully problematic. And what makes such a substitution all the more startling is that its author is one of the foremost advocates of human autonomy, to wit, Kant himself.[33]

33 Kant, *Gesammelte Schriften*, ed. Prussian Academy of the Sciences (Berlin; 1902–), VIII, 22 (subsequently cited as *Works*).

I say "painfully problematic" because I feel that, on the face of it, the substitution involves a fateful situation in which those seeking remedies for their grievances could find solace only by way of an inordinate faith in Nature or Providence as the sole providers of a reign of justice and fairness. And I say "on the face of it," because in actual fact Kant intended "cosmic" teleology to *enhance* historical consciousness as a prodder to action. The idea of providential purpose in nature and history, therefore, far from encouraging passivity, was to serve as an inducement to actively seeking the enlargement of the humanly achievable. Moreover, the effectiveness of the stimulus was to be furthered additionally by another hidden force that Kant put forward, namely, the ongoing operation of "asocial sociability."[34]

It is most likely that his cosmic-teleological idea, no less than his philosophical anthropology, was an outgrowth of his critical reassessment of reason and his oft-disclosed lack of trust in *popular* enlightenment. These, together with his resigned acceptance of an endemic impasse in politics – due to deep-rooted human deficiencies – led him to the conclusion that if any reforms were to have the slightest'chance of success, they would have to be initiated from above.[35] Analogously, Kant had little faith in public expressions of self-enactment within society at large in the absence of promptings by supra-human or "cosmic" forces. Still, given such promptings, Kant was convinced that people would want to create for themselves a republican *Rechtsstaat*, because he felt that most people seek to pursue ends of their own in conformity with law – even though they might doubtfully do so for its own sake – because they would come to realize that, for the most part, it actually paid them to do so. Hence, however gloomily he viewed the prospects of human teleology in the absence of stipulated modes of cosmic teleology, he would have shrunk from replacing human striving with acquiescent passivity, or from portraying history as the realm of randomness in place of consciously purposive self-enactment.

Most probably, too, he would have done so on grounds very little different from those which induced Collingwood to posit purposive reasons as the dominant source of meaning in the world of action and human history. For Kant's scheme of historical causation essentially sought to combine cosmic and human teleology in a kind of symbiotic interdependence, designed to augment humanity's faith in the gradual empowerment of its own self-enactment.

34 I discuss this point in the chapter on Kant below.

35 To posit popular enlightenment as the condition of political reform amounted to putting the cart before the horse. (Kant, *Works*, VIII, 366–7.)

It is hard to deny the inner logic of Kant's projected teleological symbiosis, but it is no less difficult to free oneself entirely of the naggingly
troubling apprehensions intimated earlier. No doubt these arise, in the
final analysis, from a stubborn, yet deep-seated, resistance to combining
actual purposes *in* history with putative purposes *of* history, as though
human and cosmic teleology formed one and the same seamless whole.

2

Reasons in Politics:
Explanation and Commitment

WHILE DETERMINING THE CAUSALLY DECISIVE in any sequence of historical occurrences is nearly always a contentious issue, the vital point in this chapter is not so much the particular weighing of what could be looked upon as causally decisive, as what is to be made of reasons as credal or compelling grounds for action. Yet, even thus delimited, reasons, to have any significance in the realm of political activity, must, I shall argue, have causal *relevance*.

However, to have *any* relevance at all, giving reasons as explanations or justifications presupposes the asking of questions. In contrast to a traditionalism of acceptance without any questions being asked, the practice of raising questions as a characteristic *Lebensform*, or mode of discourse, invariably involves the reopening of issues. It is presumably in keeping with a tradition of questioning that the youngest child capable of posing questions is *expected* to ask questions during the Passover meal, so that reasons for Israel's exodus from Egypt can be given. Much the same, perhaps, could be said of Plato's *Dialogues*, for whatever can be learned from the answers derives its point from the kind of questions that are raised. Or, again, Rousseau, who requires in the *Social Contract* that the general will be routinely questioned to ensure its genuine presence in whatever the citizenry is deliberating or deciding upon. That there may be an element of ritualism in such practices does nothing, I feel, to make them any the less relevant to the causality of core beliefs or credal commitments.

As a rule, the less familiar the causality of things seems to us, when we reflect upon them, the more eagerly we wish to enquire into their origins, into the particular causal reasons that have given rise to them. Perhaps that is why the foundational importance of *arche* (in its Aristotelian understanding) is considered so vital in the assessment of a state's legitimate existence, if not indeed as the very hallmark of a political community, *per se.*

The possibility of reasons doing their job in this direction presumes, however, that the relation between reasons and the actions they are meant to illuminate is other than purely accidental; in other words, that reasons are *constitutive* of whatever has been said or done. I shall maintain, accordingly, that unless reasons perform a mediating role in this structural-conceptual sense, they are unlikely to provide a credible source in accounting for actions, let alone in justifying commitments to actions. Their persuasive, explanatory, and justifying propensity hinges, therefore, on their presumed immanence within actions. This immanence is, as it were, the core of their causal validity.

REASONS, SELF-DIRECTION, AND DEMOCRACY

Giving reasons in politics is generally associated in our day with the norms and practices of democracies in which public accountability constitutes a defining quality. But that the practice of giving reasons exists at all implies. I have suggested, the context of a culture in which reasons are sought for what is said and done. Conversely, this usually implies that actions are held to occur for particular reasons, in terms of which they can be explored and potentially justified. And we have seen that these understandings are not infrequently linked with the assumed capacity for rational self-direction. Politically, democracy is often presented as the recognition of this capacity, as well as the optimum instrument for its public expression and further development. Are these linkages, however, well-founded? Surely, *having* reasons is not tantamount to having *valid* reasons, anymore than acting upon one's own reasons is to act rationally.

The close linking of autonomous self-direction with the capacity for acting on and being moved by reasons – and, in turn, the joining of either or both with political democracy – is not, therefore, beyond dispute. Acting on reasons is not a sufficient warrant for autonomous action; nor is the giving of reasons by governments sufficient evidence for the existence of democratic regimes. Ever since the European Enlightenment – whose legacy these linkages for the most part are – doubt has supplanted faith. Even those who have not questioned the underlying assumption that humanity has come or is coming of age have been far from certain about the implications of that assumption, notably its political implications. Rousseau's attempt to demonstrate a necessary (moral) identity between individuals attaining personal autonomy as humans and political autonomy as citizens-in-assembly has undoubtedly been a most ingenious endeavour, although he made no secret of his own doubts about the chances of this fusion.[1]

Kant, one of Rousseau's greatest admirers, could likewise not conceal his lack of confidence. In his essay "What is Enlightenment?" he openly admits that *Mündigkeit* – the reaching of adulthood and, with it, the capacity to speak for oneself – does not necessarily signal the end of social and political tutelage. Far too large a proportion of humans, he observes, sadly lack the resolve and courage to make *public* use of their *Mündigkeit*, which "makes it all too easy for others to set themselves up as their guardians." Hence even a revolution, although it may conceivably put an end to autocracy, does not necessarily bring about "a true reform in ways of thinking," for new prejudices may come to serve "as a leash to control the great unthinking mass."[2] In other words, being able to speak for oneself does not necessarily imply being able to think for oneself, just as it does not carry with it the desire to make civic use of it.

Accordingly, tutelage and paternalism do not disappear with the collapse of autocracy; class societies do not cease with the end of hereditary privilege, nor do despotism and servitude necessarily vanish with the emergence of popular rule. Kant's fears in this direction are echoed in Tocqueville's worries about democracy. The fact that democracy provides "some of the external forms of freedom" does not mean that the danger of manipulative tutelage has passed. The opposite may indeed be closer to the truth. For, while people under the despotic regime of an emperor would generally be aware of their servitude, they would not necessarily notice the far milder form of paternalism in a democracy. And even if they did, they probably would not mind their will being constantly "softened, bent, and guided." Although not tormenting them, democratic tutelage could nevertheless degrade humans just as much, if not more so.[3]

The causal links, then, among acting, the giving of reasons, autonomy, democracy, and the demise of paternalism would appear to be

1 Jean-Jacques Rousseau, *Social Contract*, bk. II, ch. 7. (*Oeuvres Complètes*, ed. Pléiade, Paris, 1959–69), III, 381–4.

2 Immanuel Kant, "An Answer to the Question: 'What is Enlightenment?'" in Hans Reiss, ed., *Kant's Political Writings* (London: Cambridge University Press, 1970), 54–5.

3 Alexis de Tocqueville, *Democracy in America*, ed. J.P. Mayer (New York: Doubleday, 1969), vol. 2, IV, ch. 6, 691–3.

less direct – or a good deal more tenuous – than champions of democracy liked to deduce from Enlightenment principles. But, whether or not their belief in humanity's power of, or desire for, self-direction was misplaced, the root idea that inspired their belief, the idea that humans, in acting upon reasons, are capable of understanding reasons, is basic to the democratic practice of giving reasons. However, since acting usually occurs not in isolation from others but with or among others, reasons given, to be intelligible to others, require a certain commonality of meaning. What makes sense to me must make sense to others also. Political action, above all, involves the existence of others and consequently demands a shared context of meanings; what Kant called "ways of thinking," Tocqueville often referred to as "social mores," and Heidegger rather aptly expressed by the notion of "*Mitsein,*" the consciousness of sharing a world with others.[4] It is possible that cultures and traditions are what they are and have the identity they have, *because* of certain continuities in affinitive modes of thinking, speaking, feeling, and acting.

Undoubtedly, the status of "giving reasons" is not unaffected by the incidence of mendacity within a particular public culture, insofar as it both reflects and bears upon the quality of mutual trust and, thereby, upon mutual understanding. Yet the possibility that reasons are used to mask what is true or authentic does not rule out the possibility that reasons could truly account for what people do or aspire to. There is no ground for assuming that because people do not always tell the truth, the distinction between truth and falsehood is lost, or that all reasons are mere rationalizations. What appears more basic than the incidence of mendacity, I wish to suggest, is whether or not people view reasons as playing a mediating role in human agency. Clearly, if people felt that whatever reasons are given had nothing at all to do with the events they are meant to explain or justify, not necessarily or chiefly because reasons are used to mislead but because people cannot conceptualize any link between reasons and actions or, at best, only the most tenuous link, then, any accounting in terms of reasons would be rendered totally otiose. Under such circumstances, rationalizations as make-believe would be as pointless as reasons embodying authentic truth (as I remarked in chapter 1).

The burden of argument rests, therefore, on disclosing in what sense, if any, the immanence of reasons *in* action constitutes an integral re-

4 Martin Heidegger, *Vom Wesen des Grundes* (Halle, 1929), trans. Terrence Malick, *The Essence of Reasons,* bilingual ed. (Evanston, Illinois: Northwestern University Press, 1969), 100.

quirement for the possibility of their accounting *for* action. In the sections that follow I want to focus, accordingly, on two interrelated questions or conditions that bear decisively on the way we usually think of human action, that is, as a deed carrying meaning for its author. The first question has principally to do with the extent to which we are free to choose whatever we wish to bring about for reasons of our own; for it determines how far we can appropriate actions as our own and, in turn, can account for them. The second question concerns the credibility, and hence the acceptability, of the reasons we offer as having given us cause for acting. Directly or indirectly, answers in the light of these questions should also provide clues for viewing reasons *for* acting as commitments *to* acting.

BOUNDARIES OF SELF-DIRECTION

In attributing a deed to certain persons we not uncommonly wonder how free they were in bringing it about. And, when we think of freedom in this context, we generally do so in the way Hobbes did, by envisaging freedom as having "two faces," one glancing backward to antecedent causes, the other looking ahead to what is projected. We now tend to distinguish between these two faces of freedom in terms of negative and positive freedom which, I believe, is liable to confuse a half-truth with the whole truth. But, whether I am right in this or not, I prefer to follow Hobbes, for whom both faces are comparable to two sides of one and the same coin, or, to change metaphors, two dimensions of a single phenomenon. One tells us about the presence or absence of external impediments, the other about the extent of one's internal power of reason and judgment "to do what he would."[5] It is the second, or internal, dimension of freedom, the doing of what one would, that is the major concern of this section. Only if people at least some of the time wish to do "their own thing" is there a sense in conferring upon events the status of *action*.

Whether opportunities for acting in this sense exist is clearly a question inseparably connected with the context in which humans find themselves, for context provides the space of self-enactment, as it also structures in part its range and distinctive style. Human agency, therefore, in requiring a context, is at once exposed to its positive and negative influences, to its promptings and its hazards. All the same, the

5 Thomas Hobbes, *Leviathan* (New York: Dutton, 1950), pt. I, ch. 14; see also part II, ch. 21, esp. 106, 177.

external conditions that promote or hinder our insertion into events do not in themselves constitute sufficient conditions for the occurrence of action, in that they leave wide open the question of our internal source of acting. Wherein lies this source? This question was, I believe, the pivotal consideration that Rousseau addressed in his political philosophy, Kant in his moral philosophy, and Herder in his philosophy of history – just to name three major thinkers of modernity – as it occupied Hobbes before them. Directly or indirectly, this issue bears upon three core ideas relevant to this discussion: (i) the idea that persons view themselves as agents who can say or do things for reasons of their own; (ii) the idea that they are capable of recognizing alternative ends or purposes between which to choose; and (iii) the idea that existential givens, though they delimit the range of human control or mastery, do not thereby render humans' understandings of themselves as autonomous agents invalid or largely fanciful. They are *core* ideas because in their operative absence we would be hard pressed to make sense of the demand for rational accounting.

Clearly, as a matter of common experience, people find it difficult, if not impossible, to "own up" if they cannot appropriate the reasons for which they do something as their own reasons. Under these circumstances, the only reasons they could give would have to refer to psychic or physical states of one sort or another *from* which they acted, as distinct from reasons *for* which they acted. In the former case what happened was not "minded," in the sense of contemplated, but the work of emotional stress, intoxication, or plain absent-mindedness. Not being consciously aware of any particular reason for acting in the direction of attaining certain ends or purposes, they are consequently unable to render account in purposive terms. The essential basis, therefore, for offering an explanation in these terms is the existence of reasons other than those referring to antecedent psychophysical states that "make us do" what we evidently manage to do. And what distinguishes these other reasons is their consciously purposive direction. So, unless we think of human agency as deeds routinely carried out under some "veil of ignorance," we cannot but postulate an element of intentionality that implies the notion of an end and of reassons for attaining it.

It is, I believe, this inner awareness of the what and the why of acting that prompted Rousseau and Kant to pursue further the idea of a "performative" freedom that centres on choice, seen as will combined with judgment to do what one would. Only they felt fit to add to this idea an expressly *moral* dimension: civil freedom, a liberty *sui generis* which, within relations in society, demands the self-imposition of a constraint ·

unknown in the state of nature. In so arguing, however, they added a notoriously troubling quality. I find it "troubling" because, as I indicated earlier, this addition tries to do too much by conflating the idea of freedom with an end whose causality is of value in its own right. I feel that by virtually identifying freedom with something else, they run the risk that Hobbes circumvented; namely, that of rendering freedom as such highly problematic. Clearly, freedom, essential though it is as the condition for acting morally, does not instruct us what we ought to do. I doubt, therefore, that loading freedom in this or any other manner adds force (let alone clarity) to Hobbes's intent to define a person's capacity to choose *in and for itself.*

Accordingly, inner awareness of the ability to choose one's own ends as an expression of freedom is one thing; and using one's freedom to do what one ought to do in the light of moral precepts quite another. And the latter, therefore, is neither an extension nor an entailment of the former. Rousseau, to be sure, did think of "moral freedom" in a special, and politically illuminating, way, but this hardly alters the fact that, as a concept, it is not the happiest of phrases. He was also enough of a realist, as was the older Kant, to recognize that freedom in civic society was not purely a matter of willing morally, however interpreted. Rather, it was a matter of coming to terms on an ongoing basis with a contextual self-location that includes the existence of others and, with it, the need for reciprocal constraints, which, to be duly taken cognizance of, potentially demand the backing of coercive law. In short, both realized that morality had to be supplemented by a context of legality.

In effect, therefore, with all their reservations about Hobbes's political philosophy (and its underlying assumptions), Rousseau and Kant had to acknowledge his insight that, while external conditions do not in themselves *determine* one's internal will to do what one ought – since contexts are not causes – they are nevertheless significant boundary lines of what one can or cannot do within society. Still, circumscribing human purposes (including moral ends), or embedding them within existential givens, does not make purposes causally derivative in the way an oak is derivative from an acorn. Nor is guidance comparable to the instructions of a manual. What I called *minding* earlier is therefore no more dispensable here than the weighing and evaluating of alternative choices.

What Hobbes made so emphatically clear – and Rousseau's "moral freedom" is liable to obscure – is that purposes are not chosen within a vacuum, and that realizing ends requires a *space* in which teleological reasons *can* operate, regardless of their moral content. The great merit of Hobbes's formulation of freedom lies, therefore, in calling attention to inherent limits. External conditions, though they are not purposive causalities, nevertheless bear upon the scope of human agency. Hence, perceiving oneself as a self-directed or autonomous agent, free to pursue ends of one's own, is not the same as *being* free in any absolute sense, in the absence of existential boundaries. Just as our self-understanding as rational agents does not logically entail the possession of *moral* knowledge, as Rawls seems to suggest,[6] so the ability to make choices of our own does not logically entail total independence or absolute mastery. That is why I earlier urged that it is only by keeping in mind the limits of what we *can* account for that we avoid the danger of taking on more than we can hope or expect to accomplish; that we escape the risk, that is, of personal or political irresponsibility, of uttering words or committing deeds that we can neither acknowledge nor honour in the private or the public realm, inside or outside politics. And I believe Hobbes's conception of the two faces of freedom helps us to recognize that *in* choosing there are limits *of* choosing.

Not all external conditions, admittedly, are constraints. We can, for example, hardly deny that language, though originally external to us, most profoundly helps us to be what we internally are and to express it in speech and thought. Either way, however, we do not cease considering ourselves to be autonomous agents because we act within given contexts, need guidance from others, or indeed depend on others to do for us what we cannot do by ourselves. All the same, there is a lingering tension in modernity between self-mastery and self-vulnerability which escaped neither Rousseau nor Kant.

Rousseau attributed this bipolar tension to the gulf between the growing wants of humans and their waning capacity to meet them; while Kant ascribed it to the astonishingly rapid advances of science which (as we noted earlier) he found to bring about a simultaneous increase and decline in humankind's consciousness of freedom.[7] In light of such observations, it looks as though even the most optimistic assessment of the positive dimension in Hobbes's two faces of freedom fails to support an

6 John Rawls, *A Theory of Justice* (Cambridge: Harvard University Press, 1971), 142–3, 144–50. Can "rationality" thus be stretched?

7 This is one of Rousseau's central themes in *Emile*; for a more detailed discussion of it, see F.M. Barnard, "Will and Political Rationality in Rousseau," in Jack Lively and Andrew Reeve, eds., *Modern Political Theory from Hobbes to Marx* (London and New York: Routledge, 1989), 129–48. Regarding Kant, see my "Self-Direction: Thomasius, Kant, and Herder," *Political Theory*, 11 (1983), 343–68, and ch. 7 below.

unconditional faith in human mastery. If, therefore, a sense of control over nature, here and there, does boost modernity's pride in itself, the underlying evidence for it may inadequately rest on sound footings. As Hans Blumenberg has argued, it may be closer to the manifestation of increasing self-assertion than to self-foundation.[8]

But, however we search for surer foundations, it soon emerges that verifying modernity's belief in human self-direction is an undertaking that differs markedly from the kind we normally associate with discovering factual-empirical sources. This is so, we found, because the causalities in question are *conceptual* causalities, demanding methods of *accreditation*. Notably, such methods involve the application of evaluative standards designed to uncover the combined conceptual workings of will, contemplation, and judgment within the human mind. Clearly, what makes accrediting methods necessary is the recognition that purposive reasons engaged in action simply do not do their job in the way a knife cuts bread. Rather, they disclose a mode of causality that, being highly mediated, is also highly complicated, and not least so because of its inherent contingency. The bee knows perfectly well how to build her first cell, while human action is, in its uncertainty, closer to fumbling in the dark, in spite of – or because of – its immanent processes of thinking and willing. And it is perhaps this "structural" difference that principally renders causality in the human realm so doubtful an analogue of causality elsewhere.

RATIONAL CAUSALITY IN POLITICS

Coupled with the causal difference in the working of purposive reasons, there is a no less problematic source of difficulty in their cognitive "rationality." I touched on this issue earlier, and sadly admitted the trouble I have with defining whatever *substantive* meaning it so worryingly begs.[9] I have, however, little difficulty with agreeing that, in its political applicability, rationality commonly implies intentionality, that is, the operation of purposive thinking in a particular direction. I feel that in this role and context its cognitive status may be viewed in a more attenuated or

8 Hans Blumenberg, *The Legitimacy of the Modern Age*, trans. Robert Wallace (Cambridge: MIT Press, 1982).

9 A purely formal or analytically instrumental definition, clearly, is one thing; but to merge it (as Rawls appears to do – see note 6 above) with inherently persuasive definitions that stipulate all kinds of substantive characteristics is an entirely different matter, as I argued in the previous chapter.

delimited sense; to wit, as a *modality* only. "Having reasons," accordingly, is not tantamount, in this "thinner" version, to having good or valid reasons, let alone reasons that possess indisputable truth content. Yet, surely, "meaning less" is not the same as being "meaningless." Indeed, lacking indisputable truth content may be judged a political virtue, in that it renders political discourse rational without foreclosing its contestability. Admittedly, modal rationality must contain reasons that are inter-subjectively intelligible; it must therefore be distinguishable from purely personal whims, even though it commands a degree of objectivity that cannot make the kind of generally valid truth or knowledge claims that *substantive* rationality is purportedly able to make. It must, that is, minimally contain what makes public discourse *communicable*: it must make sense. And in politics it must also avoid appearing blatantly self-serving, at any rate within a democratically open society. Private whims will not suffice because, not being capable of rational justification, they are not open to rational contestation either. Being prone to the temptation of solipsism, they not only fail to serve as a recognizable basis for yielding credible accounting but they also, and more seriously still, court the risk of making people lose sight of the fact that a political order is a *public* order.

To be sure, in owning up by giving modal reasons, we do not of necessity justify what we have said or done. We merely acknowledge authorship of word or deed; we stand up to be counted, but we do not place ourselves beyond challenge or censure. In contrast to substantive rationality, which definitionally implies indisputable validity, modal rationality gives no guarantee of intrinsic rightness or unchallengeable authenticity. Nonetheless, as I suggested, these defects may turn out to be merits in a discursive type of politics since, whatever positional claims may be made are open to the cut and thrust of public debate and its challenges. All the same, modal rationality in terms of "having reasons" calls for some further spelling out.

Two things above all need elaboration. One is that "having reasons" does not exclude the possibility that the reasons being offered are not the same as those which in fact caused an action to occur. Indeed, in an age and culture in which the giving of reasons is expected, the tendency to invent *post hoc* reasons may be widespread. However, unless rationalizations of this sort assume proportions that render reasons indistinguishable from brazen lies, we need not conclude that the giving of reasons is utterly pointless. Only when we are convinced that we are persistently fed with fibs do we start to discount what is said. We then also stop asking questions, being is no mood to listen to a string of untruths; dialogue simply becomes pre-empted.

Second, the fact of having reasons for acting does not carry with it any certainty of the actual occurrence of action, since "having reasons" does not imply a commitment to act. This is so because action-promoting reasons, as we noted, do not operate like mechanical causes. We are not compelled by some inner necessity to leave a political party once we have good reasons for doing so, having discovered the lying, the corruption, the brutality, and so on, of its leading functionaries. For, just as we may act blindly by not knowing what we ourselves are doing, we may turn a blind eye to what we know about others.[10] Possibly, we do not *mind* enough what we come to know; or, possibly, we are conscious of strong counter-reasons that prevent us from acting on what we know. We can never blandly assume, therefore, that our perceptions of reality, and the beliefs and reasoned judgment we form in the light of our perceptions, have direct causal power regarding our propensity to act. There is simply no inexorable causal continuity between reasoned judgments and practical decisions. Since decisions often involve choice, and choice often means deciding between conflicting reasons as precepts, such as between telling the truth and saving the lives of innocent people from arrest by an unjust power, acting on reasons may turn out to be a very complicated business which, because of its complexity, not infrequently involves procrastination if not total indecisiveness.

But, if having reasons for acting is not causal knowledge, does this mean that reasons have no causal power whatsoever? No doubt, if the possession of motivating reasons invariably failed to move people to act, we could not conclude otherwise. As it is, the position is considerably less straightforward. For, do we not, as the previous chapter indicated, find the same reasons (or the same knowledge) variously effective at different times or with different people? Yet, puzzling though the lack of rational causality, or its evident fickleness, may appear, no contradiction need necessarily be involved. Instead, we are forced to wonder whether a large part of the seeming perplexity should not be attributed to drawing too tight a connection between having reasons for acting, and acting upon them. Some philosophers go further by denying any causal connection, and therefore argue that it might be best to

10 In the previous chapter, I cited Paloczi-Horvath's account of his decision to take part in the Hungarian Revolution in order to demonstrate that the knowledge of the corruption in the Communist party and its use of terror did not itself move him to act for quite some time.

abandon the notion of rational causality altogether.[11] I am reluctant to accept this argument, since I cannot help feeling that people would not insist on speaking of this or that as a *reason* if they thought it had absolutely nothing cognate to do with causing things to happen; nor would they be asking for reasons if reasons never grounded their own decision to act.

It therefore seems to me less odd or abnormal, if not, indeed, closer to the truth, to recognize that just as reasons are no less rational for failing to be indisputable, so rational causality is no less real for failing to operate like mechanical causation. No doubt, there are dis-analogies. Thus, unlike mechanical causes, the same reasons do not invariably have the same effects, in view of which we are tempted to dismiss them as a causality, or to despair of their vexatious fitfulness. Conversely, mechanical causes, unlike directional reasons, cannot be viewed as good or bad, profound or shallow. On the other hand, there *are* obvious analogies. Humans strike bargains, commit crimes, go into politics for reasons, and so on. Surely, what makes an utterance a *reason*, is its explanatory or justificatory propensity, which it would sarcely have if people never acted upon reasons. All the same, to affirm the possibility of reasons' being viewed as causes is not to imply that rational causality is inextricably tied to the principle of so-called law-governing uniformities, since to find a reason being the necessary condition of an action is not the same as to claim that an action must inevitably occur or that it could not possibly have occurred under different conditions or for different reasons.

What the causality of acting on reasons *does* imply is intentionality, and this in turn implies that whatever is done is done on purpose; that is, for a reason that carries meaning for the actor. And this inherent meaning, we noted, cannot be disclosed as a causality in the way one uncovers psychophysical or sociological grounds for acting. For what these grounds would reveal would be of an altogether different order from what agents themselves see in what they do as self-acknowledged authors of an action. They could explain only what the agents could *not* rationally account for, what they *failed* to recognize as giving meaning to their grounds for acting. Such agents, though still blameable (as well as responsible) for what they evidently have brought about, could

11 See, for example, Kurth Baier in *The Moral Point of View* (Ithaca: Cornell University Press, 1958). Cf. Hume, (*Treatise of Human Nature*. 3, 1), who argued that "reason of itself is utterly impotent" to guide actions.

nonetheless hardly be expected to appropriate what they have done as their own actions, if they had not remotely contemplated them.[12]

What principally matters, therefore, is that reasons entailed in actions can be viewed as *intentions*, for agents to be expected to render a rational account. As such, reasons as entailments are not, however, antecedents in the customary sense; rather, whatever meaning they yield consists of *conceptual* properties within "minding" which behaviour as purposive action must possess. Whether reasons are "there" is, accordingly, a question not of physical fact but of reflective perception. At the same time, this conceptual form of comprehension is not devoid of factually critical components – a circumstance not without relevance to political discourse. Clearly, if reasons given in it are found to be factually unconnected with what has been said or done, they will simply be ignored and their causality will be empty of communicable meaning.

REASONS AS BELIEFS AND COMMITMENTS

By way of summing up the argument so far, four salient points seem worth recalling. First, I identified as "action" whatever people do when they act for reasons of their own choosing. Action is accordingly characterized by autonomous choice and its immanence of accountable reasons. Second, because of the internal merging of reasons and action, I spoke of a "rational structure" of action, by virtue of which it is explicable, discussable, and contestable. Third, I suggested modal rationality in preference to substantive rationality in reasoned *political* discourse, in that it is *inherently* challengeable. Admittedly while serving optimally as a medium in public debate, modal rationality is as different from intrinsic truth as it is from non-contradiction in logic. Finally, I referred to "rational causality" as that conceptual power possessed by directional reasons by means of which human purposes are articulated as well as mediated.

Although I stressed that reasons do not operate in the manner of mechanical causes, I by no means questioned their efficacy as intelligibly

12 "Reasons from" can perhaps at times be redescribed as "reasons for," as, for example, "acting out of gratitude" might be said to be no different from "acting to show gratitude"; I am not at all sure, however, that the two statements mean the same. There is a fairly voluminous literature on this sort of philosophizing. See, e.g., Alan R. White, ed., *The Philosophy of Action* (London: Oxford University Press, 1968), 167–71, or Glenn Langford, *Human Action* (New York: Doubleday, 1971), with an extensive bibliography, 107–34.

viable causes, regardless of their validity as truth or knowledge statements. I did doubt, however, the possibility that persistently fabricated
reasons could serve as politically employable reasons beyond that credibility threshold at which they cease to count as plausibly causal explanations or feasibly convincing justifications. And this applies equally, I
believe, to reasons as beliefs as to reasons as commitments, at any rate in
principle; in practice, admittedly, the degree to which it does may vary
with people and circumstances.

Supposing, however, that reasons *are* used to deceive and, in being accepted as true, generate false beliefs, does it follow that mistaking false
beliefs for true beliefs is a case of distorted consciousness that should be
viewed, as Hannah Arendt has done, as a form of self-deception, as "lying to oneself"?[13] To be sure, I may decline to abandon beliefs subsequently found to be false but, as I argue in the next chapter, I then
merely pretend to believe what I know to be incorrect. In that event,
though, I am not lying to myself, I am simply lying. If, conversely, I do
believe what is false, out of ignorance or inflexibility of thinking, I can
be said to be deceived, but not lying – to myself or anybody else. Lying
obviously is a deliberate move to deceive, but accepting as true what
happens to be untrue is manifestly nothing of the kind. There might, of
course be neurotic states of delusive thinking, but this does not alter the
fact that "lying to oneself" is a most problematic way of speaking.[14]
Being enveloped in fog or manipulated by fabricated smoke-screens is
undoubtedly going to blur my vision in the manner drugs change perceptions, so that whatever I see, think, or do then springs from distorted
sources of my consciousness. Acting from them, I certainly would be acting from what might be described as false consciousness. However,
"false consciousness" in the way Marx and Engels applied it to "ideology" (in *The German Ideology*) entails not merely cognitive characteristics, as forms of befuddlement, but also possibilities of being used as a
manipulative device. Perhaps it may not have served their polemical
designs to distinguish all that meticulously between delusions and deceptions, yet nothing but confusion ensues from conflating being
deceived with deceiving.

However, whether beliefs rest on delusions or deceptions, they do
not in themselves entail commitments to action. Thus, in spite of

13 Arendt, "Truth and Politics," *Between Past and Future*, 253–4.

14 The phrase raises problems not only of meaning regarding states of mind
but also of the identity and continuity of a person's self.

whatever action-compelling qualities are claimed for the possession of a revolutionary consciousness, there is nothing in the nature of beliefs as such (we found) that warrants an unbroken continuity between *holding* them and *acting* upon them, regardless of their ideological orientation. What is it, then, that helps to bridge the gap between having reasons and being moved into action, between, say, believing something to be unjust and translating this belief into a form of protest? What kind of rationality is capable of causing the leap from belief to commitment? Alternatively, what sort of soul-searching, metamorphosis of consciousness, or will does this transition involve? Or, again, is it simply a burst of personal courage or, conceivably, an act of sheer desperation, going *beyond* reasoning of any kind?

I doubt that there is a generally satisfactory answer to these questions. But I do wish to suggest that the switch is so bafflingly radical because it is not so much a change in degree as it is a change in kind. I used the term "metamorphosis" since I cannot see that the change can simply be equated with a sharpened form of recognition; we do not suddenly see what we have not seen before, in the way a biologist discovers new data under the microscope. And this may be so, because the change is not a strictly cognitive change at all. Hence, to find injustice *unbearably* abhorrent does not require us to gain additional knowledge; as I put it earlier, we do not have to know more, but know *differently*. Also, *how* we come to think and feel now is in its genesis strikingly unlike drawing logical inferences. Evidently, a sense of commitment cannot be *deduced*.

I must confess that I am unable to account for the transformation from belief to commitment in general terms. It could well be a matter of external moulding, if not manipulation; or it could, on the other hand, result from an inner conversion of experience – comparable to that of St Paul. But I very much doubt that the decisive source lies in a specific property of reasons themselves that qualifies them as either reasons *qua* beliefs or reasons *qua* commitments. Similarly, though regrettably, I hesitate to express an opinion as to whether the switch is more likely if people draw on authentic information instead of being the victims of misinformation, since it might be altogether independent of its causal origins. A sense of commitment, to be sure, seems inseparable from a sense of conviction; and to be genuinely convinced of a reason one presumably has to believe it to be true. Still, here again, the conviction itself, even if it rests on beliefs held to be true, tells us nothing about the actual truth content of its supporting reasons. In the final analysis, therefore, the metamorphosis from belief to commitment – from *having*

66 *From Historical to Revolutionary Consciousness*

reasons and *doing* something about them – may result from an act of personal discovery that is as mysterious in its coming about as it is in its potentially heroic, redemptive, or destructive outcome.

But whatever it is, precisely, that is capable of effecting the changeover from one to the other, it would be rash to suggest that it depends solely or chiefly on the intensity of our convictions. And this, I think, holds true of moral as well as political beliefs regarding their causal efficacy in spawning commitments to action. If I may, perhaps rather improperly, borrow here from theology, *faith* may not be enough; whatever merit deeply felt beliefs may have as personal convictions, they will produce scant ripples in the waters of political activity if they fail to produce recognizably practical achievements. But, if mere dedication to "faith" may be found wanting, total dedication to "works" could effectively render reasons as principles altogether inoperative in politics. Once again, a rather fine balancing act seems clearly called for, since a purely *ad hoc* pragmatism could easily signal the end to discursive politics of any kind, apart from creating a degree of cynicism that has been know to backfire.

I tentatively conclude, therefore, that, while reasons as purposive convictions are in themselves no warrant for active commitments, and though there may be a great variety of motivating grounds for the switch from one to the other, as well as diverse forms or senses of "commitment,"[15] any principled and publicly discursive form of politics could scarcely be sustained without them. The dominant sense in which I have been approaching the conversion from reasons as belief to reasons as commitments is closest to Hannah Arendt's portrayal of the American Revolution, which she speaks of as one of the rare moments in history when the power of words and the power of action coincide.[16] For, conceived in this sense, reasons as beliefs are ideally meant to possess a causality that not only can account for actions but also can beget their enactment.

THE UNITY OF THEORY AND PRACTICE

To state an aspiration, or possibly a requirement, is not, however, to provide a blueprint for its attainment. Similarly, to argue (as I have done) that actions demand that reasons be entailed in them is not the same as

15 I return to the variety of meanings of "commitment" in chapter 8. See also Raymond Geuss, *History and Illusion in Politics* (Cambridge: Cambridge University Press, 2001), 36–7.
16 See note 6, ch. 4, below.

to maintain that reasons and actions form a seamless whole in the manner of the unity of theory and practice. My speaking earlier of a rational structure of action should therefore not be construed to imply a necessary reversibility or symmetry between reasons and actions, so that, because actions entail reasons, reasons of necessity entail actions. Nor do I wish to suggest that actions in any fashion confirm or deny the validity of reasons, and thereby establish their substantive truth or falseness. I make this point rather emphatically in order to establish unequivocally that the position I take is wholly at variance with that form of cognitive realism which insists on the necessary coincidence between purposive commitments and purposive attainments as conclusive proof of the former's conceptual authenticity.

Even when "ideology" is viewed, along the lines of Kant's categories of thought (*Gedankenformen*) or Max Weber's pivotal perspectives (*Gesichtspunkte*), as a guide helping us to focus on things as well as prompting us to do something about them, there is no ground for expecting the kind of epistemic-practical unity implicit in the Marxian notion of "true social consciousness," which corroborates the claimed unity of theory and practice. Hardly any belief informing a purposive commitment has been known so far, in which creed, commitment, and action coalesce in such a direct causal continuity. And therefore, to credit any set of political beliefs with so total a fusion of cognition and reality is to come alarmingly close to making claims comparable to those in which Wittgenstein's observation that "the limits of my language mean the limits of my world" has been grossly overworked.[17] For rarely are we so completely captives of our language, our categories of thought, or our perspectives of vision as to be blinded to a reality that escapes the lenses of these constructs. Custodians of ideologies, who are determined to correct people's vision of reality, may therefore do worse than ask themselves whether they are not sooner liable to entrap themselves than those they address.

No doubt, reasons as political beliefs, in seeking to rally support for concerted action, potentially effect a type of unity between individual purposes and collective purposes, but this in itself still proves nothing about the theoretical status of such reasons. For, clearly, the "theory" involved is not somsething that "practice" validates in any sense analogous to the sense in which experimental testing associated with scientific procedures (such as they are) supports or negates a theory. Nor is theory

17 Ludwig Wittgenstein, *Tractatus Logico-Philosophicus*, trans. D.F. Pears and B.F. McGuinness (London: Routledge, 1961), 6.

evidently seen here as being valid *independently* of its practical use.[18] In the second place, whatever "unity" comes into being is highly ambiguous if it is meant to imply *both*: credibility as a belief, by virtue of its inner coherence, as well as the power to move people into action, by virtue of its external appeal. For, clearly, the two need *not* coincide.

Interestingly, not only Marx but Kant as well makes use of the unity postulate by variously employing a "scientifically" empirical or "philosophically" logical approach in his "Theory and Practice."[19] In either case, the ambiguity is more serious still in political action, because it may give rise to the illusory substitution of inexorable "determination" for what in truth is contingent "enactment." Likewise, the idea of "unity" may conceal the fact that vision does not entail implementation any more than credal agreement on generalities rules out fierce disagreement on specifics, in politics, at any rate.[20]

Thus, while individual and collective purposes may coincide in general terms or, at any rate, not be found doctrinally incompatible, discrepancies *can* emerge about their practical interpretation, causing their unity to evaporate. The burden of choice then lies between allegiance to a common cause in its basic generalities and wholly opting out – a decision not easily made. A further discrepant source may be a lack of shared standards regarding the *morality* of political means. History demonstrates that, once issues reach the implementational stage, some have serious reservations about means chosen that, in private life, they would consider highly unethical. Bedevilling though such an eventuality

18 It may be worth noting that "theory," in its original meaning, had a cognitive status of its own, independent of the uses to which it was put. Significantly, R.G. Collingwood made clear that the role of theory is not to solve problems but to remove or, at least, to uncover the misunderstandings that foreclose their solution. See his "Political Action," *Proceedings of the Aristotelian Society*, 29 (1929), 158.

19 In the third section of "Theory and Practice" Kant argues that a general acceptance of the thesis that progress is inherent in nature and history cannot but promote action directed toward the moral improvement of humanity. (*Works*, VIII, 308–9).

20 The scope for bridging differences is a central theme in Paul Hirst, *Associative Democracy: New Forms of Economic and Social Governance* (Amherst: University of Massachusetts Press, 1994) and in Ralph Grillo, *Pluralism and the Politics of Difference* (Oxford: Clarendon Press, 1998). See also Thomas Christino, *The Rule of the Many: Fundamental Issues in Democratic Theory* (Boulder, Colorado: Westview Press, 1996), 165–99.

is in its effect on the continuity between purposive vision and political enactment, it is not strictly relevant to the point under discussion.[21] For this point is not whether *moral* reasoning converges, but whether the parallelism between individual goals can be such as to ascribe to it the character of an integral *unity*.

The problem for the most part undoubtedly lies in the use of the concept of unity *per se*; for, even if we accept the possibility of individual goals' converging, such convergence would hardly demonstrate the alleged oneness of theory and practice, let alone serve as a yardstick for measuring the validity of its underlying reasoning. Thus, while I do not in the least question the possibility – or, indeed, the desirability – of individual ends' coalescing, such coalescence in itself tells us little or nothing about their conceptual foundations as a source that would establish the authenticity of a common genus. Rather, what it possibly *could* point to is a sort of dialogical coming together, comparable to what Hannah Arendt describes as representative thinking, by way of shared modes of transpersonal striving.

JOINT AGENCY
AND POLITICAL SELF-UNDERSTANDINGS:
CONCLUDING REMARKS

Supposing we grant the possibility of a structural analogy between individual and collective purposes; the question then arises as to how such a common genus of directional agency, if transferred to collective decision making, might affect political accounting – a question Tocqueville is best known to have seriously worried about. Were this the case, could any individuals be held severally responsible and accountable for collective decisions reached at the politically administrative level? More worryingly still, could it in the event of discrepancies at the implementational stage between originally shared purposes and subsequent policies cause citizens to lose every sense of continuity between public events and their own individual thinking and feeling?[22]

21 John Plamenatz interestingly observes that some of the vilest actions are not privately or selfishly motivated but done on public grounds of one sort or another. In *Democracy and Illusion* (London: Longman, 1973), 158–9. See also Thomas Nagel, "Ruthlessness in Public Life," in S. Hampshire, ed., *Public and Private Morals* (Cambridge: Cambridge University Press, 1978), 75–91; and Joseph Raz, *Ethics in the Public Domain* (Oxford: Clarendon Press, 1994), 102–9.

22 Tocqueville, *Democracy in America*, II, ch. 2.

Developments since Tocqueville raised these questions bear ample witness to his sagacity and the importance of his forebodings. I have no wish to belittle these developments, or the rise of organized deception attending them, together with the dissemination of slogans whose ellip- tic meanings are intended to serve a wide range of promotional designs, causing people to lose the capacity to form views of their own. But there is always a chance that over-steering can backfire, that slogans can be- come empty catch phrases or, like over-worked clichés, cease to convey the intended message; or, again, that they acquire meanings altogether different from what they literally say, as when "frank and honest discus- sions" means that no agreement has been reached, or when "heroically fighting troops" has unmistakably obituary connotations.

Also, I do not want to exclude the possibility of newly emerging forms of *self*-generated expressions of political thinking and participa- tory acting. With such trends in mind, I earlier suggested that levels of purposive striving be extended beyond a rather parsimonious confine- ment to exclusively individual goals, on the one hand, or highly gener- alized collective aims, on the other. But I do realize that any such departures from stereotypes would demand added channels of public discourse, a greater sense of civic inclusiveness, and new understand- ings of associative action in political life.[23] As things are, however,

23 I make an attempt in this direction in *Democratic Legitimacy: Plural Values and Political Power* (Montreal: McGill-Queen's University Press, 2001). See also Stephen Macedo, *Liberal Virtues* (Oxford: Clarendon Press, 1990) and William Galston, *Liberal Purposes* (Cambridge: Cambridge University Press, 1992). Collingwood echoes Tocqueville when he writes: "The centre of gravity of political life lies not in the group, but in the individual ... Political activity therefore proceeds not from outside inwards – from the group to the individual – but from inside outwards, from the individual to his fellows; it is the understanding what another's purpose is, and the making that purpose one's own." "Political Action," 169–70. For self-consciously liberal visions in this direction, see A. Margalit, *The Decent Society* (Cambridge: Harvard University press, 1996), and R. Geuss, *Morality, Culture, and History* (Cambridge: Cambridge University Press, 1999). Of further general interest in this connection is J. Raz, *The Morality of Freedom* (Oxford: Oxford University Press, 1986), F. Hayek, *The Constitution of Liberty* (Chicago: University of Chicago Press, 1960), which could be viewed as a classic by now, although social democrats (in the broadest sense) may prefer Rawls's philosophical exposition of political liberalism in Rawls, *Political Liberalism* (New York: Columbia University Press, 1993, 1996), and Will Kymlicka, *Liberalism, Community and Culture* (Oxford: Clarendon Press, 1989).

vastly more sophisticated devices now exist, not only for the fabrication of reasons but also for making them eminently more credible. For, coupled with these new manipulative techniques, there is a marked decline in cognitive sensitivity, helping to make spurious reasons every bit as effective as authentic reasons – at any rate, in the short run. Hence, instead of the emergence of greater openness and truthfulness, we may find more rationalizations taking the place of genuine reasons, and more skilful "damage control" taking the place of candid owning up.

Why, then, do we still uphold the idea of reasons' being inherent in actions as their defining quality, as well as the condition of meaningful accounting? The answer might well be that we do so because, once again, we are caught on the horns of a dilemma. For any alternative to the belief in an essentially rational structure of action would call for a total reversal of human experience, if not for the abandonment of judgment itself. Actions and reasons would no longer have anything in common and, thus rent apart, reasons would no longer be able to serve as *reasons* in a causally intelligible sense.

A prospect such as this would clearly demand modes and categories of thinking so different from the aspirations of modernity's Age of Enlightenment, that I frankly find them impossible to fathom. Discourse, if not rationality itself, would be emptied of whatever meaning it has come to have, and the notion of principled conduct, in which particularity joins with universality, would likewise prove vacuous. The unique and the universal, like word and deed, far from converging within the culmination of a shared purpose, would each follow an entirely separate path. Actions, then, would not only speak louder than words; they would speak an altogether different language.

For a discerning analysis of the extent to which liberalism depends upon pluralism, see Richard Vernon, "Moral Pluralism and the Liberal Mind," in J.M. Porter and Richard Vernon, eds., *Unity, Plurality and Politics* (London: Croom Helm, 1986), 143–61. For an alternative to both liberal and communitarian approaches, see Philip Pettit, *Republicanism: A Theory of Freedom and Government* (Oxford: Clarendon Press, 1997), esp. 180–205, and ch. 8.

3

Reasons, Ideology, and Politics

ONE WONDERS AT TIMES if modernity is overarticulate, and at other times one feels it suffers from a dearth of vocabulary to give expression to shades of perception. Not infrequently, moreover, words are confused with things, giving rise to the belief that every addition to the stock of language is tantamount to the birth of a new phenomenon. Even as sensitive a writer as Hannah Arendt, for instance, appears to have been taken in by the word "ideology." The word, it is true, is undeniably fairly recent, but it can hardly, in many of its stipulated connotations, be said to be "a very recent *phenomenon.*"[1] Surely, neither terror, nor the despotic regimes of a Stalin or Hitler – which provided the exemplars of her notion of "totalitarianism" as much as of her interpretation of "ideology" – can be viewed as new phenomena. There is perhaps more than a modicum of reductionism in such a conception of ideology as well as more than a hint of its heavily leaning on wholly pejorative uses of the word. And it is, I believe, this reductionist tendency which, in the main, compounds the task of disentangling implied meanings.

A NEW ANCHORAGE FOR IDEOLOGY?

Apart from mistaking a new word for a new phenomenon, there is the snare of confusing the word and the concept, on the one hand, and the concept and its multiple understandings, on the other. Here I am not concerned with tracing the origin of the word "ideology" itself – this has

---

1 Hannah Arendt, *The Origins of Totalitarianism* (Cleveland: World Publishing Company, 1958, 1966), 468.

been done often enough – but rather with the polarity of meanings it has acquired in its political career. Thus, at one end of the spectrum, ideology is identified with deception within warlike strife, while at the other it is seen as the key to one's view of the world and one's sense of sharing it with others.

Either way, what is involved is not simply a linguistic muddle, but rather a profound conceptual hiatus between bases of purposive meaning as well as functional relevance. Hence, as a concept, the anchorage of "ideology" is in question to an extent that calls for a radical overhaul of its cognitive status. I make no claim, however, that the following discussion at all adequately meets this need. Its aim is more limited; principally, it seeks to dispute the close linking of ideology with totalitarian regimes by pointing to an alternative interpretation. I am suggesting the possibility of associating ideology with forms of politics typified by principled argument – in the sense in which Collingwood identified the latter with genuinely *political* thinking – within contexts of *plural* voices. That is to say, I query approaches that dismiss ideology as empty rhetoric, if not as the device of spreading twilight meanings within one-party regimes, designed to pervert truth and blur the contours of reality.

In a real sense, therefore, this chapter picks up where the previous one left off, by returning to the question of whether political action can be viewed as structurally akin to individual action. And, since political action, especially within democracies, is not confined to deeds attributable to "great men" or hereditary notables, but is composed of multiple degrees of joint endeavour, the central issue appears to revolve around the possibility of individuals' acting in concert with others, and yet finding themselves able to appropriate collective reasons as coinciding with their own.

In an attempt to address this issue, I shall propose that whatever makes an analogy between individual goals and collective goals potentially tenable rests chiefly on two considerations, both of which received earlier mention. One is that, in principle, there is nothing in the nature of a human purpose that precludes it from serving as a ground for joint commitments. The other is that, given that agents in politics are identifiable agents, there is no reason why they could not be held to account for what they jointly bring about. This line of thinking in turn presumes that political actors do what they do for reasons which they are able and willing to appropriate as their own; so that, within the limitations of time and place, they are playwrights as well as players.

The extent to which collective purposes can ever be made to wholly coincide with individual purposes is, admittedly, not solely a matter of writing the right plot or finding the right players. But insofar as joint purposes and collective problems are amenable to conceptual and organizational processes that are not simply bureaucratically imposed but are associatively generated, the mediation of shared understandings, whereby people could act jointly and yet be severally accountable for what is done, should not prove impossible.

Given these assumptions, I want to put forward the mediation of political ideology (as interpreted here) as being instrumental in effecting the marriage of individual and collective reasons for action. The point to note, however, is the proviso that a group not see itself as something distinct from shared understandings but as *constitutive* of them. In other words, associative groups are what they are *because* of their shared understandings; they *express* a common transpersonal view. Coupled with this proviso, I wish to claim that political ideologies should be capable of being seen as causal rather than as merely reductively caused. Notwithstanding, therefore, that ideologies might be said in some sense to "reflect" social structures, communal values, or economic interests, it is imperative for my argument that ideologies themselves be taken for causal agents in political development or political change of one kind or another. For example, rather than looking upon the spread of ideologies from the West as the *result* of the disruption of traditional societies, I contend that it is perfectly feasible to view ideologies as having themselves critically helped to generate the disruptive change.

Furthermore, although I do not deny that political ideologies borrow from broader philosophical *Weltanschauungen*, I am suggesting that it is not *Weltanschauungen* in themselves that give rise to ideologies but that ideologies, conceived as guides for and explanations of courses of political action, merely draw on broader belief systems as they serve their organizational and policy needs. For belief systems have an existence independent from the use to which they are applied, while ideologies come into their own as *political* principles and active causalities only within specific contexts of cultures, organization, and argument. They constitute, so to speak, the element of universality within the particularity of situations and actions.

Finally, since I regard political ideologies as capable of serving as causal agents in processes of policy implementation, I want to reiterate that I am using "cause" in a sense closer to its legal use – as giving grounds for acting – than to its use in mechanical causation or scientific language generally.

IDEOLOGICAL FUNCTIONALITY:
THE MARXIAN THESIS

Discussions not uncommonly concentrate on the instrumentality of ideology within a given political setting, on what ideology *does* to secure its "system maintenance," without unduly bothering (conceptually) with what it actually *is*. Indeed, it looks as though it is not worth trying to shed light on its cognitive status because there is none to shed light *on*. Being thought *inherently* vacuous as a moral concept and spurious as a rational concept, its moralizing and its rationalizing both have but a hollow ring. For many, therefore, political ideologies simply have no cognitive status; they are purely manipulative tools; and all they do, and are meant to do, is to pull wool over people's eyes.

That certain modes of speaking and acting serve as masking instruments has of course been known before Marx. Without going further back, we find the theme of corrupting perceptions and distorting consciousness in the works of Holbach and Helvetius, while the notion of alienation is prominent in the writings of Diderot, Rousseau, Herder, and Schiller, in which it is used in regard to strictures of modernity and intended to characterize the onset of social and cultural decadence. Said to have been brought about by changing economic and political institutions, massive alienation is alleged to have caused people to lose their sense of reality as they became prey to a degree of self-delusion that obscures the difference between what is and what merely appears to be. Marx was, however, the first of modern thinkers to speak of a total *separation* of consciousness from social existence. The doctrinal impetus seems to have been a play on the word *Bewusstsein*, which combines "consciousness" with "being." Delighting in semantic games, Marx pounced on the purported split between the word's constituent parts, claiming that consciousness and being had been rent asunder, causing consciousness to have lost its moorings; free-floating, it wholly contaminated whatever it came in contact with – morality, law, philosophy, the arts, and thought itself – begetting a superstructure bereft of infrastructure and creating the phantom of a politics devoid of inner life and social substance. As he put it in *On the Jewish Question*, "The political state, in relation to civil society is just as spiritual as is heaven in relation to earth." Its members are "imaginary members of an imaginary sovereignty, divested of real individuality and infused with an unreal universality."[2]

2 Karl Marx, "Bruno Bauer, Die Judenfrage," in T.B. Bottomore, ed. and trans., *Karl Marx: Early Writings* (New York: McGraw-Hill, 1964), 13–14.

Granted that there is more than a little plausibility in Marx's critique of the state viewed as the arbiter, if not the very embodiment, of justice, presenting it as a wholly fraudulent consecration of what in truth is a device for exploitive domination. Nevertheless, resting his theory of ideology as false consciousness on this critique is not beyond challenge, chiefly perhaps because of its sweeping use of the notion of "determination." Engels later sought to remedy this defect by way of causal interaction; while social existence remains a basic cause of social consciousness, it is now also influenced by it in turn. And he points to a number of Marx's writings, notably his *Theses on Feuerbach*, to make his case that Marx indeed stresses the interplay between existence and consciousness. All the same, there is a studied ambiguity on the issue of false consciousness *before* capitalism and the extensive division of labour, as to whether "false consciousness" already then pervaded religion, art, science, philosophy, or law. Although rather reticent on this issue, Marx makes clear that the owners of the means of production are no less affected by false consciousness than the non-owners – the bourgeoisie no less than the proletariat. Yet the proletariat, in its struggle for liberation from the alienation of the work process, is to gain glimpses of true reality, whereas the bourgeoisie has a vested interest in preserving a spurious reality as a smoke-screen, so as to make non-owners believe that they share a common concern with the owners, their employers. Thus, they strive to salvage their privileged position, together with a legal superstructure that ensures their continued right to productive ownership.

Marx prophesied that the eventual victory of the proletariat over the bourgeoisie would herald the end of the state and of ideological (that is, deceptive) politics, since he regarded both as the corollary of class societies. In coming to power, the proletariat, the last historical class, would abolish itself as a class and usher in the classless society, a society no longer ruled by any one class, and hence in no further need of a state or an ideology. Many commentators have argued that Marx was totally wrong in this prophecy; for, they object, have Communist societies not maintained class rule and the state apparatus, and did they not resuscitate ideology as their *official* doctrine? These commentators are right, of course, in pointing to discrepancies between what was said before the establishment of a Communist state and what happened subsequently, although a good deal may have been the work of events overtaking intentions, possibly as a result of the operation of the "cunning of reason." Be that as it may, "ideology" ceased to be synonymous with class terror, and "statehood" with class oppression.

Ultimately, however, it is less significant whether Marx was right in predicting one thing or the other; what matters more is whether his class analysis and his notion of false consciousness at all corresponded to historical and conceptual realities. For, once his concept of statehood is questioned and redefined as a locus of laws, rights, and freedoms, ideology assumes a different complexion as well, together with the meaning of political *party*. In what follows, by way of reinterpreting "ideology," I therefore suggest an alternative to Marx's theoretical scheme.

IDEOLOGICAL FUNCTIONALITY:
AN ALTERNATIVE THESIS

The conception of political ideology that I wish to put forward owes more to David Hume and Alexis de Tocqueville than to Marx. Of course, Hume did not use the word "ideology," but he was the first of modern thinkers, as far as I can tell, to speak of philosophical ideas as possible *tools* in the service of political parties. To quote his own words, taken from his essay "Of the Original Contract": "As no party, in the present age, can well support itself without a philosophical or speculative system of principles annexed to its political or practical one, we accordingly find that each of the factions into which this nation is divided has reared a fabric of the former kind in order to protect and cover that scheme of actions which it pursues."[3]

Unlike Marx, Hume did not suggest that parties and their respective philosophies were locked in irreconcilable struggles that could be resolved only by the total victory of one and the total defeat of all the others. The notion of an official party doctrine that brooked no rival, by using government-sanctioned terror to this end, was equally repugnant to Hume's thinking. In this regard, he wholly shared the sentiments of his contemporary and fellow-Scot, Adam Ferguson: "If, in matters of controversy, the sense of any one individual or party is invariably pursued, the cause of freedom is already betrayed."[4] If, therefore, politics by definition is viewed as "a matter of controversy," no party can claim a monopoly on the truth for its ideological or philosophical principles.

In this blending of philosophy and politics by making use of general principles in the pursuit of party ends, the intention may well be to

3 *Political Discourses*, 1752; in *David Hume's Political Essays*, ed. Charles W. Hendel (New York: Liberal Arts Press, 1953), 43.

4 Adam Ferguson, *An Essay on the History of Civil Society* (1767), Part VI, Sect. 5.

protect partisan interests, as Hume observes. But this surely does not mean that "covering principles" are nothing but crafty rationalizations; nor does Hume mean to imply that it in fact does. What he does affirm, however, and most remarkably so, is that "in the present age" the legitimation and grounding of claims in politics require methods of authentication that emphatically differ from those based on tradition or command. The "fabric" that a political party must rear to support its scheme of actions demands forms of *rational* authentication; that is, reasoned arguments, and not simply precepts hallowed by time, or decrees backed by force.

Tocqueville, who is closest to Hume in promoting this kind of interlacing between philosophy and politics, entirely agrees that philosophical ideas that embody core values could serve political purposes, even to the point of being abused as rationalizations of "petty and transitory ambitions and interests."[5] But he too refuses to *identify* philosophical principles, when applied to political action, with self-serving goals or the sheer trimming of sails. He refuses, not only because this identification debases the status of politics, but also, if not chiefly, because it fails to correspond to experienced reality. Principled argument, he insists, does have efficacy in political discourse, even when it does little to convince opponents; for, at a minimum, it makes reasoned discourse in politics *possible*. The alternative to principled argument, on the other hand, may mean the demise of politics as *communication*. For Tocqueville, cultures and periods in which principles carry no weight accordingly coincide with cultures and periods that are utterly "barbarian."[6] But, although a politics of sheer practice approximates for him to a politics of mindless doing, principled arguments in politics must nonetheless be distinguished from philosophical theories; at best they are "metaphysical conversions" of these, while frequently they are just "general ideas," or abridged "conceptions," saving citizens from "wasting time considering particular cases."[7]

5 Alexis de Tocqueville, Letter to Beaumont (22 April 1838), *Oeuvres et correspondence inédites*, II, 83–4, cited in Jack Lively, *The Social and Political Thought of Alexis de Tocqueville* (Oxford: Clarendon Press, 1962), 58.

6 Tocqueville, *Discours prononcé à la séance publique annuelle* (3 April 1852) *de l'Académie des Sciences Morales et Politiques, Oeuvres* (B) IX, 123, cited in Lively, *Social and Political Thought of Alexis de Tocqueville*, 61.

7 Tocqueville, Letter to Corcelle (16 October 1855), *Oeuvres et correspondance*, II, 301, cited in Lively, *Social and Political Thought of Alexis de Tocqueville*, 59; see also his *Democracy in America*, 442.

Thus viewed, an ideological politics could be described as a *style* of public communication that puts a premium on adducing *reasons*, which derive their general explanatory and justificatory force from broadly philosophical arguments. And whether they are meant to protect or conceal vested interests, such reasons have to formulate their purposive intent in the mould of *propositions*, for only in this mould are they inherently discussable and, thereby, at all employable in an ideological style of politics that is *contestable*. Four sets of comments may help to clarify this point.

IDEOLOGY, PRAGMATISM, AND COMMITMENT

First, then, an ideological politics, thus understood, involves making public utterances; whatever is being argued is argued in public. In this sense, politics is no different in its form of expression from a public lecture, a book, or a newscast. But while not every book, lecture, or newscast is bent on persuading people, on rallying support by striking a popular chord, every public utterance of ideological politics is designed to achieve action-promoting attitudes toward given objectives. Its effective dissemination, therefore, aims not only at conveying a message but also at evoking a response; accordingly, it has to relate to people in particular situations, helping them to make manifest what may or may not be latent. In practice, no doubt, responses could be newly aroused instead of merely awakened, involving a radical shift of public thinking. But in either case there is a measure of interplay at work in the framing and expounding of this form of politics, which, of necessity, must take into account the audience aimed at, in particular the difference between committed supporters and uncommitted, and, thus, merely potential supporters.

It follows that, while ideologically based political utterances are public pronouncements, they are not scientific propositions; and, while derived from philosophical arguments, they are not philosophical theories. For both scientific and philosophic claims depend for their soundness on intrinsically self-sustaining criteria such as substantive consistency and independent verifiability. Popularity in no way elevates the status of scientific discovery or philosophic scholarship. While a degree of consistency is required for any form of reasoned discourse, internal coherence is not the sole, or necessarily the decisive, criterion of what is or is not a viable style of ideological politics. Its substantive content will, in other words, not be wholly detachable from extrinsic appeal, from its capacity to generate certain results. An ideology's external "appeal" component, therefore, inevitably influences its internal "logic" component; and, in view of this, "coherence" could be said to refer as much to extrinsic relevance as to intrinsic meaning.

This said, a caveat is nevertheless in order. The emphasis on extrinsic appeal must not be carried so far as to suggest infinite possibilities of adaptability or flexibility. There are clearly limits to the degree to which an ideology can depart from its founding principles without losing its identity and whatever internal coherence it needs so as not to endanger the loyalty of existing adherents. Parties of all shades of the political spectrum that involve ideological principles have had to learn this to their costs. Emphasis on the appeal component, therefore, cannot be carried to excess; flexibility in an ideological style of politics is bounded in a way an *ad hoc* style of "pragmatic" politics is not. However opportune ideological revisions may appear to party functionaries, they must not cause core meanings to change to an extent that threatens the balance (or difference) between a principled and a non-principled style of politics or proves counter-productive to the preservation of a measure of party unity. Although ideological principles, to be politically viable, demand "refraction" from strictly philosophical principles, they cannot go so far as to yield *infinite* adaptability.

The second, though related, point refers to the element of "commitment." It, too, presupposes that an ideological politics is conducted openly in and through public utterances. So conceived, every public assertion of ideological principle potentially constitutes a binding commitment, and does so in a two-way manner. For, on the one side, it encompasses party leaders and, on the other, it encompasses party followers. The constraint of publicly declared principles could therefore be as stringent upon party leaders as the commitment to adhere to them is binding on party followers. And, if so, such constraints clearly set boundaries to the range of elite accommodation, to the wheeling and dealing of party bosses. Unless, therefore, party members feel pledged to unconditional loyalty to a party leader, the latter can ill afford to turn a blind eye to principles he or she has publicly announced and has vouched to honour. Contrary to some views on ideological politics, there is accordingly no obvious warrant for believing that this style of politics induces leaders to be dictatorial, irresponsive, or irresponsible.[8]

---

8 In this connection an observation by Edmund Burke is not without interest: "Those who will lead, must also, in a considerable degree, follow" (*Reflections on the Revolution in France*, 47).

My third point is to question a widely held belief that ideological politics is "closed," whereas non-ideological politics, involving the give and take of pragmatic negotiation or bargaining, is "open." An ideological style of politics, viewed as principled discourse, is admittedly less flexible or manipulable than a non-ideological style; and, for this reason, non-ideological politics could be said to be more open, particularly at the elite level. On the other hand, the public complexion of discursive ideological claims confers upon the political process an openness that is conspicuously lacking in non-ideological forms of elite accommodation, since it would prove dysfunctional to its mode of negotiation. Which of these two styles is more "political" may perhaps be an arguable question; surely, however, one could scarcely maintain that a non-ideological politics is inherently more compatible with *democracy*, at any rate with a democracy of plural voices, public debate, and political accountability.

Fourth, it could be argued that a pragmatic style of politics, not being constrained by doctrinal considerations, is better fitted to deal with factual reality and with what needs doing here and now. On the face of it, there is plausibility in this argument. On closer examination, however, it is in truth beset with serious flaws, and is so for chiefly two (closely interrelated) reasons. One is that, however factual a given reality may seem, it is almost invariably projected into the future and is therefore faced with uncertainty. The other reason is that "factuality" itself is rarely, if ever, self-explanatory in politics and hence is open to different interpretations or assessments, neither of which render public discussion superfluous.

I shall comment further on the association of "factuality" with veracity in the next section. Here I confine my remaining remarks to the idea of pragmatic political realism as such.

Undoubtedly, if ideological politics is identified with unchallengeable doctrinal fundamentalism, any discursiveness is virtually unthinkable. It is no accident, therefore, that both Hume and Tocqueville envisioned principled discourse as politically viable only if it was publicly contestable. Conversely, this means that no political system can claim to be a system open to discursive challenge unless it rests whatever policies it seeks to put forward on principles, however weakly they are upheld, or however abridged they may be in substantive content. A political system that makes a virtue out of having *no* principles at all therefore not only raises serious problems of self-validation for itself but also implicitly removes an essential basis for public debate.[9]

9 Giovanni Sartori, "Politics, Ideology, and Belief Systems," *American Political Science Review,* 63 (1969), 398–411, esp. 404–11.

This is not to deny, as I conceded earlier, that a pragmatic style of politics, unfettered by principles, has a marked rhetorical advantage. For it can claim in its favour that, since it does not rest on doctrinal assumptions or historical analogies as validating rationales, it is in a better position to cope with the uncertainties attending political processes. And pragmatists, presenting themselves thus as avowed enemies of "causes," conceptual "commitments," and "utopian" ideas, who make no excessive demands on the citizenry by indulging in fanciful vagaries that are out of touch with political reality, undoubtedly succeed generally in making sizable tactical advances. Especially in times of political crisis such a posture may prove highly opportune.

All the same, this brand of pragmatic rhetoric is not as well founded as its (somewhat tautological) plausibility might suggest. For, as a rule, modern governances, expressly pragmatic or not, are in the habit of using the promotional language of "innovation," "reform," or "change," as their sales pitch, and hence scarcely escape the risk of having to face the unanticipated. Consequently, they can never be certain not to create a gap between what they aspire to and what they can accomplish that simply resists being bridged by cognitive foresight. Evidently, policy making within any context of modern governance, being *inherently* chancy, is more akin to *giving cause*, to merely providing (contingent) guidelines, than to *directly causing* (certain) outcomes. In sum, *policies* that are ideologically or pragmatically offered cannot eschew the unexpected.

Provided, then, that political ideologies make no excessively peremptory claims – by pretending to be blueprints rather than purposive visions – the occasional occurrence of gaps between aspirations and achievements need cause less perplexity among their adherents and sympathizers than an overly self-assured pragmatic style among its supporters. Thus, as long as it is possible to avoid "blind consistency," that is, a doctrinal rigour that ignores the limits of the politically demandable, an ideological style could prove a lesser threat to the survival of a regime, in the event of implementational shortcomings.

Claims purporting that a pragmatic style confronts "reality on its own terms" (Arendt's phrase), may therefore turn out to be rather hollow once the phrase carries *prospective* meaning, and reality is no longer viewed from the perspective of a completed (historical) event.[10]

Pragmatists are no doubt right in saying that there are some indisputable facts. The invasion of Belgium by Germany (Arendt's example)

10 Arendt, *Crisis of the Republic* (New York: Harcourt, Brace, Jovanovich, 1968), 40.

could be held to illustrate such a factuality, able to stand on its own.[11] Yet, clearly, this factuality tells us only so much, leaving questions of reasons, circumstances, and meanings unanswered. It also yields little scope – as a past event – for weighing *purposive* visions within the prior political debate. In short, once "confronting reality" is viewed prospectively, it calls (I maintain) for a strategy altogether different from that of historical assessment, by involving the need to exercise reasoning in the choice between specific policy options, a reasoning that includes consideration of consequences in their wider repercussions. Democratic governments, especially, are not uncommonly held accountable for these consequences, whether or not they intended or could foresee them. And, if this is so, a discursive ideological style of politics might arguably induce governments to act more responsibly, notably if their manner of accounting critically affects their chances of survival. Would it, however, also ensure greater veracity? And, if not, can one at all speak of *ideological* rationality?

RATIONALITY, VERACITY, AND MEANING

To pose these questions is undoubtedly to raise fundamental issues, although veracity and rationality are concerns pertinent to *any* politics, pragmatic or ideological. And, in attempting to deal with them, I may as well confess from the start that, while I believe that an ideological style – in the sense discussed here – proves more rational because of its greater openness to contestability, I could not convincingly substantiate my added belief that it is also more truthful. And this is so chiefly in view of the difficulty of defining not only rationality but truth itself.

It might perhaps be of interest in this connection to adduce the Weberian distinction between value rationality and instrumental rationality, in order to see if it could shed added light on the validity of speaking of ideological rationality. At first blush it seems that whatever rationality an ideological style can disclose cannot qualify as value rationality in any substantive sense. Even as a formally rational body of propositions, it is not infrequently rejected as an essentially rhetorical device that dispenses with the most minimal truth content, if and when the latter clashes with ideologically held partisan claims. Others go further still and wholly question not only the truth content but *any* expression of rationality, by viewing ideology principally in terms of psychological drives

11 Arendt, *Between Past and Future* (New York: Viking Press, 1961), 227–64, esp. 239.

in the way Pareto refers to "residues." For them, ideologies are purely means of disguising the irrational as rational, in contrast not only with substantive (value) rationality but with any form of actual reasoning.

Although instrumental rationality seems less complex than substantive or value rationality, it is in truth not unproblematic either, in that it can properly be attributed only with the wisdom of hindsight, *ex post facto.* Only after the event can we know if the means chosen were the right means. On the other hand, it could be argued that, in view of the operation of unintended consequences, what counts is the instrumental rationality contained in the intentions themselves, that is, the reasoning underlying the choice of ends, and not the actual outcomes. Yet, besides the fact that intentions carry less weight in the assessment of political actions than in the assessment of moral actions, instrumental rationality in politics almost invariably involves elements of value rationality concerning the pursuit of ends as such. Given, therefore, that means and ends are rarely separable in politics, a case could be made for not overdrawing the contrast between value rationality and instrumental rationality, however much practitioners of *Realpolitik* are wont to stress consequentialist evaluations of political agency only.

All in all, it appears, accordingly, a moot point if much is to be gained in political coinage by applying the distinction between *Wert* and *Zweck* rationality on Weberian lines. Indeed, in the final analysis, some may wonder if anything truly meaningful is to be derived from using "rationality" in either sense as a decisive criterion of what is acceptably "ideological" in political claims. Not surprisingly, they ask whether we may not do just as well, or just as badly, without it. All the same, it is worth keeping in mind the alternatives which both Hume and Tocqueville so forcefully call to our attention. Ideological argument may lack impartiality or indisputable rationality, yet, being embedded in a matrix of general propositions, it does employ reasoned statements in place of sheer *ad hocism,* appeals to hallowed traditions, or the use of edicts backed by physical force. Clearly, one cannot easily undo traditional habits of thinking or argue with brute physical force. Any *discursive* politics, therefore, cannot sever ideology from rationality, however conceived precisely; especially "in the present age," as Hume points out, because reasoned argument is then expected, if not demanded. And, that the rationality at work is *disputable* can only help to enhance the challengeability of ideological discourse in a politics of *arguable* truth, in which "rationality," therefore, makes no *substantive* claims of the kind adduced in the previous chapter.

Still, this does raise the troubling issue of "truth" as such – a notion no less perplexing than that of rationality. Arendt's essay on truth and politics bears this recognition out most strikingly. Indeed, it touches depths of thought that in themselves provoke reflection, albeit not without a fair dose of puzzlement.[12]

Arendt approvingly quotes Hobbes's confrontation of two allegedly opposite faculties, the faculty of "solid reasoning" and the faculty of "powerful eloquence." Now, few would deny that eloquence and sound reasoning may make strange bed-fellows; but are they so incompatible that they could never share the same bed? Could sound reasoning never be eloquent, or eloquent reasoning sound? Eloquence is admittedly of greater political appeal than sound reasoning, but is this invariably so? Could not a political ideology *fail* to be effective precisely because it strikes people as too smooth or simply too good to be credibly true? Moreover, does "soundness" unequivocally stand for one and the same thing wherever it is applied? Is soundness in political judgment, for example, the same as soundness in mathematics, in grammar, or in civil service understandings? And why should "solitude" improve soundness and the quality of thinking in general, bringing it closer to epistemic truth than shared thinking by the "plurality" of numbers? We may readily agree that the sharing of opinion by numbers contributes to its credibility rather than its truth, since truth is perfectly capable of standing on its own, regardless of numbers. We may also grant, therefore, that credibility and truth are entirely different animals and that, of the two, credibility is of greater importance for the success of a political ideology. Why, however, should truth be *incompatible* with numbers, or indeed be *incommunicable* among the many, and inherently defy being shared? Surely, to say that the intrinsic quality of truth makes it independent of the many, is one thing, but to deduce from this that truth faces destruction in the company of the many is clearly quite another.[13]

Similarly, Arendt maintains – rather startlingly – that lying to others is a lesser threat to truth than lying to oneself.[14] First of all (as I mentioned earlier and further discuss below), "lying to oneself" – which Arendt identifies with self-deception – is a most problematic way of speaking, since in a case of *lying*, that is, the deliberate presentation of an untruth as a truth, whatever is held to be true is not lost, because the

12 F.M. Barnard, "Hannah Arendt on Politics and Truth," *Canadian Journal of Political and Social Theory*, 1 (1977), 29–57; and "Hannah Arendt in Retrospect," *Deutsche Vierteljahrsschrift für Literaturwissenschaft und Geistesgeschichte*, 69 (1995), 546–69. I return to this in chapter 8.

13 Arendt, *Between Past and Future*, 235–8.

14 Ibid., 254.

liar knows the truth he is wilfully distorting. Thus, if self-deception is indeed a form of lying, the truth, surely, cannot remain unknown to the lying self. But, no matter what precisely the phenomenon of self-deception is, it is not an instance of deliberately presenting an untruth as something truthful *to oneself.* Even on the assumption that self-deception is a variant of lying, there is little ground for thinking that it is more damaging to the survival of truth than lying to others. Clearly, as long as I know what is what, no lying to myself presents any real danger to truth. It is only if I am deceived because I do *not* know what is what, that I can rightly be said to be a victim of delusion. But, then, as I argued earlier, I can hardly be held to be untrue to myself; whatever the truth is may escape me, but this does not stop me from believing truly what I happen to believe.

Second, and perhaps more important, why should *meaning* itself be threatened by self-deception? I may have my facts wrong, but that does not render them meaningless. Nor can I see why it should be of such *political* significance, as Arendt claims. Who else is affected by what I think or fancy, as long as I keep such thoughts or fancies to myself? Even adherents of a delusive ideology, analogously to those who have their facts wrong, need not give cause for concern, unless they also profess total indifference to whether or not reality matters, or to the difference between falsehood and truth.[15] Quite conceivably, Arendt has in mind here citizens living in countries where the official ideology is backed by terror. Even they, however, may only pretend to believe what they in fact do not believe at all, for a variety of reasons, such as self-protection, lack of trust, or sheer opportunism. But, one way or another, it scarcely follows that a non-ideological or pragmatic politics would be less of a breeding ground for mendacity than principled forms of ideological discourse on Humean lines.

To be sure, a political ideology that has become synonymous with official lying fails to command credibility.[16] In that case, however, the ideology has ceased to be politically relevant, and it is really a matter of indifference whether its official exponents themselves keep believing in its truth. From the perspective of causal efficacy, the degree of credal conviction on the part of leading officials is simply neither here nor there.

Truth, of course, may at times be stranger than fiction and, for this reason, less credible than fiction. On the other hand, fiction, though

15 Ibid., 236.
16 Ibid., 251.

other than factual truth, is not necessarily bereft of expressions of meaning or authenticity – a point to which I return below. By the same token, unvarnished truth is often less palatable than embroidered truth, or the whole truth less politically sagacious than the half-truth; but neither the embroidered truth nor the half-truth necessarily lacks meaning. Surely, if that were the case, both would prove entirely counter-productive, and no less so than total lies, persistently employed, or even, possibly, total truths.

Moreover, and somewhat more problematically, truth may not only be less credible than fiction but it may also be in conflict with a politics of plurality, in that the identification of value claims with total and absolute truth could implicitly deny their contestability. In that case, in the event that truth claims could brook no rival, this could spell the doom of politics as the realm of public discursiveness and erode the possibility of thinking of political ends in plural terms – precisely what Hume, Ferguson, and Tocqueville feared. Any attempt to absolutize "truth" could therefore empty "democracy" from being the idea of plurality, choice, and debate, of an arena, that is, in which there is room for contending goals and meanings. No less worth reiterating, however, is the qualifier that, *contra* J.S. Mill, the sheer existence of plural goals and meanings need do nothing to enhance the discovery of truth. If this claimed rationale for political pluralism were valid, then, analogously, multiplying ideologies could not but aid the emergence of "the truth." Unfortunately, this pluralist thesis is sadly ill-founded. While pluralism is a well-grounded acknowledgment of the reality of multiple human values, it is no royal road to veracity. Augmenting ideologies may just as feasibly augment lies as it may promote the recovery of truth.

IDEOLOGICAL COMMITMENTS
AND PUBLIC CONSTRAINTS

Yet, even if it is granted that pluralism is not quite what it is made out to be, this does not justify its dismissal as "old hat," especially within the context of the argument put forward here in support of a pluralist conception of ideology. Clearly, an old hat, if signifying the upholding of pluralism, could turn out to be a good deal less restrictive than a brand-new strait-jacket parading as the "real truth." Pluralism may fail to uncover such a truth, but there is little to encourage the belief that a non-pluralist, non-ideological or "pragmatic" approach would be more likely to deliver it. For there is little in pragmatism as such, any more than in pluralism, that qualifies it for begetting the truth. Nevertheless, there is a widely held view that, whereas the ideologically committed is bound to feel constrained from shouting the truth from the rooftops, the pragmatist would feel free to let the chips fall where they may. Plausible though this view sounds, the following examples only partially tend to corroborate it.

The first example is that of Alfred Rosenberg. He, as the creator of "philosophical" Nazism, reportedly believed in the truth of the "Protocols of Zion," which detail the alleged strategy of a Jewish world conspiracy. After publishing his racist treatise, however Rosenberg, expressed doubts in private about the authenticity of the "Protocols," but decided against making his doubts public, for fear of harming the cause in which he believed and to which he felt totally committed.[17] As a result, Rosenberg moved from the category of truth-believer into the category of truth-suppressor. But, when he published a revised edition of his treatise and blatantly repeated what he now knew to be a concoction, Rosenberg moved into the category of the liar who wilfully fabricates untruths that he presents as truths.

The second example is that of Lenin who, during his exile in Switzerland, frequently described socialists as traitors and lackeys of capitalism. After giving a speech in Zürich, he was approached by one of his supporters by the name of Angelica Balabanowa. She asked why he accused fellow socialists, whom he knew to be persons of the highest integrity, of treachery. "In the struggle for power," Lenin replied, "all means are legitimate." Whereupon Balabanowa tartly enquired whether this included fraud and defamation of character. Lenin then assured her that he had no wish to imply that the men he attacked were as individuals dishonourable; all he wanted to express is the view that their political posture caused them to be traitors in the objective sense. When reminded that ordinary working people would not see the distinction he was making, Lenin merely shrugged.[18]

Believing himself to be acting in the service of a superior cause, Lenin, like Rosenberg, showed little scruple in his disregard for the truth. At the same time, he professed to uphold a truth – such as the existence of a classless humanity – which transcended conventional truth claims.

In such a situation, therefore, the relation between commitments seems more complicated than in the Rosenberg example, in which it is essentially a conflict between a particularist ethic, such as Aryan race

17 See Kurt Lüdecke, *I Knew Hitler* (London: The National Book Association, 1938), 433.

18 *Neue Zürcher Zeitung,* 16 October 1973.

purity, and a universalist ethic of truthfulness. For now the clash is within a hermeneutic hierarchy of two *universal* ethics: the ethic of "humanity" and the ethic of "truth."

The possibility of conflictual commitments to veracity arising out of diverging ethical principles within contexts of essentially pragmatic (and only obliquely political) thinking, is rather tellingly illustrated, I believe, by the example of Voltaire. Intimately associated with the emergence of the European Enlightenment, the last thing he wished for was *popular* enlightenment. "When the people meddle with argument," he felt, "everything is lost."[19] Eager enough to speak freely to his fellow intellectuals, he nonetheless saw no point in parading the truth. Thus, whatever he himself thought of the existence of God was one thing; but what he wanted the bulk of humanity to think was evidently quite another. God, or more precisely the belief in Him, was to him not so much a matter of truth as it was a matter of social necessity: "I want my lawyer, my tailor, and even my wife, to believe in God; for I imagine that I shall then not be robbed or hoodwinked as I would otherwise be. Therefore, if God did not in truth exist, He would need to be invented."[20]

Now, was Voltaire, who had no party-political axe to grind, hypo-critically deceitful or merely "pragmatically" circumspect in keeping the truth, as he saw it, to himself? For, although he was neither suppressing the truth nor distorting it, he nevertheless declined to reveal it to all and sundry, partly because it conflicted with his self-interest and partly because he feared for the consequences of publicly doing so. By no means a fanatic or an ideologue, he was perhaps of that breed of public figures who draw a sharp line between what is to be said in the open, when and to whom, and what is better left unsaid, but do so on grounds that rely on no recognizably doctrinal source. There may be something distinctly enigmatic about their self-location within humanity at large, but the driving force of their self-commitment as of their general line of thinking about their place and role within the public realm is squarely pragmatic.

19 Voltaire, Letter to Damilaville, 1 April 1766, cited in Harold J. Laski, *The Rise of European Liberalism* (London: Allen and Unwin, 1936), 215.

20 Voltaire, *Oeuvres*, XL, 134; see also *Dieu et les Hommes. Oeuvres*, XLVI, 102, cited in Laski, *Rise of European Liberalism*, 213–14. For an illuminating contrast between Voltaire and Rousseau on this point, see Judith N. Shklar, *Men and Citizens: A Study of Rousseau's Social Theory* (Cambridge: Cambridge University Press, 1969), 123–4.

AUTHENTICITY *SUI GENERIS*

It seems, then, that it does not require a recognizably ideological frame-work of thinking for truth to be clouded. At the same time, there is a form of truth, identifiable with authenticity, that may also be hidden, but which is there for all to discern who have the conceptual sensitivity or imagination called for. I have in mind truths within myths and anec-dotes, as well as, possibly, by extension, in political ideologies. Hannah Arendt comes close to such understandings of truth in her interpreta-tion of stories.[21]

Particularly since the Age of Reason, myths have been treated as wilful distortions intended to beguile the ignorant many for the benefit of the educated few. A notable exception to this attitude has been J.G. Herder, for whom myths contained profound truths that had long lived in the consciousness of mankind and given people a sense of order and pur-pose. Although he conceded that shamans, priests, and despots had made use of them, he emphasized that they were not invariably cheats, since they themselves believed in them as a species of reality which, if not true in a factual sense, nevertheless was not false or fabricated either.

Suffused though they frequently are with accretions, myths uncannily lay bare the inner spirit of times, cultures, and nations, their peaks and valleys, and their heights of pride and triumph, no less than their depths of sadness and humiliation.

Certain anecdotes, I would suggest, are made of similar stuff, however amusing they appear on the surface. Usually, like court jesters, they can get away with expressing things which, in any other form, could be told only at fearful risks. Two anecdotes, chosen from dark times of the not so distant past may illustrate this.

In the (then) Soviet Union, during the seventies, there was an open-line program on the radio. One listener wanted to know why the Rus-sians were still in Czechoslovakia even though the situation was reported to be "normal" again. Answer: "They are there because they are still searching for those who had called for their assistance." The second an-ecdote goes something like this: A new political prisoner has just arrived at a camp in Siberia. All the older inmates crowd around him for the lat-est news of the outside world. Is it true, they ask, that the Russians and

21 Arendt, *Between Past and Future*, 248, 262–3. In politics, some of the most important myths concern the emergence of states, citing heroic figures, real or imaginary, who are said to have laid the foundations of states' original coming into being.

the Americans are now friends? Yes, it is true, the new inmate confirms. And is it true that Nixon and Kissinger came to Moscow? Yes, this is correct, he replies. And that Brezhnev visited Nixon at San Clemente? Yes, yes. And, say, who lost the chess match between Fischer and Spassky? I lost, explains the newcomer.

Now, both anecdotes, though not strictly true as factual accounts, nevertheless yield, like myths, profoundly authentic glimpses of the truth of deeply distressing times. And, like myths, far from being overtaken by science or technology, they may well outlive, in their creative authenticity, the "post-modern" quantum leaps of either. At any rate, those searching for "authenticity" may do worse than take anecdotal stories of this genre seriously; they reveal truths that defy being uncovered in more direct ways, whether or not they make people laugh and cry at one and the same time.

A similar degree of authenticity could, I believe, be established, or queried, once political ideologies are exposed to open debate within pluralist modes of governance, provided positional claims are presented as propositions that contain general principles of justification, and are not exclusively or transparently only forms of special pleading. Perhaps this could be made clearer by underlining the distinction between the *formulation* of claims and their *motivation*. If, for example, the opposition is pressing the government to spend more money on armaments, it would have to mount a general argument in support of its demand by way of demonstrating urgent requirements with respect to the defence of the realm. Clearly, only such an argument lends itself to public debate regarding a country's defence needs; simply making added demands on the public purse in order to please a foreign power, because that power is an important market for goods in which the opposition party has a vital interest, would hardly qualify for authenticity as a *general* political claim, and simply would not wash, *politically*. The crux of authenticity here, therefore, is revealed by the formulation of ideological positions. Without comprising principles of intelligibly general validity, any party's claims, by not transcending self-serving goals, would (on this view) fail to make any mileage in political terms.

If, however, the possibility of combining positional claims with standards of general validity is dismissed as wholly unrealistic, because such claims would thereby risk being unduly watered down, then ideological contestation of the type I sought to portray seems virtually foreclosed. But could similar objections not also be raised against parties claiming *national* status? For, as long as parties are being launched as entities professing to be other than *segmental* lobbying groups, they surely are expected to combine general principles with partisan goals, in order to provide a recognizable basis for contest within a public forum of discursive politics. The only alternative would be forms of contention that *defy* debate. Positions could then be affirmed or rejected, but they could not be *argued*. Such an alternative, however, suspiciously resembles contexts in which, owing to the absolutist character of authorizing as well as wielding governmental power, no explanations or justifications are strictly necessary and, consequently, no mode of ideological persuasion or accounting either.

It follows that it is only a context that yields the opportunity for offering explanations and justifications of a principled kind in open debate that yields room for the mode of ideological contestation I am suggesting, as also for the emphasis I put on its expression, by way of the *formulation* of ideological claims. Clearly, in view of both features – the context as well as the mode of expression – the suggested reappraisal fundamentally departs from approaches to ideology that principally focus on ideologies' meeting primordial psychological (motivational) needs, such as those in connection with *Gemeinschaft* analyses, or those which concentrate on the extent to which ideologies reflect social mentalities, such as sociological analyses or, again, those which look upon ideologies as devices to conceal dominant self-serving interests, notably economic ones, as in Marxist analyses. In essence, what therefore specifically differentiates the suggested approach is its advocacy of a symbiotic-like inter-penetration between *quasi* universal principles and particular or "positional" purposes, by means of which a given political ideology communicates, as well as authenticates, its grounds for entering public space.[22]

22 Clifford Geertz, although foremost among those who seek to get away from the purely functional approach to ideology, at times misleadingly suggests that the real significance of ideologies lies in their functional role in periods of historical crisis, in bringing the issues involved to the surface of political consciousness. This is meant to account for the fact that ideologies find fertile ground in cultures or traditions undergoing severe breakdowns. See, for example, his "Ideology as a Cultural System", in David E. Apter, ed., *Ideology and Discontent* (New York: Free Press, 1964), 47–76. By contrast I am arguing that ideologies *themselves* are active (and originating) agents in this disruptive process. Similarly, on the more positive side, they can be as stringent upon leaders as upon followers, I suggested, in their bearing upon political commitments. In this respect, I feel, few political theorists have been as fascinated by the interplay between leading and following as Edmund Burke has been in his reflections

At heart, this approach is closely in line with the political thinking of Hume and Tocqueville, according to which a politics, lacking such conceptual structuring, is bound to prove operationally sterile as a *discursive* politics. This is not to deny, however, that, whatever conceptual-credal causality an ideology contains, may fail to make it an operable *political* belief system, unless it has the capacity to convert aspired ends into tangible outcomes. Precisely in view of their contingency as implementational devices, therefore – no less than in view of their discursive challengeability – ideologies have merely hypothetical validity, unlike the categorical validity of moral or logical theorems.

On the other hand, by not commanding categorical validity, principled claims, as presented in my argument, make possible the existence of *plural* rights of affirmation, together with plural choices. Indeed, by their *lack* of logical or moral self-evidence, they remarkably reverberate Hannah Arendt's emphasis on the absence of finality as the critical quality typifying the authenticity of political *action*. Similarly, by demonstrating, despite their failure to present indisputable truth claims, the indispensability of general principles, they echo Collingwood's thesis, in accordance with which unprincipled action disqualifies itself as *political* action.

PLURALIST DEMOCRACY AND POLITICAL IDEOLOGY: CONCLUDING THOUGHTS

On the assumption that political parties will continue to characterize mainstream democracies, ideological principles, as proposed, could offer a *modus operandi* for regimes in which plural voices are able to engage in open debate. For they yield an opportunity to express divergences to an extent that is virtually unthinkable in non-discursive

on the French Revolution (see note 8 above). As for motivational-sociological approaches and *Gemeinschaft* analyses, I still find Edward Shils's "Primordial, Personal, Sacred and Civil Ties," in *British Journal of Sociology*, 8 (1957), 130–45, one of the most elegant, instructive, yet succinct, expositions, relating empirical studies and reflective theories. Further, for an excellent account of the problem of cognitive distortion, first acutely recognized by Francis Bacon, see Hans Barth, *Wahrheit und Ideologie* (Zürich; Rentsch, 1961), 32–60. Willard A. Mullins explores most thoroughly and perceptively ideology, juxtaposed with other cultural or symbolic forms, in "On the Concept of Ideology in Political Science," APSR, 66 (1972), 498–510, and in J.M. Porter and Richard Vernon, eds., *Unity, Plurality and Politics* (London: Croom Helm, 1986), 12–37.

governances, which rest on the unquestioned acceptance of time-hallowed traditions or on the uncritical submission to absolutist commands of philosopher-kings, super-technocrats, or military rulers. And, although not designed or expected to *bridge* differences, but rather to *articulate* them, ideological principles could, through their public openness and their element of generality, more appropriately act as instruments in their *mediation* than, as under command structures, in their *elimination*.

On this interpretation, therefore, what qualifies an ideological style of politics as authentically discursive is not its capacity to stake irrefutable truth or knowledge claims, but merely its amenability to *argument*. Embodying a sort of marriage between philosophical precepts and practical policy, in the manner Hume and Tocqueville foreshadowed it, "ideology" combines general core values with particular political options. And it is this attempted fusion that, I argue, could be a binding link between ends that are individually cherished and ends that are jointly pursued as *political* goals.

It could no doubt be objected that a politics of plural options could be discursive without being ideologically positional. Only it is not easy to imagine how a party-structured democracy could be non-ideological in this manner. Admittedly, expressions of further democratization of society might involve the extension of participatory activities outside party-political channels, and for such activities new forms of associative principles could well be pressed into service. I am not at all sure, however, how they would differ from ideological principles of the kind envisaged, since they, too, would need to combine positional particularity with discursive universality, and persuasive appeal with performative causality, in the way any principles, to be politically viable, must contain reasons as beliefs that are potentially convertible into reasons as commitments.

But, whether I am right or not in believing that parties will go on being dominant channels for articulating pluralist-discursive purposes, they most probably will undergo significant change. For much has altered in terms of democratic perceptions and socio-economic stratification. While, hitherto, political contestation and party differentiation were mainly bound up with class rivalry (or loyalty) and group interests on essentially economic lines, new segmental entities may increasingly emerge that cluster around subjects which have no, or little, resemblance to the cleavages that originally prompted the rise of political parties.

Changes of this order can be expected to enhance the recognition of previously ignored or marginalized concerns, if not, indeed, to give birth to new understandings of democracy altogether.[23] But, regardless of whether an ideological style of politics would drastically alter people's vision of political reality or their sense of civic belonging, it might succeed in minimally establishing that the quality and stability of a democratic ethos was *not* necessarily a matter of the number and distribution of automobiles, refrigerators, or computers. Also, by focusing on issues rather than personalities, it could assist to de-emphasize the role of money or the paramountcy of advertising party functionaries; and, if so, an ideological politics might *extend* the range and character of principled debate rather than *displace* it.[24] Cumulatively, I wish to suggest,

23 I have touched on this point in *Democratic Legitimacy*, esp. 57–61. The burgeoning emphasis on party financing, as much as the lack of inner democracy in party structures, has contributed to quasi-dictatorial leaderships, notably within governmental parties. As a frequent upshot of these shortcomings not only has public debate suffered – and, with it, the nature of discursive democracy – but also, and no less tangibly, a growing number of people have come to feel excluded from the democratic process by the marginalization or total cold-shouldering of their views and interests. Apart from marginalizing trends, there has also been a pronounced denigration of principles as such, as proponents of "deliberative democracy" keep reminding us. (I have stressed this in *Democratic Legitimacy*, especially in chapter 8.) That is why I regard Collingwood's insistent call for a return to principled political action both pioneering and timely. Among the best-known recent "followers" of Collingwood and deliberative democracy is John Rawls, especially in *Political Liberalism* (New York: Columbia University Press, 1993, 1996) and "The Idea of Public Reason Revisited," *University of Chicago Law Review*, 64 (1997), 765–807, and Charles Taylor, *Multiculturalism and the "Politics of Recognition"* (Princeton: Princeton University Press, 1992; see also Philip Pettit, *Republicanism: A Theory of Freedom and Government* (Oxford: Clarendon Press, 1997), esp. 180–205, and ch. 8. For influential studies on deliberative democracy, see Bohman and Rehg, eds., *Deliberative Democracy* (Cambridge: MIT Press, 1997).

24 Since the "end of ideology" theme as such is not really my concern in this discussion, I may perhaps be forgiven if I merely mention some of the authors who, in the early 1970s, wrote on it, such as Daniel Bell, John Plamenatz, Wolfram Burisch, Jakob Barion – just to name a few within a fairly extensive literature I was most familiar with at the time. There were also several collections ("readers"), such as that edited by M. Rejai, *Decline of Ideology?* (Chicago/New York: Aldine-Asherton, 1971). Among the "classical" authors on the subject of ideology as a broadly cultural phenomenon, I found Gustav Bergmann, in

such institutional changes might revitalize the public domain and help transform politics from essentially being a race, a game, or a performance – largely intended for spectators – into the kind of joint endeavour Hannah Arendt had in mind, in which people, in their plurality, actually participate, and not merely watch.

To put it slightly differently: Granted that political ideologies are less than timeless foundational ideals – in the way noble myths are – as well as less reliable than road maps or performative blueprints, they are not therefore tantamount to merely "optional extras," let alone to fanciful lies (the now common interpretation of myths), wholly designed to cloud, if not entirely to distort, the world of political purpose and civic engagement.

addition to Clifford Geertz, of particular relevance to my reference to myth. See especially, Bergmann's "Ideology," *Ethics*, LXI (1951), 205–18. As for the extension and reappraisal of ideology in the direction I have suggested, I see a significant beginning toward a form of principled as well as discursive politics in the founding of the Cooperative Commonwealth Federation (CCF) in Canada during the worldwide depression of the 1930s. As Professor Walter Young has perceptively pointed out, taking this direction *encourages* the expression of plurality rather than suppressing it, or muffling it (as political *parties* typically do). "Ideology," writes Young, *invites* dispute ... and argument rather than political organization." See his *Democracy and Discontent* (Toronto: McGraw-Hill Ryerson, 1978), 62 (italics are added). The proliferation of parties in Canada, together with trends toward articulating differences within existing parties *publicly*, possibly bears witness to an unprecedented emergence of ideological-principled thinking. The most prominent example of the latter in recent years has been the revival of *progressive* conservatism by David Orchard – another seminal impetus originating in rural Saskatchewan. Regarding my discussion of pragmatism and democracy, a very recent book by Richard A. Posner, *Law, Pragmatism and Democracy* (Cambridge: Harvard University Press, 2003), focusing on Joseph Schumpeter's thinking on democracy and ideology, seems to me of considerable interest. I am indebted for this reference to Professor Ernest A. Menze.

4

Revolutionary Purpose:
Rational and Natural Necessity

WHETHER OR NOT "REVOLUTION" ULTIMATELY is little more than a metaphor, taken as a concept, it absorbs meanings as eagerly as a sponge absorbs water. Hence, whatever is said in general terms is either equivocal or platitudinous, or both. Even when confined to the political sphere, as in this chapter, it is a highly slippery notion, and a definition is at best stipulative. Revolutions are commonly contrasted with gradual or evolutionary change, that is, with change that does not involve the violent and non-constitutional replacement of one government by another. At the same time, revolutionary change implies not merely the violent takeover of governmental power but the creation of a new *modus vivendi*, a new social order, with another set of normative perspectives.

Yet, regardless of the particular shift in the currency of values, the rhetoric of revolutionary change rarely makes its pitch without invoking terms such as purpose or growth. Principally, therefore, what the following pages attempt is a closer look at the causality claimed for purposive change, as a matter of both rational and natural *necessity*.

THE MARKETING OF REVOLUTION

The idea of rational necessity, or natural necessity, seems to find its way as easily into "regressive" conceptions of revolutionary change as into "progressive" conceptions; one putting a golden age into the past, the other into the future.[1] And both tend to combine the negation of

---

1 Both conceptions could be viewed as utopian if conceived as a timeless "ought" in a purely general sense of moral justification. At the same time, however, they can serve as a *motive* for acting (as distinct from a definite plan or blueprint) restoratively as well as progressively.

the status quo with the affirmation of its successor. But although the negation may bring with it much destruction, it is not necessarily followed by the projected transformation. The negation, it is true, need not invariably involve in its starting point the violent or unconstitutional seizure of governmental power. In either case, however, the skills employed in destroying (or non-violently terminating) an order are not the same as those required for effecting a "turn." For the transfer of power may be carried off *within* a political framework, and yet leave wide open whether, or how far, it succeeds in consummating its revolutionary goals.

In Czechoslovakia or Chile, for example, a perfectly legal takeover was accomplished via the so-called parliamentary road, by Marxist parties' gaining the greatest percentage of votes in regular, free elections, thereby assuming power constitutionally.[2] In both cases, the constitutional takeover was to form the overture, so to speak, of subsequent measures intended to alter the existing order more or less drastically. Yet, in point of fact, it emerged that winning power was not the same as winning the revolution. In Czechoslovakia the two forms of winning coincided, in Chile they did not. External factors unquestionably had something to do with that, but this is not at issue in citing these cases as examples.

What *is* at issue is to emphasize that a revolution is successful only if it can put its purposive scheme into operation *authoritatively*. Much, no doubt, depends on opportune timing and, subsequently, on a revolutionary regime's ability to shape the course of events it has unleashed. But a good deal hinges also, in the first place, on how its purposive reasons are put forward. They can add considerable revolutionary momentum, for example, if they succeed in combining the force of "rational necessity" with that of "natural necessity," since such a combination undeniably injects powerful causal ingredients that enable the revolutionaries to stake the claim of being in a position to accomplish what

2 Although this mode of gaining power does not typify Marxian thinking about revolutionary practice, it is not entirely ruled out by Marx in advanced parliamentary systems. In the majority of cases, of course, rebellion is seen as the struggle between irreconcilable class foes. The crux of the matter, as I see it, is whether or not a parliamentary or democratic road *to* Marxist socialism would be pursued further *under* Marxist socialism, with the continued existence of a parliamentary opposition, capable of forming an alternative government after subsequent elections (if any). The extreme case of using democracy to destroy it was undoubtedly the Nazi seizure of power.

Condorcet had merely attempted: the assimilation of social laws to natural laws. For, by such a move, they could invest social laws with the regularity and determinacy of cosmic processes.

In point of fact, however, such rhetorical affirmations, designed as they are to suggest that there is nothing haphazard about the nature of revolutionary activity, cannot hide the truth that revolutions are highly unpredictable affairs. Lenin, for example, had no inkling whatsoever of the outbreak of the Bolshevik Revolution six weeks prior to it, for at that point he doubted that it would come about during his own lifetime. The Petöfi Circle in Budapest, generally credited with having triggered the Hungarian Revolution in October 1956, scarcely foresaw in June of the same year, let alone planned, its violent burst into reality.

Not surprisingly, there are sharply contradictory theories about what conditions are most likely to spark a revolution. Edmund Burke, for instance, traces revolutionary origins to conditions that make insurgency inescapable. Revolution for him is an event that is not chosen but one that chooses itself: "a necessity paramount to deliberation that admits no discussion, and demands no evidence."[3] Nor is there agreement about what precisely creates such inevitability, whether it consists of periods when conditions generally improve, creating incessantly rising expectations (as Tocqueville argued), or periods in which there is persistent escalation of misery and "social degradation" (as Marx maintained). Or, again, albeit using more "scientific" vocabulary, sociological analyses speak of disequilibrium in the social system, aided or caused by administrative chaos and/or military defeats, and then go on to explain these conditions in turn as essentially "functionalist" breakdowns.[4]

I fear that these prognoses imply a degree of determinacy that simply is not to be had. They suggest a knowledge about historical sequences and the timing of occurrences which, in truth, renders them neither more explicable nor predictable. At the same time, undue emphasis on antecedent circumstances is liable to obscure the *purposive* content of revolutions, the reasons which *prospectively* seek to justify them, and, thereby, to atomize the terms upon which they are held inexorably necessary. In essence, the difference is one between reasons *for* which a revolution is set into motion, and the reasons *from*

3 Edmund Burke, *Reflections on the Revolution in France*, ed., William B. Todd (New York: Holt, Rinehart and Winston, 1959), 118.

4 See, for example, Chalmers Johnson, *Revolutionary Change* (Boston: Little Brown, 1966), esp. chs. 4 and 5, a "classic" approach to revolution from a sociological perspective. See also note 20, below.

which it happens to occur. And it is principally the former, the reasons *for*, that are the major concern of this discussion.

Subsequent sections, therefore, focus on the justifying authenticity of professedly purposive reasons, both as the source of meaning attributable to a revolution and as authorizing grounds for its occurrence. Admittedly, the results of acting need not coincide with the reasons for acting, so that outcomes may clearly diverge from purposes. To decry purposes entirely would, however, shroud whatever point the struggle is claimed to have as a *moral* struggle. And any political revolution bereft of a moralizing rationale would surely prove a very hard sell indeed.

It was precisely the discrepancy between revolutionary outcomes and revolutionary claims which Burke fastened onto in order to puncture the rationalizing moral pretensions of the French revolutionaries, presenting them as the blatantly marketing rhetoric of sheer sales talk. "France," he charged, "has bought undignified calamities at a higher price than any nation has purchased the most unequivocal blessings."[5] Evidently, notwithstanding the validity of Collingwood's fundamental thesis, purposive principles *may* be thought hollow in retrospect.

REVOLUTIONARY CAUSALITY

Granted, then, that purposive principles do not rule out unintended consequences or, indeed, spurious claims, does this justify abandoning the idea of acting on purposes? Arendt, in her reflections on the American Revolution, roundly dismisses such an alternative. For her, we noted, the Declaration of Independence captures precisely the culmination of a revolution inspired by a self-sustaining purpose, and symbolizes those "rare moments in history" when the power of words and the power of action coalesce. The grandeur of this culmination "consists not in its philosophy and not even so much in its 'bringing an argument in support of an action' as in its being the perfect way for an action to appear in words."[6] This oneness of purposive thinking and purposive acting erects for her a unique monument to revolutionary causality *par excellence*.

Similarly, Marx would scarcely have put as much emphasis on revolutionary *consciousness* had he doubted that purposes shape actions in history or that, in the moment of choosing, they coincide. Revolutionary consciousness, therefore, formed for him a continuum with historical

5 Burke, *Reflections*, 43.
6 Hannah Arendt, *On Revolution* (Harmondsworth: Penguin, 1963), 130.

consciousness – a view that Collingwood boldly carries one step further: "The revolutionary can only regard his revolution as a progress in so far as he is also an historian, genuinely re-enacting in his own historical thought the life he nevertheless rejects."[7] At times, however, Marx came close to identifying this twofold consciousness with the possession of performative *knowledge*, thereby converting purposive *vision* into purposive *certainty*. Yet, however profitably this conceptual leap from what Herder and Hegel meant by historical consciousness may augment revolutionary support, it is apt to backfire once discrepancies between rhetoric and reality can no longer be hidden or explained away. Purposes, in short, if dressed up as certain knowledge, can prove highly perilous. Not all that surprisingly, therefore, Marxist "revisionists" like Eduard Bernstein advocated the retention of revolutionary rhetoric in combination with modifications in its practical *modus operandi*. This, too, however, has its dangers; for, as I wondered in the previous chapter, how open can an ideology be, or flexible, without becoming indistinguishable from *ad hoc* maxims or from principles so general that it ceases to possess any positional identity of its own? Clearly, "pragmatizing" ideologically credal convictions is like mixing oil with water.

The trouble with trying to fuse revolutionary rhetoric with pragmatic positiveness is that it inadequately takes into account the difference between *sequences* that (unpredictably) happen and *consequences* that an ideology seeks to predict. Obviously, for sequences and consequences to coincide, revolutionaries would have to *know* at the time of agitating for support that what was intended must of necessity materialize, and do so exactly the way it had been plotted. Since, however, the cognitive calculus available at the time of plotting can only accommodate probabilities that are foreseeable, it is by no means impossible that the *im*probable could in reality prove the most decisive; for, surely, nothing is less uncommon than the totally unexpected. An inordinate faith in ideologies to have the causal power of invariably transforming aspired purposes into tangible attainments would therefore have to hinge on an equally inordinate faith in the operation of self-fulfilling prophecies. Should, however, either faith be wearing thin, the ethic of the revolution itself may start to crumble, if not the revolutionary enterprise as a whole. Thus, just as the unthinkable may in fact happen, the thinkable may never materialize. Boundaries in the propagation of the ideologically

7 R.G. Collingwood, *The Idea of History* (London: Oxford University Press, 1961, originally Clarendon Press, 1946), 326.

thinkable are therefore as politically important as those of the tangibly attainable. In other words, ideologically believing that conditions should be other than they are carries with it no blueprint of how they could be changed and politically appropriated. Negative seeing simply is not positive knowing.

But stating what at heart is a truism should not detract from the importance of historical consciousness *per se* as the indispensable basis of thinking in terms of multiple alternatives and, hence, in terms of choice, itself, in the charting of history and politics. A strictly tradition-bound society would be unable to entertain ideas that projected alternatives to its way of life and its understanding of political authority. For it, therefore, not merely would the *outcome* of change be incalculable but the very concept of change would be unthinkable. The dimension of purposive choice simply would have no place in its vision of the future; things could not be imagined other than they were and had always been. Any discontent with the status quo could, accordingly, not be channelled into imaginary projects of change, let alone into acts of revolutionary transmutation.

While the capacity to envisage alternatives may correctly be said to distinguish modern societies from traditionalist societies, it is not the same as the possession of some definitive knowledge about the degree of "rational necessity" needed to act as a causal force. Consciousness of choosable alternatives in the form of purposive reasons is not, in other words, tantamount to having a precise road-map guiding us to a predetermined destination. Furthermore, the rationality of revolutionary causality is not the rationality of calculus or syllogistic deduction. Perceiving the need for revolutionary action, accordingly, demands a broader understanding of "reason" as its embedment, an understanding which does not rule out Rousseau's "reasons of the heart," or Hume's "sensitive part of human nature." Although, in suggesting this widening of reason I am not unduly anxious to pursue or advocate an emotivist approach to revolutionary causality, I cannot conceal my sympathy with the mode of thinking of Hume or Moses Hess or, for that matter, Edmund Burke. For all three felt that people are most likely to defy the given when they find it abhorrent to their moral sensitivity rather than because it fails to conform to principles of rationality. I do not dispute that what motivates action is open to profound differences of opinion, but simply to assume a necessary causal relation between the rational and the moral is to beg rather critically the question of a currency shift from a rational calculus to a moral commitment. And I cannot help feeling that those who maintain that moral willing derives from "truly rational" thinking overestimate the rational as a bridge to the moral.[8]

CAUSALITY AND CONTINGENCY

Most problematic, however, from the perspective of this chapter, is the linking of choice with *natural* necessity. This linking, not uncharacteristic of revolutionary rhetoric, in adroitly substituting natural for rational necessity, in effect renders choice empty of meaning. For it virtually amounts to saying that revolutionaries have *no* choice. Admittedly, the "no choice" position confers upon revolutionary action the character of inexorable inevitability, comparable to organic growth. Yet, at the same time, what is lost in this metamorphosis is the indispensable basis of purposive action itself. For when purposive contingency becomes wholly absorbed by the existentially certain, the idea of choosable alternatives has no intelligible moorings.

To be sure, there are contingencies in nature; an acorn may *not* grow into an oak in barren soil, or might grow merely into a sickly one; nonetheless, an acorn cannot grow into a plum tree. If, therefore, there is contingency in nature, it is radically different from contingency in society. With the sole exception of a *totally* traditionalist way of life, there is no such thing as a social order that is forever programmed to be one thing and no other. And even if modern societies do retain elements of traditionality to preserve their continuity as distinct societies, this does not amount to their institutions and ways of thinking being fixed and unalterable. Moreover, if not most significantly, continuities as much as changes are in society characterized by

8 Apart from underestimating the self-sustaining causality of moral indignation, there is thus also the opposite risk of overestimating its strictly political force; for it is not at all obvious how the currency of moral determination is to be converted into the currency of political action, revolutionary or otherwise, without loss of tolerance and humanity. This is a predicament, from which both neither the onset of tyranny nor the use of violence (especially in revolutions) can be excluded, as Plato, Machiavelli, and Rousseau, made clear (and not only Robespierre or Lenin), regarding the founding of new political institutions or the undoing of corrupt ones. In short, the idea of not being able to make an omelette without breaking eggs, as applied to revolutionary violence, is not exactly a new one. (I return to revolutionary violence below.)

modes of causality that are altogether different from those within the realm of nature. For, involving *values* and the contingency in their workings, they cannot but bring with them a high degree of endemic uncertainty and irregularity.

No doubt, events attributed to providential design or "cosmic teleology" could be said to rule out any such uncertainty or irregularity. But, whether this might be so or not, I prefer to follow here thinkers such as Spinoza or Hegel, who *categorically* declined to apply the terminology of purposiveness to non-human or supra-human agency. Otherwise (they gave us to understand), there was a danger of committing a sort of double conflation of mistaking outcomes of natural or divine forces for outcomes of human design and human action; or the other way around, human deeds for supra-human intervention. It looks, therefore, as though we can have certainty, and little or no scope for making purposive choices, or purposive choices and uncertain outcomes; but we cannot have both.

Nevertheless, there have been those who want it both ways. Edmund Burke, for example, seriously toyed with the idea of merging the necessity and spontaneity of natural (supra-human) forces with deliberate (human) modes of purposive shaping, by fusing the notion of organic growth and intrinsic evolvement with extrinsic constructional images. Thus, after making ample use of "growth" and "coming of age" when dealing with the early fortunes of the British Constitution, he seems less eager to use biological imagery once it had attained "maturity," since this would either have to imply that maturity had not really been achieved or that decay was looming ahead. Neither alternative appealed to him; at this point, therefore, he abandons organic metaphors in favour of mechanical metaphors such as keeping buildings in good repair. Deliberately preserving the Constitution replaces the spontaneity of natural growth as the process of political legitimation.

It is patently true that political institutions, like other human artifacts, are a complex amalgam of conscious purposes and non-conscious processes, of intended and unintended consequences, of accident and design; but to concede this does not dispose of the question as to whether acts that unmistakably involve the mediation of ideas, interests, and values are properly located in explanations of unmediated natural processes. Why, then, does "growth," a term borrowed from a non-normative universe of discourse, figure so prominently as an explanatory and evaluative category in claims made on behalf of revolutionary change, despite the fact that the latter is marked by (often violent) forms of *dis*continuity and, above all, by an arsenal of normative justifications?

When Aristotle employed the metaphor of growth to typify not only the biological dynamic of intrinsic unfolding and continuity but also the most perfect marriage of spontaneity and necessity, he certainly had no political revolutions in mind. This, however, did not stop revolutionaries from finding this line of thought of immense manipulative possibility. Nor, for that matter, did it fail to have tremendous appeal to those anxious to defend gradual and non-revolutionary change. In neither case, however, does the claimed merger of persistence and change give any indication of meaning or value. As Friedrich Meinecke, the prominent theorist of historism, has made clear, equating revolutionary or non-revolutionary change with natural growth and processes of inexorable unfolding does not escape the burden of *evaluation*. Echoing this view, Collingwood maintains that progress in history, if taken for "improvement," implies a "standard of valuation" for which "there is no natural, and in this sense, necessary law of progress in history." Precisely for this reason, Meinecke warned against subordinating human purposes to naturalist causal understandings, since human purposes are not like the fruit produced by the seed and growth of a plant; for, almost invariably, they occur and operate in new and predominantly unforeseeable ways and expressions.[9]

NATURAL AND RATIONAL NECESSITY

It is not surprising that Meinecke nevertheless did not disparage the idea of intrinsic unfolding (*Entwicklung*), in that such unfolding illustrates change generated by immanent purposes. Following Herder's emphasis on the inner sources of human creativity, he saw it as a counter-paradigm to mechanical causation and the external relationship of cause and effect. The emphasis on internal unfolding, characteristic of growth, furthermore, was not only the bedrock of anti-mechanical theorizing or the stock in trade of Romanticism in its critique of the "vainglorious Enlightenment"; it was also a spur to sociocultural censures, in that it opposed the spontaneity and authenticity of the natural and organic to the artificial, contrived, and stereotyped that, in its phoneyness, stifled vigour and muffled true liberation from the conventional.

That the apotheosis of the natural, or organic, was not supported by anthropology, philosophy, or religion, or that biology offered no more of a social and political ethic than the mechanical sciences, was scarcely

9 Friedrich Meinecke, *Zur Theorie und Philosophie der Geschichte* (Stuttgart: K.F. Koehler, 1965), 107, 375; Collingwood, *The Idea of History*, 321, 323.

taken into account. What mattered was to puncture the complacency of the age and to create a consciousness bent on change, on unmasking and unmaking the status quo, so that its pretensions could be seen for what they were, and true reality could be what it was meant to be: self-generated, intact, and, above all, authentic. Somehow human growth got stunted, people's development warped, and authenticity lost. What was needed, therefore, was to return to nature and recover the true and the genuine beneath the mechanical and the artificial, the conventional and the feigned, and retake possession of one's cultural heritage. Although it was rarely made clear why the recovery of the past should help to give birth to a better future, *change* was the unequivocal answer to all that was wrong in the present.

How, precisely, nature was to be distinguished from convention, moreover, was a question that generally was glossed over. If and when critics did face up to it, the ambiguity of the word "nature" as a norm or ideal confronted them as starkly as it had confronted Aristotle before them, although the distinction between *physis* and *nomos*, between nature and convention or law, was not unknown to Aristotle and other Greek thinkers a century or so before him.[10] But, unlike modern critics, pre-Aristotelian philosophers did not endow nature with ameloriative properties or moral qualities. Nature was nothing more than what was original or primitive. Only after Aristotle did nature assume a moral connotation, suffused with the striving for perfection, with an inner dynamic toward moving from the potential to the actual, or from what is to what ought to be. And it was *this* conception of nature from which revolutionary thinking has drawn its doctrinal normativeness and rhetoric appeal.

However, this metamorphosis of the natural deprives choice of its ontological basis, as we noted earlier. It was no doubt of advantage to the revolutionary cause to appropriate the language of immanent purpose in terms of organic growth, as long as nobody bothered to ask why the natural or organic ought to be possessed of moral purpose or, indeed, or any *purpose* whatsoever. Hegel certainly *did* ask this awkward question, and the answer he gave to it was perfectly clear. A machine, he observed, can more correctly be associated with the notion of purpose than an organism.[11] Organisms have no purposes; they do what they do because

10 See Ernest Barker's introduction to The *Politics of Aristotle* (Oxford: Clarendon Press, 1946), xlviii.

11 G.W.F. Hegel, *The Phenomenology of Mind*, transl. J.B. Baillie (London: 1931; Torchbook ed., 1967), 299–300.

they are what they are. "What is produced is as much there *already* as produced"; the end is not determined *by* the being, but *within* it. The "very end shows itself to have been also the beginning."[12]

Interestingly, Marx, although he was not above marrying purpose with growth, nonetheless followed Hegel in setting apart natural necessity from rational necessity. In a striking passage in the *Critique of the Gotha Programme*, for example, Marx expressly distinguishes between natural growth and the process of conscious creativity by contrasting the *emergence* of Communist society "from the womb" of capitalist society, "still stamped with its birthmarks," to its deliberate rationally-purposive *development*.[13] Collingwood almost echoes Marx, if less vibrantly, in distinguishing progress in history from progress in nature, to the latter of which he refers as "evolution" *only* if and when it does bring "into existence new specific forms."[14]

That revolutionary changes – as historical events in general – are not wholly the outcome of deliberate (purposive) action, has been conceded. But this, surely, in no way implies that we can think of purposes other than as aims that we consciously pursue. At any rate, that has been the burden of my argument so far; and it is in its light, I believe, that we generally differentiate *actions* from mere *events*. The possibility, therefore, that outcomes may fail to correspond to intended purposes, need not belie the latters' existence. Revolutionary change, unlike biological growth, does not just happen; it is *made* to happen, in the sense of "making" that Vico proclaimed to be the core characteristic of the human world, by virtue of which this world is a *creation*, consciously intended and retrospectively knowable, in ways in which the realm of nature is not.

Indirectly, Vico's celebrated dictum indeed provides a conceptual foundation in support of the linkage between historical consciousness and revolutionary consciousness, unintended though it clearly was. For although his philosophy of history, reinforced by Herder's theory of human creativity, was solely designed to enable us to feel ourselves into the *past* in an attempt to re-enact it,[15] it nevertheless opened up new visions capable of serving as revolutionary paths into the future.

12 Hegel, *Phenomenology*, 297, (author's translation).

13 Karl Marx, *Critique of the Gotha Program*, in Lewis S. Feuer, ed., *Marx and Engels: Basic Writings on Politics and Philosophy* (New York: Doubleday, 1959), 117.

14 R.G. Collingwood, *The Idea of History*, 321.

15 For an interesting elaboration of this point, see Isaiah Berlin, *Vico and Herder: Two Studies in the History of Ideas* (London: Hogarth Press, 1976).

Unwittingly, therefore, both thinkers made significant inroads into ways not only of *understanding* history but also of *transforming* it.

CONSCIOUSNESS, VIOLENCE, AND MORALITY

Unlike revolutionary *consciousness*, however, revolutionary *violence* yields no clue toward a revolution's purposive thrust, or the sincerity and intensity with which it is envisioned. What it may disclose, though, is the absence of channels for non-violent forms of change and, thereby, the need for *revolutionary* change. Even so, there are no ways of measuring the rationality or irrationality of revolutionary violence *per se* any more than of assessing with certainty the rationality of revolution as such. Nor can one predict how many people are required to perceive conditions to be intolerable enough to engage in it and to commit acts of defiance involving wholesale destruction of lives and belongings. Of course, numbers alone do not necessarily determine revolutionary action or the intensity of violence. But, supposing a revolution is to be *democratically* justified, numbers cannot entirely be a matter of indifference. At least a majority must then sufficiently experience discontent with things as they are to turn to revolutionary dissent. Revolutionary elites may have to twist people's perceptions to bring this about, but they can never be certain when such a metamorphosis of consciousness had occurred or has optimally ripened, since there are no unequivocal pointers to guide them. This, possibly, is one salient reason for why timing a revolution is such a tricky thing; additionally, it may also account for the difficulty of containing violence once it has been unleashed – a potentially troubling matter for revolutionary leaders after their seizure of power.

The effect of violence, intended or not, is an issue that revolutionary leaders can only calculate with a minimal degree of accuracy when setting off a revolution. It is a burden they cannot easily divest themselves of; nor can they be free of the responsibility for the way both the cost and the result of violence may bear upon the ultimate fortunes of the revolution. And, if they present themselves as democratic leaders, they may not all that self-assuredly be able to rely on self-justifications – their motives or intentions – however noble these in themselves may be. For, like any other democratic leaders, they must "reckon with consequences" – the ethic of responsibility, in Weberian terminology. Even if creating disarray may be part of revolutionary strategy, eventually the aim must be to forge order out of chaos and, above all, to remain in control of events, rather than be overtaken by them. Similarly, revolutionary leaders, like non-revolutionary ones, must guard against raising their moral purposes to a pitch that escalates expectations to a level they know they cannot attain, lest they themselves become trapped within the wheels of their rhetorical excesses. For, to de-escalate expectations is vastly more difficult than to escalate them.

I can offer no irrefutable prescription for guarding against unduly raising expectations, but it may be worth keeping in mind that revolutionary change involves at least three distinct stages which, inherently, are independent variables within the total process, in that one stage does *not* necessarily lead to the next. They are: (a) the stage (or phase) of revolutionary agitation; (b) the stage of seizing power; and (c) the stage of transforming a given order. And, even if (a) and (b) harvest success, (c) need not materialize, if revolutionary regimes find the task of actualizing their self-justifying (moral) purposes intractable. In that event they in effect face a situation not basically different from that which any other regime faces that fails to make good its electoral hype. Hence, whatever moral goals justify the seizure of power, if the latter is not followed by an authoritative turning around of things, the revolution may be said to have misfired. For no revolution is politically meaningful if the acquisition of governmental authority does not lead to the replacement of one order by another. Losing sight of the need for *political* implementation, is therefore tantamount to losing sight of what a political insurgency is about.

Thus, it is one thing to expect a revolution to be morally justifiable; but it may be potentially disastrous to envision revolutionary action as *entirely* moral. For this comes close to viewing revolutionary actors as actors in a purely theatrical sense, engaged in a play of political fiction, be it a tragedy or a farce. Whether or not it stirs feelings to the extent of transforming calm waters into turbid streams will have little to do with altering their flow in reality. Thus, although it makes perfectly good sense to speak of a "moral revolution" in order to describe a radical change in ethical thinking, or to maintain that, *formally*, any revolutionary claim is a moral claim insofar as it posits what ought to be in place of what actually is, it hardly follows that the *means* of carrying off a revolution can be wholly moral in substance or form. Hence, even if revolutionary aims are not conspicuously vague but offer instead concretely articulated moral objectives, translating these into political reality, *and* fully preserving them as moral phenomena, seems empirically unachievable.[16]

16 Collingwood is most explicit on this point in "Political Action," *Proceedings of the Aristotelian Society* (1929), 159–60.

If this indeed be the case, it is so, not because integral moral purposes are unreal or unimportant, but rather because, as *implementational* goals, they demand *political* translation. And, in view of it, the historical dimension of a given situation resists being disregarded. Although a revolution is directed toward the future, it is manifestly rooted also in the past, simultaneously a component of an existing continuum *and* the source of its transformation. Marx, one of the foremost revolutionary theorists, saw this very clearly. "Men make their own history," he wrote in *The Eighteenth Brumaire*, "but they do not make it just as they please; they do not make it under circumstances chosen by themselves, but under circumstances directly found, given and transmitted from the past." And he relates this insight expressly to "such epochs of revolutionary crisis" in which, thinking that they are creating something entirely new, those engaged in revolutionary action "anxiously conjure up the spirits of the past to their services."[17] The past, however, also demonstrates that every political creation has coercive power at its disposal, so that (once again), while conjuring up the noble spirits of the past may undeniably help to moralize a revolution, it cannot thereby obliterate its politically-coercive dimension. Thus, whether or not revolutionary elites themselves believe in the authenticity of moral aims as basic causalities, it usually, sooner or later, becomes evident that such aims are used principally as devices of rationalization and legitimation; that is, as mere instrumentalities, functionally comparable to the use of violence, and therefore that, teleologically, purpose and function coalesce.[18]

FUNCTION, PURPOSE, AND ORGANIC GROWTH

This running together of purpose and function was, I believe, a major cause of the demise of East-European communism, and it gathered force from a long-standing doctrinal crisis (arising mainly from Marx's "super-structure" philosophy of politics) as well as from a mounting sense of betrayal by those who had taken the revolutionary ideals seriously. For, increasingly they found that these ideals carried in practice little, if any, authentic meaning for the revolutionary leaders, and that, consequently, terror acts of unprecedented brutality, coupled with cynicism and corruption, had to be viewed as part and parcel of a revolution, whose roots were in the historic soil of despotic forms of (Russian)

17 Marx, *The Eighteenth Brumaire*, ed., Robert C. Tucker (New York: Norton, 1978), 595.

18 It is a position that is (rightly) identified with Lenin's interpretation of Marx's revolutionary thinking.

governance. This realization was articulated most clearly by the Petöfi Circle; its members demanded in effect the reversal of history as much as the reversal of doctrine. Truth was to be recognized as an independent authority, the press was to be free to express it, and the rule of law was to be restored in place of faked trials under courts, created by, and subservient to, the ruling Party.[19]

Here is a telling example in support of the thesis that purposes are not reducible to functions but have an independent cognitive and moral life of their own, a rationale and an ethic *sui generis*. On this thesis, there must be values other than those which derive from class or group interests, and criteria of rightness and justice that stand on their own. Clearly, in the absence of such self-sustaining standards, there are no recognizable benchmarks for appraising the meaning, validity, or integrity of revolutionary claims (or any claims at all) in order to establish what is what and to distinguish between the delusory, the deceitful, and the genuine. Moreover, revolutionary (or any other) purposes, once they are reduced to functions, make it chancy whether they are causative forces in themselves or mere by-products, accidental outcomes that somehow follow in the train of disruption and chaos. For, in the latter case, purposes can hardly be said to have prefigured a new social order as independent causalities that have, as sources of the transformation, any explanatory power whatsoever. Not being self-generated and self-sustaining reasons *for*, they simply are *in*authentic purposes, since they lack the essence of a *telos*, properly so called.[20]

It is of poignant interest, therefore, that what chiefly sparked the searching reappraisal of communist thought and practice in Eastern Europe revolved in essence as much around the difference between

19 See Michael Polanyi, "The Message of the Hungarian Revolution" in Tomas Aczel, ed., *Ten Years After: The Hungarian Revolution in the Perspective of History* (New York, 1966), 9.

20 Oddly enough, although Chalmers Johnson acknowledges the distinctness of a "system's value structure," the explanation and meaning he attaches to value-oriented conduct conflicts with his acknowledgment (*Revolutionary Change*, 32–3). As a result, purposive actions are essentially viewed by their effect on the overall functioning of the "system." (ibid., 46.) This, however, seems to ignore the difference between the *scope* of an explanation of value and the *nature* of an evaluative explanation. Hence the possibility of *intrinsic* values is in doubt. For a similar criticism, more specifically from an historical perspective, which questions the idea of *deriving* evaluative explanations from a system itself impaired by revolution, see John Dunn, *Modern Revolutions* (Cambridge: Cambridge University Press, 1972, 93–9, 274–5.

self-sustaining purposes and derived functions as around whether the purposes themselves rested on perceptions based on authentic information or were in fact pseudo-purposes based on perceptions that had been systematically corrupted by feeding people with lies. Unfortunately, all of this took on meaning only *ex post facto*, after years of official deception, although a fair dose of *self*-deception played its part as well, with people *wanting* to believe what they were told.

On the other hand, it is possibly a moot point whether revolutionary commitments can at all be generated within most social and political cultures in the absence of twilight meanings or manipulative contrivances of one kind or another. Besides, even if there is no deliberate distortion of reality, it might in practice be virtually impossible to maintain not only identity between moral vision and political outcomes but often also the continuity between original goals, whatever they are, and their actualization, since goals, in non-revolutionary politics as much as in revolutionary politics, may undergo almost a self-enstrangement in the course of political implementation. Still, it is important, I believe, to distinguish analytically between the absence of clear enough objectives, to start with, and the failure to attain objectives, owing to the operation of historical-situational contingencies and political-implementational crises.

Equally, however, it is necessary to keep in mind the difference between a lack of perfect continuity and the occurrence of persistent *discontinuity*. For, in the latter event, the very idea of reasoned purpose, let alone the notion of rational necessity, is at risk. In other words, while occasional lapses in purposive attainments may be taken in stride without impairing the authenticity of envisioned goals, recurrent lapses could fatally undermine the intelligible meaning, validity, or integrity of purposive claims, revolutionary or otherwise, as they could play havoc with assigning praise or blame, if not with the operation of rational causality and rational accountability altogether.

Evidently, whatever the authenticity of original revolutionary purposes, there is need for *some* recognizable continuity amidst inescapable implementational contingencies.[21] Organic growth has the appeal it has because it most strikingly conveys the interpenetration of persistence and

21 The French Revolution, through the constant civil strife and fighting between factions and, finally, the emergence of a military dictatorship, epitomized a rampant degree of discontinuity. For an insightful account of it, see Tocqueville, *The Old Regime and the French Revolution*, trans. Stuart Gilbert (New York: Doubleday, 1955), 203–11. See also F.C. Beiser, *Enlightenment, Revolution, and Romanticism* (Cambridge: Harvard University Press, 1992), 363–5.

change, of identity within the flux of multiplicity. Furthermore, since "growth" typifies also the dynamic of internal unfolding, if not indeed of self-directed activity, its impressive plausibility and popularity can hardly be gainsaid. Regrettably, however, both the plausibility and the popularity of the concept succeed in masking the fact that organisms have no purposes and that revolutionary change is man-made, and not the product of nature. Thus, although there has to be an internal relationship between widespread discontent and militantly defiant dissent to make revolutionary activity at all feasible, the source of its determinateness is not the causal force of organic growth but the inner unfolding of historical consciousness. In short, the causality of "becoming" in each case is vastly different.

The heuristic value of "growth" as a paradigm of persistence within change does not, it is true, demand exact analogical fit. Yet, if a paradigm is intended to clarify meanings, the areas of its applicability must share certain essential characteristics. Since, however, what is constitutive in one area is wholly non-constitutive in the other – one being governed by determinate necessity, while the other by indeterminate contingency – the possibility to derive regulative guidance from the former seems logically foreclosed; there simply is no basis for it.

CONTINUUM AND TRANSFORMATION: CONCLUDING THOUGHTS

It was not the intent of the preceding discussion to make any startling discoveries on the idea of revolution as such. Its aim was at once more limited and more specific. It focused principally on the rhetoric of revolutionary agitation and its tendency to blur the causality of purposive human action. Such blurring, I suggested, incurs the risk of conflating purpose with function, value with fact, and the contingency of rational determination with the necessity of natural determination.

I would summarize three themes as most closely aligned with my central concern: (i) the idea of revolution as a turnaround; (ii) the mistaken identification of revolutionary *consciousness* with performative *knowledge*; and (iii) the question of purposive continuity.

First, then, I maintain that "revolution," as a conceptual metaphor as much as a political-historical phenomenon, implicitly demands the transformation of an existing order of governance and pattern of society. Hence, whatever the reasons *from* which a revolution takes its origin, its reasons *for* must include the seizure of governmental power and the turning around of the status quo. The incidence of violence, in both its negative (destructive) phase and its positive (constructive) phase, though undoubtedly a serious matter, in itself does not invalidate the thesis of a necessary turnaround as the condition of a revolution proper.

Second, while I agree that a revolutionary consciousness is unthinkable in the absence of an historical consciousness, I nevertheless try to make it clear that accepting this link as an essential link is not the same as identifying the existence of a revolutionary consciousness with the possession of a blueprint that tells one exactly what to do. For this would involve an unwarranted leap from rational *choice* to rational *certainty*, from contingent causality to necessary causality, or from conjectural to ineluctable reality. Antecedently computing the cost of revolutionary change thus amounts to a type of calculation that is little different from engaging in a game of chance; far from being a case of physical *determination*, therefore, even as conceptual *enactment* it is almost haphazardly elusive.

The third salient theme, being in its way perhaps the dominant theme of the discussion, takes up practically the bulk of the chapter. Contrasting derived function with underived purpose, and necessary outcomes with contingent outcomes, it reaches the conclusion that the meaning of revolutionary purpose is not enhanced by paralleling human action with organic growth, or historical continuity with processes of spontaneous unfolding in nature. Nor is much gained, I argue, by drawing analogies between enquiries into non-human occurrences and enquiries into human occurrences; for, whatever laws natural science derives from observing causal regularities yield no basis for the evaluation of purposive human choice. Such strategies might possibly be of assistance whenever human behaviour defies understanding in terms of conscious choice, or be of use in explaining circumstances occurring within the contextual grain of history, whose origins are closer to causes operating in nature.

However, even if it is granted that the paradigm of growth helps explain odd behaviour, or occurrences, which elude intelligibility as instances of human purposiveness, its value seems to me worryingly problematic. For it is liable to obscure basic differences between change in which decision and choice have little or no relevance, and change in which decision and choice are of the essence. Thus, whatever we make of revolutions as societal turnarounds or of their degree of continuity as historically causal processes, we could not even begin to fathom their coming into existence as *political* events, that is, as the work of human action, if they were wholly reducible to, or entirely explicable by, sources virtually unconnected with the reasons, visions, expectations and choices, that we usually associate with modes of human self-enactment. Clearly, in the absence of understanding their historical roots as conceptual origins or their purposive direction as conceptual objectives, we would have no intelligible causalities to draw on. And, without such causal-conceptual mediation, we simply could not make the least bit of sense of how revolutionary activity might arise in the first place, or go anywhere, in the second place. Its exertions would be as bereft of recognizable drift, in practical terms, as its credal professions in conceptually-principled terms. Possibly, it was this combined poverty of meaning that marred the coherence, continuity, and eventual outcome, of two great revolutions, the Russian, as before the French.

Although they succeeded in shaking existing institutions, both revolutions failed to take in the most urgently pressing priorities, as they were perceived at the time. Foundering to connect with these, they also failed, in their constructive phase, to create the needed faith in their ability to meet the expectations they had raised. They were "great experiments," which, for the most part, ended in fiasco.[22]

To be sure, even if both revolutions had not misread the pressing priorities that the pre-revolutionary situation called for, or had had more realistically focused policy objectives, it may not have been enough to consummate both revolutions to the full, politically. Still, a more convincing manner of connecting with the present and of plotting the future would have provided valuable clues, whereby to assess their activities as *politically* revolutionary activities. And this would be so because, as Collingwood emphasized, they would yield the only paths to understanding history as *human* history, and politics as the work of human creation and, hence, as *purposive* activity.

As purposive activity, moreover, it is also, Collingwood makes clear, structured by the consciousness of a particular *order* people share, or want to share, in the world they have in common. Indeed, the added combination of "purpose" and "order" underlies his conception of "political

22 As a result, Habermas observes, "we have lost our confidence that conditions can be changed by revolutions." See his "Popular Sovereignty as Procedure," in Bohman and Rehg, eds., *Deliberative Democracy* (Cambridge: MIT Press, 1997), 39. I have touched on the disenchantment with revolutionary change in Czechoslovakia in *Socialism with a Human Face: Slogan and Substance* (Saskatoon: University of Saskatchewan Lecture Series, 1973) and in *Pluralism, Socialism, and Political Legitimacy: Reflections on "Opening-Up" Communism* (Cambridge: Cambridge University Press, 1991).

action" as much as the merger of particularity and universality.[23] Hannah Arendt most memorably mirrors this merger, in conjunction with "purpose" and "order," in her portrayal of the inauguration of a new political order by the American Revolution. For, as we noted, it marks for her that rare moment in history when word and deed, as well as particularity and universality, come together within a shared purpose, and, in their oneness, give birth to a transmuted order of civic mutuality.[24]

"Order," as such, to be sure, entails no ideal, and a new order may fail to be a better order. Yet, while an order provides no guarantee for the "good society," or the "just society," it sets the minimal conditions for *any* society, by demarcating its rights and freedoms, as much as their protection and constraints. All this is of course no less true of orders created by non-revolutionary action than of those created by revolutionary action. Only what makes a not negligible difference is the price at which revolutionary change is purchased; and all the more so if its success demands, as Friedrich Engels has stressed, a decidedly authoritarian direction.[25] Clearly, whether the price is worth paying is, to say the least, a difficult question to resolve, if it can be resolved at all. The most one can confidently assert is that combining the problematic notion of rational-purposive *necessity* with the even more problematic notion of organic-*purposive* necessity may not be a very promising way of getting correct answers. For, given the argument put forward in the preceding pages, it involves not only a fearful mixing of terminology, but also, if not chiefly, a fearful mixing of wholly disparate species of causality.

23 Collingwood, "Political Action," 161–2. On this view, there can be no meaningfully *political* revolution, if it fails to project an alternative societal *order*, although it is highly doubtful whether it could ever be an entirely new order, since it then would lack originating or purposive intelligibility. As Collingwood argues in *The Idea of History*, 326, a revolution, and the order it creates, has to *connect* with what went before, if it is to *contrast* with it, and thus make it historically understandable.

24 See above, note 6. Arendt attributes the success of the American Revolution to its having been entirely *political*, not attended (or deflected) by recognizably *social* considerations or by purposes of an idealistic (abstract) nature, as the French and Russian revolutions were. (In "What is Authority?" BPF, 140.)

25 Friedrich Engels, "Über das Autoritätsprinzip," *Die Neue Zeit*, 32, 1 (1914). See also Introduction (above), note 23.

PART II

From Public Reason
to Representative Thinking:
Four Voices

5

Practical Reason and Civic Mutuality: Christian Thomasius

IN HER ACCOUNT of the emergence of the American republic, Hannah Arendt cites the central principle on which it was founded as that of mutuality. And she emphasizes that it was a mutuality characterizing the relation of citizens among themselves, as distinct from a mutual pledge by subjects to their monarch. One promises a common life of "fortune and sacred honour," to be shared by fellow-citizens, while the other constitutes a vow of submission by loyal subjects.[1]

It is the mutuality of citizens that this chapter is about. And it traces the idea to a seventeenth-century thinker who contrasted it not with the mutuality of subjects in their submission to a monarch but with the mutuality of communal fellowship. Whereas, for him, civic mutuality involved an "extrinsic" ethic derived from reasoned understandings of reciprocity, communal fellowship involved an "intrinsic" ethic derived from motives of disinterested amity. And while civic reciprocity demands, as it presupposes, prudential reasons of deliberation among a plurality of disparate individuals, leading, explicitly or tacitly, to contractual forms of agreement, communal fellowship rests on prior ties that are valued in themselves, and demand no further grounding. In effect, this twofold understanding of mutuality makes a pointed distinction between mediated civic bonds and instant communal bonds, between a oneness that is only contingently consensual, and a oneness that is spontaneous and implicitly consensual.

An essential component of Thomasius's theory of civic mutuality is the concept of *decorum*. Neither strictly moral nor strictly legal in its

1 Hannah Arendt, *On Revolution* (Harmondsworth: Penguin Books, 1963), 130. See also regarding this principle in action, Arendt, "What is Freedom?" in *Between Past and Future* (New York: Viking, 1968), 152–3.

source, decorum is meant to serve as a distinctly *civic* means of alliance. Its intended habitat being the political domain, it bears specifically on humans in their reciprocity as citizens. As opposed to conduct in private life, it is to govern what Thomasius calls *vita civilis.*

Its theoretical merits apart, Thomasius's notion of a specific civic ethic of mutuality helped to launch a highly novel *style* of acting in the public forum, including a sort of new language in which to think about politics; a language not confined to the few, but one intended to be generally accessible, in order to make politics a fit subject for public debate. This, in its time and place, was no less than a revolutionary idea, because hitherto the notion of a "public" itself was virtually unheard of.

THE CREATION OF "PUBLIC REASON"

Christian Thomasius (1655–1728), I know, is not a familiar name in the English-speaking world. There are certainly not many who have more than a nodding acquaintance with him, while most, not to put too fine a point on it, have simply never heard of him. That he has not been altogether forgotten is the merit of notably one man: Leonard Krieger. In an enviably concise manner his *German Idea of Freedom* portrays Thomasius's political thought and deftly pinpoints "tension" as its dominant characteristic[2] – a characteristic that, I am suggesting, colours in several respects the *Aufklärung,* the German Enlightenment, as a whole.

Overshadowed by Locke (whom he profoundly admired), as well as by his own countrymen of the stature of Leibniz, Pufendorf, and Christian Wolff, Thomasius was nonetheless in his day unusually popular.[3]

2 Leonard Krieger, *The German Idea of Freedom* (Boston: Beacon Press, 1957), 59–66.

3 Thomasius was profoundly admired by such thinkers as Lessing, Herder, Goethe, Schiller, J.C. Gottsched, and the historian A.L. Schlözer, but above all by Samuel Pufendorf and Immanuel Kant. Undoubtedly, his decision to use German, and his determination to write in a manner intelligible to the layman, accounted for the popularity of his writings, many of which were republished in several editions. Not since the days of Martin Luther were the works of a German scholar so much in demand by people of all walks of life. His most immediate impact was on his students at the university of Halle, then the chief training ground of the newly emergent, and soon widely acclaimed, Prussian public service. For an early account of Thomasius's influence, see Heinrich Luden, *Christian Thomasius* (Berlin, 1805). See also Erich Wolf, *Grosse Rechtsdenker des deutschen Geistes* (Tübingen, 1951), ch. 10, and Werner Schneiders, ed., *Christian*

Jurist, philosopher, and, above all, astute publicist, Thomasius was a rather exceptional scholar, a scholar without peevishness, *ein deutscher Gelehrter ohne Misere*, as Ernst Bloch has aptly called him.[4] Unlike Pufendorf and Leibniz, who favoured "discretion" and addressed themselves for the most part to the learned few or the politically eminent, Thomasius chose to argue his case publicly by founding the first popular journal in Germany, in which he and others strove to write in a way anyone able to read could understand. Feared and loved, persecuted and admired, Thomasius created something unknown, or practically non-existent in his homeland: the beginnings of what Rousseau was to call "public opinion," in which he saw the essential bedrock of true political freedom. And, in order to arouse such a civic consciousness among people who hitherto knew and cared for nothing but their private concerns, Thomasius took up issues few dared to touch upon, and his language was bold and incisive. Not surprisingly, Pufendorf, discreet diplomat that he was, could not help wondering if his friend and disciple "was not tearing down more houses than he could ever erect in their place."[5] Abolition

Thomasius (Hamburg: Meiner, 1989), 1–20. Unfortunately, Thomasius's intense popularity disseminated his ideas so widely that, by the time Kant wrote, he as many others, were not always aware of their borrowings from him, as Werner Schneiders points out.

4 Ernst Bloch, *Christian Thomasius, ein deutscher Gelehrter ohne Misere* (Frankfurt: Suhrkamp, 1961).

5 Emil Gigas, ed., *Briefe Samuel Pufendorf's an Christian Thomasius (1687–93)* (Munich and Leipzig: Oldenbourg, 1897), 73. The letter is dated 20 May 1693. In an earlier letter Pufendorf writes to Thomasius: "You have the courage to put into print views which I wholly share, but which I did not have the nerve to express publicly." The letter is dated 25 February 1688. (Ibid., 14.) Samuel Stryk, one of the most renowned jurists of the period, introduced Thomasius to Pufendorf and, by the time he took his doctorate in 1678 (at the age of 23), he had become one of the most enthusiastic supporters of Pufendorf, who, together with Grotius, was out of favour at the university of Leipzig at the time. Thomasius himself met with a similar fate when, after a few years as a practising lawyer, he followed in his father's footsteps and joined the faculty of law and philosophy at Leipzig, in 1686. For his "heretical" views soon brought him into conflict with his more conservative colleagues. Estrangement was followed by hostility and then by open persecution. In 1690, with the help of Pufendorf and the Prussian Court, Thomasius was invited to Halle, then in process of becoming a new university. And it was above all at Halle that Thomasius published his most outspoken censures of contemporary legal practices.

of torture, an end to witch trials, toleration of religious minorities – Thomasius expressly included Jews among them, an intrepid act in his day – attacks on hereditary privileges and advantages of wealth, pleas for equal treatment before the law and, not least, equal access to education for men and women: these are some of the issues that demanded, Thomasius felt, a public airing, a degree of exposure capable of generating public debate.

To political theorists and historians of ideas, Thomasius is best known as the successor to Pufendorf, who completed what the latter had started, by severing the ties between theology and political thinking, and between divine law and positive law. While this view is not mistaken as a generalized statement, it nonetheless conceals the inner tension that Thomasius had to contend with in moving toward his rationalist voluntarism from his Pietist beginnings, beginnings that, as Krieger correctly observes, were not very different from the traditional-religious interpretation of Natural law.[6]

It appears that in order to come to terms with this tension, if not to resolve it, Thomasius needed a middle category between positive law and moral law, between the enforceable *justum* and the unenforceable *honestum*. This category should comprise a property that was less formal than positive law and less exalted than moral law, but yet, at the same time, was able to engender a needed measure of civility in public life. The concept of decorum might do this, Thomasius felt, by steering between commands of divine source and commands of human source, embodying an ethic of mutuality based on prudential reasoning and an ethic of obedience based on the conditionality of civic authorities. Interestingly, in the course of advancing such a rationally rightful (*rechtmässiges*) decorum, Thomasius also managed to transform the meaning of "reason" itself. This, perhaps, more than anything else, in strictly philosophical terms, earned him the parenthood of the German Enlightenment in the sense in which it was subsequently interpreted by Kant.[7] From serving chiefly as a *method*, as with Descartes, reason was now intended to serve as a *criterion*, an evaluative standard. By transforming it from a tool of theoretical enquiry into a tool of practical thinking, Thomasius in effect made rationality an essential constituent of human agency. Moreover, the close linkage between reason and action was expressly meant to turn thought toward

6 Krieger, *The German Idea of Freedom*, 61–2.

7 Immanuel Kant, "An Answer to the Question: 'What is Enlightenment?'" in *Kant's Political Writings*, ed. Hans Reiss (Cambridge: Cambridge University Press, 1970, 1991), 54–60.

performative ends within the *public* domain, with a view to generating interest in political concerns and in a distinctly *civic* morality.

The transformed meaning, as well as the transformed use, of rationality was essential for Thomasius's project to convert *decorum* from an innocuous, if not trivial, attribute of conventional propriety into an ethical principle of civic mutuality. Yet, it was above all this conversion which occasioned his agonizing conflicts about taking a step that could not help laying bare his loss of faith in the traditional understanding of Natural Law as an ordering maxim of public conduct. While he still expressed the hope that "sparks" of the moral *honestum* would survive, his new faith in *decorum* had by now effectively replaced his old faith as an operative ethic of civic relations and as the ultimate (extra-legal) touchstone of *legitimate* legality.[8]

Although in stressing the *prudential* component of rationality Thomasius seems closest to Locke, he was in fact drawing chiefly on more distant sources, on sources nearer to the classical period of Rome. By the same token, although there are undeniably close and significant affinities between Thomasius's thinking on *honestum* and *justum* and strands of seventeenth-century moral and legal theorizing, his conception of *decorum* discloses an impressive degree of originality.[9] The basic philosophical assumptions bolstering this conception found principal expression in his *Vernunftlehre*, his *Introduction to the Theory of Reason*. In its central thesis Thomasius attempts to fill a new page, as it were, in the annals of "reason" by insisting that there is more to reason than purely theoretical understanding. In effect, reason is to be extended into an instrument of practical judgment along the lines ordinary people apply their own sound (*gesunde*) reasoning.[10] But, to bring about

8 For the regulative principles of *honestum*, *justum*, and *decorum*, as interpreted by Thomasius, see his *Fundamenta Juris Naturae et Gentium* (Halle and Leipzig: Salfeld, 1705), I, cap. 6, paras. 40–2.

9 Thomasius himself traces his empirical orientation to the Aristotelian dictum in Aquinas's *De Trinitate* (I, 3): "Nihil est in intellectu, quod prius non fuerit in sensibus." See Thomasius, *Introductio ad Philosophiam Aulicam* (Leipzig, 1688), cap. v, para. 34; see also *Einleitung zu der Vernunftlehre* (Halle: Salfeld, 1691), 170, (hereafter cited as EV).

10 Thomasius, EV, 84–8. The concept of "civic humanism" encapsulates aptly the rational-prudential ethic that Thomasius postulates as the foundation of morality in civic society. On the history of the concept, see J.G.A. Pocock, *The Machiavellian Moment* (Princeton: Princeton University Press, 1975). See also Thomasius, *Ausübung der Vernunftlehre* (Halle: Salfeld, 1691), 16, 43–50, (hereafter AV).

this extension, reason has to undergo a marked broadening of meaning in itself. Toward this end Thomasius suggests three transforming processes, in and through which reason could act as a solvent, a ferment, and a self-corrective.

To extend its action to being a solvent, reason first had to purge itself from "prejudice," as well as liberate itself from subservience to "authority." For only by thus effecting its own emancipation could reason claim general validity and demand recognition by everyone, regardless of rank, sex, wealth, or education. Reason, in this broadened sense, Thomasius called "sound reason," by means of which all were in principle able to submit beliefs, requests, and opinions to the test of reasoned inquiry. As a result, the entrenched would never be beyond challenge, but forever open to debate and, potentially, to being transmuted.[11] Before acting as a ferment of change, reason accordingly had first to serve as a solvent. And it was by means of both these processes that reason came to be in a position to be critically conscious of itself.

The main avenue toward the transformation of reason, in Thomasius's thinking, could therefore be likened to what Hegel was to call the dissolution of unreflective life. For, either way – as a solvent or a ferment – reason was no longer merely a tool for testing the logical consistency of propositions; rather it was intended to evaluate the content of thinking as such, in its bearing upon action, with a view to confirming or questioning its appropriateness. Hence, coupled with its critical-cognitive function, reason was now meant to serve as a check upon itself as a practical causality. With respect to action (properly so called), it was accordingly as much a critical-*causal* category as a critical-*cognitive* category.

Not surprisingly, to demonstrate and emphasize the practical relevance of reason as a causality, Thomasius devoted a whole volume to the *Practice of Reason* as a companion volume to his *Theory of Reason*.[12] And the area of applying practical reason, as a solvent or a ferment, he principally associated with the realm of civil life and the diverse public or supra-personal activities in which it was involved.[13] Above all he linked it with reasoned discourse in politics. Typified by no single overarching truth, politics was for Thomasius pre-eminently the sphere of a plurality of truths, each jostling for recognition. It called, therefore, he argued,

11 Thomasius, EV, 81–8; see also Thomasius, *Einleitung zur Sittenlehre* (Halle: Salfeld, 1692), 356–8, (hereafter ES).

12 See note 10.

13 Thomasius, EV, 134; ES, 30; see also EV, 2; AV, 40–1.

for a special form of reasoning, verifiable not by logical or scientific proof, but by its possession of propositions containing a high degree of *persuasive* credibility.[14] Implicit in his argument is the conviction that once reason has undergone a suitable broadening of meaning, public debate is opened to every person endowed with sound reason. In principle, therefore, every adult is able to grasp reasons when offered, and justified in demanding that they be given if they are not forthcoming. Thus, claiming universal intelligibility for practical reasoning, Thomasius conferred upon reason an authentic *public* status, whose validity was independent of private likes or dislikes, or personal privileges of any kind. In this public sense, accordingly, reason alone was to be sovereign – but a sovereign who had to defend and justify her rule.

A CIVIC ETHIC OF RECIPROCITY

Thomasius did not expressly advance a theory of popular sovereignty, but he lost no opportunity to promote the idea that the vast majority of humankind consisted not of fools or morons but of selves who had every right to be given reasons for why they should obey any will other than their own. And it was this idea that Frederick II endorsed in his throne speech in 1740. Such was already the impact of Thomasius's theory of the conditionality of political authority and of a subject's duty to submit to it. Evidently, Thomasius had by then succeeded in transforming not only the meaning of reason but also, and for our purposes most tellingly, its performative employment in the public realm.[15]

In his political philosophy Thomasius sought to establish politics as something *sui generis*, not only independent of ecclesiastic authorities, but also decidedly at variance with relations in other spheres. It was undoubtedly for this reason that he groped for a distinctly civic ethic of public conduct and, not unlike Machiavelli, sought to separate a particularistic virtue of acting politically from the universal virtue of acting morally. Intriguingly, however, the grounds upon which he attempted

14 Thomasius, EV, 229.

15 On Thomasius's practical philosophy and the emerging "public" and public service, see my "Christian Thomasius: Enlightenment and Bureaucracy," *American Political Science Review*, 59 (1965), 430–8, and "The Practical Philosophy of Christian Thomasius," *Journal of the History of Ideas*, 32 (1971), 221–46. See also Benjamin W. Redekop, *Enlightenment and Community: Lessing, Abbt, and Herder, and the Quest for a German Public* (Montreal: McGill-Queen's University press, 2000).

the separation were markedly different. For Thomasius, we noted, contrasts not so much the private with the public as he opposes two sets of *social* contexts, the domain of a religious *community* and that of a political *society*. At the same time, in contrast to subsequent *Gemeinschaft-Gesellschaft* theorizing, he refrains from dramatically opposing the tightly-knit solidarity of the community to the anomic individualism or rationalist negativism of a wholly tradition-less society, marked by *homo-homini-lupus* type of antagonism. For Thomasius, society is still composed of "nuggets of disinterested love," although it is hardly ever wholly sustained by it as (ideally) a religious community may be, in that political society draws on sources of cohesion which, though varied, are inherently prudential and instrumental in nature.[16] Also, whereas the bonds of community, being essentially credal, are free of coercion, the contingent unity of civic society evolves within a structure of legal sanctions, capable of ensuring "judicious compliance."[17]

Nonetheless, legal sanctions do not *characterize* civic relations for Thomasius, since he refused to believe that fear of punishment could alone serve as a durable basis for their viability. It was precisely for this purpose that he introduced *decorum* to serve as a basic principle of *civic* morality *per se*. A concept inherited from a pre-modern era, Thomasius converted it, parallel with reason itself, in order to make it serve as a practical guide for conduct in public life. He saw it not so much as a replacement for *honestum* and *justum*, but rather as an operational complement, and, additionally, as an instrument for clearly distinguishing the realm of mediated relations that characterize civic society from the unmediated relations within the realm of personal friendship or communal fellowship. As developed by him, *decorum* was to straddle between outright informality and structured formality, in order to bring about a consciousness of civic rightfulness that was both extra-legal and extra-moral. In a very distinctive sense, therefore, Thomasius wanted *decorum* to be the hallmark of a *prudential* ethic of conduct among humans who have learned, in an through their "sound reason," that a mutuality of basic social decency is in their best interests as *citizens*.

His *Political Philosopher* (1724) gives particular emphasis to the need for such an in-between ethic of civic life, by making clear that politics is not principally a matter of law enactment and law enforcement. By the same token, Thomasius is emphatic about viewing political *discourse* as

16 Thomasius, ES, 93–5, 113–15.

17 Thomasius, ES, 299–310, 356–69; see also *Ausübung der Sittenlehre* (Halle: Salfeld, 1696), 10–13, (hereafter cited as AS).

something with a rationality all of its own. Specifically, he contrasts it with the nature of strictly philosophic discourse. The rationality of politics, therefore, has no more in common with the rationality of philosophy "than a policeman has with a physician."[18] In effect, this is another endorsement of his demand for a distinct autonomy of politics and its medium of communicative action, whose concerns should be those that recognizably impinge on people in general, on the life they have in common as citizens. Only then, Thomasius argues, would people come to realize that public concerns *are* their concerns and, hence, that those who govern must make sure at all times to keep in mind the welfare, safety, goals, and interests of those who have placed their trust in them. In particular, Thomasius sought to remind those wielding political power that civic trust cannot be taken for granted, and that it had to be earned in an ongoing way, by rulers giving proof, time and again, that they care about "what makes people tick."[19]

If this gives the impression that Thomasius puts maximum emphasis on "pragmatic" concerns of political governance, it doubtless gives the correct impression. For he certainly focuses on "down to earth" issues as *political* issues – the sort of concerns that Hannah Arendt (rather contemptuously) calls "life's necessities." At the same time, his thinking in this direction does not imply disregard for unmistakably normative aspects of public life. The weight Thomasius accords to *decorum* as a normative category clearly belies the impression of an *ad hoc* pragmatism. What seems closer to the truth is that he had little use for preaching in

18 Thomasius, *Der Politische Philosophus* (Frankfurt and Leipzig: Grosse 1724), Preface.

19 Thomasius, ibid.; see also *Kurtzer Entwurff der Politischen Klugheit* (Frankfurt and Leipzig: Grosse, 1713), 169–70. In another work, some time earlier, Thomasius actually tried his hand at some behavioural form of political enquiry as an aid to the study of individual opinions. The full title of the work leaves no doubts that Thomasius was consciously offering a novelty, a "new science," of which the public domain has much need: *Die neue Erfindung einer wohlgegründeten und für das gemeine Wesen höchstnöthigen Wissenschaft* (Halle: Salfeld, 1692). In its Introduction he revealingly discloses both the essence of his own critical spirit and the main impulse of his particular political reformism. Why, he asks, are the Dutch, English, and French peoples so much ahead of the Germans in all sciences? And answers: "It is the unfettered freedom which alone gives real life to the human spirit." Unlike other political jurists, Thomasius focused on changing social, educational, and legal infra-structures rather than on transforming symbolic, or even real, super-structures.

politics, of a religious or philosophical kind. For either appeared to him liable to involve the attempt to *legislate* one virtue or another, in the direction of a utopian perfectionism – a tendency he viewed as the "most baleful curse of politics." A sense of appropriateness and good taste, which he associated with decorum, therefore appeared to him much more profitably called for.[20]

But if Thomasius was forthright, he was also modest. He generously acknowledged Cicero as his "great precursor," despite the fact that he significantly went far beyond him. For while Cicero, in defining "decorum," did emphasize appropriateness, he disclosed no intention of conferring upon it any broader meaning in terms of civic reciprocity, in the light of which individuals, regardless of rank, sex, or education, were to recognize each other's worth as *citizens* subject to no authority other than that sanctioned by rationally intelligible principles. In turn, Thomasius's conception of decorum was to ensure that no citizen made any claims against another unless these could be justified *and* challenged by appeal to reason. And the "reason" in question was that of a prudential ethic of social reciprocity: "You treat others as you expect others to treat yourself."[21]

RIGHTFUL DECORUM AND A POLITICS OF ACCOUNTABILITY

Without rejecting the traditional contract theory, Thomasius nonetheless identified the fulcrum of political right-doing with governmental accountability (*Rechenschaft*). As the central element of civic decorum, it was meant to act as the legitimizing principle not only for the founding of sovereign statehood but also for the institution of governments,

20 Thomasius, EV, 4; *Kurtzer Entwurff*, 169; and *Erinnerung wegen zweyer Collegiorum über den Anderen Theil seiner Grund-Lehren* (Halle: Renger, 1702), 32–5. The idea of "taste" figures prominently in Thomasius's most mature work, the *Fundamenta Juris*, I, ch. 6, paras. 40–2; see also EV,167–8, 92, 151–2; AV, 68, 92, 267; and ES, 29, 104. With regard to his outspoken anti-utopianism – a trend which he was among the first to originate in modernity –, see Isaiah Berlin, "The Decline of Utopian Ideas in the West," in J.M. Porter and Richard Vernon, eds., *Unity, Plurality, and Politics: Essays in Honour F.M. Barnard* (London: Croom Helm, 1986), 120–42.

21 *Fundamenta Juris*, I, chs. 6 and 7, esp. ch. 6, para. 41; see also AV, 95–9; ES, 241, 248–52. On Cicero, see *De Officiis*, trans. T. Cookman (London: Dent, 1909), 7, 42–56.

whose right to rule was thereby made contingent on their fulfilling their obligation to give reasons for whatever demands they decided to make upon the citizenry. Additionally, Thomasius, in his resolve to provide an autonomously anchored standard of political legitimacy, looked upon the entailment of accountability within decorum as the rightful (*recht-mässige*) core of overall civic mutuality.[22]

In this manner, decorum is pressed into service not simply as a *modus operandi* of professional politicians or magistrates but as a way of acting together in public as citizens in what Thomasius calls the "politics of life."[23] There is, by his own account, no other medium that can effectively link people as citizens on a voluntary basis. The only alternatives could be the reign of *honestum*, in which case politics would be entirely dispensable, or the reign of *justum*, in which case politics could function in a fashion through constant fear of the law; but it would not be a politics of freedom. Decorum, by invoking prudential considerations rather than strictly moral or strictly legal reasoning, seeks to come to terms with the fact that humans "are neither beasts nor saints."[24]

Likewise, decorum is not intended to provide a blueprint for an ideal politics; all it is meant to ensure is that ordinary women and men are taken into account (as well as given account), and that their interests and well-being are borne in mind. J.S. Mill's later observation (in *Representative Government*) would therefore not be out of line with Thomasius's interpretation of the principle of decorum, in that Mill viewed political guidelines of legitimate rule less as signposts instructing men and women how they may themselves govern than as safeguards that they not be wantonly misgoverned. And, as we noted, politics was for Thomasius the most fitting area for the application of civic decorum because: (i) it was the domain of practical action demanding what he called "sound reason"; and (ii) it was the domain of a plurality of opinions and interests demanding a reciprocity of civility. As for (i), engaging sound reason in practical pursuits such as politics was not the same as engaging logical thinking proper. "There is," Thomasius firmly insists, "a great difference between logic and politics."[25] His idea of political discourse, therefore, has much in common with Aristotle's idea

22 EV, 2; *Fundamenta Juris*, III, ch. 6. Apart from Plato's idea of philosopher-kings, Thomasius rejected the belief in divine rights of kings.

23 ES, 30; *Kurtzer Entwurff*, 5.

24 ES, 233–50; AV, 267–71, 293–5; *Fundamenta*, I, ch. 4, paras. 32–64, ch. 5, para. 58, ch. 6, para. 35, ch. 7, paras. 1–5.

25 EV, 229.

of the *enthymeme*, the reasoning of rhetoric and persuasion, which people in general can follow, apply, and discuss. As for (ii), in the absence of any single overarching value or truth, more than one party could be right; dogmatic insistence on any one truth or value, however sincerely cherished, could therefore be of little *public* relevance, and perhaps even positively harmful. "Not all that is true is necessarily of benefit" in a world of plural values.[26]

Thomasius is exceptionally (and refreshingly) candid in exploding the thesis that politics is the instrument for establishing incontestable truths. Each opinion, each proposal, and each decision calls for a grounding of its own. Reasons must be given, or demanded, for why anything should be believed, agreed, or acted upon. Truth in politics, accordingly, is forever a question rather than an answer, and the way anything like an answer may be found is rarely, if ever, by absolute proof, but rather by degrees of credibility and mutual acceptance. In accounting for, or engaging in, political action, therefore, appeals to some overarching truth or system of belief simply will not do, just as whatever truth *is* established must be open to challenge and hence is forever only contingent truth.[27]

Instead of some permanent or overarching truth in politics, Thomasius posits standards of appropriateness, set by civic decorum, as the operative criteria of prudentially reasoned reciprocity and good taste. And, because, in Thomasius's thinking, every adult is in principle able to judge what conforms to such public standards, public judgment – a matter of taste as much as of reason – is in effect the ultimately supreme arbiter of rightful authority. No superior knowledge, or special appeal to holy writ, is called for to enable people to understand (or to agree) why they should do what their rulers command, in order that they comply willingly and not out of servility or fear.[28] Admittedly, this presupposes, we noted, that governments act upon purposive reasons that are of a kind most people are able to grasp, and on which they can form an opinion of their own. This, indeed, *was* Thomasius's central assumption; central, because it formed the crux of his theory of *conditional* authority.

The confidence that Thomasius professed in the intelligibility of purposive reasons in politics had its main source in the belief that almost all

26 AS, 544.

27 AV, 235–6, 294; see also AS, 544.

28 EV, 151–2, 167–8, 177, 229; AV, 68, 267–9; see also *Kurtzer Entwurff*, 169–70.

aspects of public polity, other than planning for war, had to do with one and the same thing, regardless of its particular expression: the promotion of welfare. Further implicit in this belief was the conviction that most people could themselves judge what was likely to advance or hinder the attainment of this goal, whatever their level of education. "Despair not," Thomasius therefore urges his fellow citizens: "Do not lose heart (*verzage nicht*), for it is not from books or professors that we learn how to judge these matters or form views about them, but from living and acting with others."[29]

In addition to placing this confidence in people's capacity to understand and judge purposive reasons in support of public policies, however, Thomasius puts great emphasis on the intelligibility of public language. Public utterances must make sense, so that people, in taking in what is being said, can make out the purposive meaning it carries. And this hinges in the main, Thomasius argues, on governments' using the language that people ordinarily speak, as well as the kind of reasons they themselves ordinarily give in accounting for their actions.[30]

RECIPROCITY, TRUTH, AND POWER

There can be no civil society without reciprocity. For Thomasius reciprocity is therefore the quintessential requirement of communicative language and action in the public domain; it is the alpha and omega of his concept of rightful decorum in its bearing upon governmental accountability and civic mutuality. Without reciprocity, there can be neither order nor liberty. This is the paramount thrust of his political creed, in which he strikingly anticipates not only Rousseau and Kant but also Arendt's vision of representative thinking.

At the same time, while the ethic of reciprocity is intended to sustain mutuality in civil society, it is at variance with the dominant ethic of a religious community – a difference that parallels Thomasius's distinction between citizenship and fellowship. The juxtaposition of these ethics as mainstays of human mutuality was crucially important to him, because

29 EV, 13, 76, 87, 151–2, 269; see also AV, 81. Underlying this position is the Roman adage "omnes homines beati volunt."

30 In principle, Thomasius claims, mutual understanding is possible because "we know that others are humans like us." (EV, 261.) See also AV, 165–77, 181–235. Disputes often arise, Thomasius remarks, not because parties are necessarily far apart in substance but rather as a result of verbal misunderstandings or the deliberate twisting of words. (AV, 271–2, 295.)

he feared that a communitarian ethic, with its emphasis on credal consensus, could pose a potential threat to the articulation of plural ends. Credal monism, the ideal of being of one mind and soul, desirable though it might be in religion and in affairs of the heart, appeared highly suspect to him within society at large.

As the domain of plural values, civil society was doomed, Thomasius felt, if credal monism allied itself with absolutist rule. For the conviction of having truth utterly in their possession could then turn its champions into tyrants bent on wielding absolute power. And, since absolute truth needs no justification, while power, to be absolute, needs only might to support it, the prospect for civil society seemed to Thomasius a most frightful one. This, he argued, was all the more so because absolute *power* was always a real possibility, even though absolute *authority* (in his view) was an *Unding*, a contradiction in terms. Not surprisingly, truthfulness looms far larger in his scheme of things than truth, particularly in his ethic of reciprocal decorum.[31]

The deeper rationale for this preference bears spelling out. Thomasius well knew that truthfulness was no more easily to be had than truth, yet he felt certain that persistent mendacity was bound to prove politically counterproductive, for governments as much as for citizens among themselves. Thus, while truthfulness is in principle operationally indispensable, truth as an icon (Thomasius argues) is closer to a menace. Moreover, the combination of a single truth with absolute power is as dangerous to the existence of plural *choices* as to the survival of plural values. Should absolute truth join hands with absolute power, governments could easily claim, Thomasius feared, that they "had no choice," and hence could indisputably dismiss any questioning. Reckoning with alternative consequences would thus form no part of their deliberations. *Rechenschaft*, the rendering of account, whose semantic root lies in the weighing of alternatives and its different outcomes, would no longer have any relevance. What Thomasius accordingly dreaded above all was that only one single course of action would be offered to the public. Contesting alternatives would fall by the wayside, and politics, he concluded, would cease to be the realm of plurality.[32]

But, since no absolute value – or purely quantitative calculus – can assess the varied nature of human needs and human wants, the reality of plural – and qualitatively divergent – propensities and capacities would willy-nilly be ignored. Multiple challenges would no longer exist, and

31 EV, 172–3, 193–4; see also AV, 68.
32 Ibid.

decorum, the principle of political civility, would in effect be rendered dispensable. The reign of absolute truth could, it follows, signal the demise of public discourse. The irony of this potential upshot was not lost on Thomasius.

On this view – a view which, we shall find, Hannah Arendt echoes – absolute truth as a supreme value is of doubtful political coinage. However, *truthfulness*, although a most desirable requirement in authentic accounting, may not be sufficient either. For, to act accountably, governments must have a discretionary space in which they *can* act, at least some of the time. Hence, like other genuine *agents*, they demand autonomy, at any rate within a circumscribed area, in which they are their own masters, directing whatever they wish to do or leave undone, their "*Thun und Lassen.*" For it is only self-directed actions that agents can rationally account for. And the basic objective of such actions in the public as well as the private sphere is the attainment of welfare. About this, Thomasius reiterates, there can be no doubt whatsoever. "We all know what our welfare means to us and how best to preserve it." Neither rulers nor subjects know "what *causes* them to know this; but each of them knows that it is as universal a craving as the striving for self-preservation."[33]

Similarly, even though we do not know what makes us think of ourselves as self-directing agents, we know that we can act and choose for reasons of our own. "Although man does not know what the mind is which thinks in him, he knows, without doubt or quibble, that he can grasp the thoughts that the mind produces in him."[34] In other words, while we may not know the grounds *from* which we act, we do know the grounds *for* which we do, and thus *can* truthfully account for them.

Still, while we may know what our welfare consists in, we are fully aware that we cannot bring it about entirely by ourselves alone; we need others to be what we can and should be. "Without society, each of us would be virtually nothing."[35] Even thinking itself would be of little use "if we had no one to share our thoughts with."[36] If this is a recognizably Aristotelian position, Thomasius goes beyond it. Not only would thinking be of little use in the absence of society; it would not even have arisen in the first place, had it not been "kindled" (*angefeuret*) by the existence and help of others.[37]

33 EV, 261–2.
34 EV, 262.
35 ES, 25, 89–90.
36 ES, 89.
37 EV, 291.

Moreover, it is only through living and acting with others that we discover that others think and judge similarly to ourselves. Without this discovery, there would be little point in giving or demanding reasons, for we could not know whether others understood us or we understood them. Like Vico, though before Vico, Thomasius declares that it is precisely because we are able to assume that others are like us that we can perceive what others have done in a way we can never hope to perceive or understand the world of Nature. With no other substances, Thomasius writes, "not even with those of animal creatures, can we gain a comparable insight into their inner nature."[38] To be sure, we may misinterpret meanings, wittingly or unwittingly, in view of the immense variety of motives and ways of speaking; yet, generally, we do understand reasons when they are given or explained to us, for we know that, basically, others think and reason like us.[39]

In order to render account then, people must, as Thomasius shows, have the capacity for autonomous self-direction and also be able to understand each other's way of thinking. This, however, is still not all there is to it. Autonomy, truthfulness, and intelligibility may make the operation of accountability *possible*, but what makes it *necessary* is people's consciousness of being in need of each other. Without consciousness of this mutual dependence, neither associating with, nor accounting to, others would make much sense. Thomasius is here clearly seeking to reconcile individual autonomy with mutual interdependence, and to suggest a *modus vivendi* in which individual purposes, far from clashing, could indeed coincide. Such purposes, furthermore, if perceived as *common* purposes, might assume the form of publicly shared objectives (*Absehen*) as specific *policy* goals in *vita civili*. In essence, Thomasius thereby wants to demonstrate that, although humans as individuals are distinct selves, they nevertheless need a context of others. At the same time, he is anxious to make clear that such a context need not be that of a consensual community. Despite the merits of communal fellowship, most people, he feels, prefer a mutuality that makes less exacting demands, and do so chiefly because they are as aware of their divergences as of their similarities. In view of this, the majority of humans opt for living in a society in which not only is the right to private property protected but also the right to be different. Of course, Thomasius adds, these benefits of

38 EV, 261.
39 AV, 165–77.

living in a state carry a cost, the cost of being under the dominion (*Herrschaft*) of governmental authority and its laws.[40]

THE FALSIFICATION OF CONSCIOUSNESS

Regrettably, Thomasius observes, political society suffers from defects that detract from these benefits. Such faults, which also affect the degree of its civic decorum (including accountability), stem in part from imperfections in its legality and morality; but they are largely attributable to impediments within thinking itself. Worse still, the real trouble lies not solely in the existence of such impediments, but rather in their highly insidious nature, by dint of which we are not even aware of them.[41]

Second to Francis Bacon, Thomasius is among the first of modern thinkers to dwell upon distorted modes of human consciousness, and to disclose the extent to which they can blur our vision and warp our judgment. Individual delusions undoubtedly have something to do with such distortions; for the most part, however, he traces them to deception by others, which causes us to believe not what we see, but what others want us to see. Thomasius diagnoses the principal impediment to correct vision and sound judgment as prejudice. It is prejudice that eminently lends itself to manipulation, by means of which people are made to take smokescreens for real fog. And he concludes that, thus amplified, it is massive prejudice, and not inadequate memory or logical cognition that clouds human minds.[42]

Coupled with prejudice, and possibly in part its source, are haste and impatience, defects deeply ingrained in the human makeup. We want to know and judge things before we have given ourselves time enough to *learn* to know them, and know them from the inside, from the depth of our very being, and not by blindly following others.[43] We cut corners, we short-circuit the actual *experience* of things. We insist that children learn things by heart in order to train their memory; but memorizing things

40 ES, 299–310, 356–69; AS, 10–13. Rather closely anticipating Max Weber, Thomasius states that, in modernity, authority typically assumes the form of rational-legal dominion (*Herrschaft*). This, he adds, is in sharp contrast to the intrinsic-traditional authority of the original Christian communities, which shared not only their basic beliefs but also their ownership of property.

41 EV, 100–2, 287–305; see also ES, 89.

42 EV, 76–7, 269–70, 272–85, 285–304; see also AS, 14–17.

43 EV, 296.

hardly leads to the formation of practical judgment. If only, Thomasius exclaims, we gave a fraction of the attention we give to memory training to the development of our judgment; for "one ounce of judgment (*judici*) counts infinitely more than a pound of memory."[44] There is only one cure: a determined effort to guide children in such a way that they do not judge prematurely, that they do not jump to conclusions before they have learned to weigh the evidence before them, or indeed have learned to recognize what is and what is not appropriate evidence to judge upon.[45]

Unfortunately, however, every form of guidance itself harbours the danger of disseminating prejudices, and prejudices that are potentially more destructive than those that guidance is meant to prevent. And this is so because guidance is liable to generate dependence on authorities, and these can more permanently warp our judgment than the impatience of youth. We learn to rely on others to tell us what is what, and thereby expose ourselves to being infected by their own prejudices. Dependence makes us hold on to walls, to any prop we can find, and thus risk never discovering what it is to walk on our own.[46]

It will hardly escape notice that Thomasius's idea of autonomous self-direction, of acting on one's own judgment, strongly prefigures Kant's understanding of "enlightenment." At the same time, there is an important difference in their thinking, in view of which Thomasius's individualism sharply contrasts with that of Kant. What Kant was to call self-incurred (*selbst-verschuldet*) immaturity (*Unmündigkeit*) was for Thomasius by no means *self*-incurred. Consistent with his theory of human inter-dependence, Thomasius is reluctant to blame individuals in themselves for failing to see their way to self-direction or the removal of falsifications that block their minds. He simply cannot and will not accept that people knowingly choose immaturity because it suits them to remain immature. Hence whereas Kant speaks of "man's self-incurred immaturity" as an *individual* problem, brought about and perpetuated by himself, in being the work of his own will regardless of social contexts and political regimes, Thomasius looks upon it as something that is neither self-incurred nor self-chosen. Persons do not knowingly falsify their consciousness; they do not *want* to remain deluded in the way Kant's typical humans decide to remain immature.

44 EV, 300–8, 226–7; AV, 75, 100, 270–1.
45 EV, 162–3, 294–6.
46 EV, 227–9, 293–308; see also AS, 15.

Nor is the problem attributable for him to cowardice, weakness of nerve, or sheer laziness, as immaturity is for Kant.[47]

Defects in our moral propensities may indeed, Thomasius grants, be self-incurred; more often than not, however, they are the result of external influences, be it within family life, during our days at school, within the professions, and in response to authorities generally. There is a constant tension throughout Thomasius's thinking between emphasis on independence and emphasis on interdependence, between the need for guidance and the need for distrusting guidance. In spite, or because, of this tension, Thomasius persistently pressed for reforms of external conditions that discriminate against the poor, against unpopular minorities, or non-conforming individuals, in order to promote both a more independent mode of individual thinking *and* a more interdependent mode of acting in the public realm.[48] That the bulk of humanity should *want* to be deceived, or was eager to remain permanently immature, Thomasius simply refused to accept.

REASON, WILL, AND INTERDEPENDENCE

Thomasius's propagation of reforms should not, however, be construed to imply a sanguine belief on his part that later means better, or in there being possibilities for doing the world over. Nothing, in truth, was further from his exceptionally critical mind. If anything, Thomasius was

47 See Kant, "What is Enlightenment?", in H. Reiss, ed., *Kant's Political Writings*, 54–5. Thomasius cites some telling examples of discrimination against the poor.

48 The discrimination is greatest, Thomasius declares, in the administration of the legal system, so that there is in fact one law for the rich and another for the poor. "It is hard to see," he writes, "what Christian ethics are involved in the verdicts of our learned judges or, for that matter, of our Christian pastors. A poor simple soul that allowed herself to be seduced into pregnancy is not one thousandth part as depraved (*verhurt*) as many a 'respectable' lady who for years has led an adulterous, whore-like existence. Yet the former is publicly pilloried as a whore and required to do church penance as well, while the latter is rewarded with grand titles, and occupies the most coveted pews in church. A poor soldier who has been press-ganged into war service, and who upon his release is driven by poverty and bad company into highway robbery is not one thousandth part as villainous as many a 'gentleman' who by skillful graft and doubtful dealings not only succeeds in our times and society in lining his pockets handsomely, but also in acquiring fame and respect to boot." (AS, 541–2.)

obsessed with a sense of human tragedy that, in its way, is perhaps a good deal more disturbing than Kant's lack of faith in overcoming "man's self-incurred immaturity." For while Kant for the most part blamed the individual and viewed the problem of immaturity as a profoundly personal problem, Thomasius's deep despair had its source in the idea of a fateful predicament in the human condition itself. Rightful decorum, mutual esteem, and honest accounting may never come into being, not because of this or that defect or weakness of will, but rather because no enlisting of will can deliver humans from the evil that envelops them.

All that is left is to seek divine grace, to pray for the kind of redemption which no human reform can yield.[49] Thomasius was a deeply reflective thinker, and intellectually too honest to conceal from himself or from others the extent of his agonizing doubts about the scale or duration of secular remedies. Particularly during the period in which he revised his moral theory (*Ausübung der Sittenlehre*) (1696). Thomasius underwent a severe crisis of conscience that almost made him disavow his earlier voluntarist writings.[50]

I do not intend to follow here Thomasius's understanding of divine grace or the line of thought that prompted him to disavow his earlier writings, but I am inclined to accept the view that this period of his life was more than a merely passing phase. This said, notwithstanding his mounting uncertainty about the power of reason to engage the instrumentality of will in the service of the good, Thomasius shrank from breaking the ties between reason and action or from discontinuing his reforming projects in *vita civili*.[51] It is not hard to see why this was so. Manifestly, if reason ceased to form a structural constituent of action, his affirmation of human self-direction and human accountability would be in serious jeopardy; and at this Thomasius understandably balked.

Thomasius's soul-searching about the power of rational willing was not, however, atypical of Enlightenment thinking. For, contrary to its common identification with the Age of Reason, a facile belief in reason hardly ever formed the mainstay of the *Aufklärung*. In his gropingly troubled approach to reason and will, therefore, Thomasius was very much the Enlightenment's true forerunner. Still, setting limits to the scope of

49 AV, 174; AS, 514–15; see also Thomasius, *Versuch vom Wesen des Geistes* (Halle: Salfeld, 1699), 183–4.

50 AS, 526–7; see also EV, 101–2; AV, 163–76, 181–2, 194–6.

51 AV, 174; for Thomasius's revised theory of the will, see esp. AS, 514–15 and his *Versuch vom Wesen des Geistes*, 183–4.

reason, or realizing the obstacles that impede human self-emancipation (including defects of will) did not stop him from making a dogged attempt to advance a distinctive ethic of civic reciprocity, or from breathing new life into the idea of accountable rule. And in both directions he put utmost emphasis on the creation of a level of public consciousness, in and through which ordinary people were to feel that they should demand reasons from their "betters" when called upon to serve the state and do as they are bid by its rulers. The rulers, in turn, were to take note of what was expected of them as responsible and upright servants of the state. Above all, in making the operation of rightful decorum conditional upon merit and public esteem as dominant societal values, as well as upon rationally intelligible and rationally defensible criteria of justice, Thomasius pioneered a new overall perspective from which authority could be judged and its inherent fallibility exposed. Although he stopped short of working out a constitutional framework within which rightful civility and rational accountability would be enshrined, he did lay the groundwork upon which others could build.[52]

In its general thrust, Thomasius's thinking must probably be located within the liberal tradition, although it departs significantly from the usual brand of liberal individualism in its stress on *public* goods and *social* interdependence. On the other hand, his insistence on two *distinct* ethics of mutuality, and his sharp separation of communal fellowship from societal citizenship, might make him suspect to communitarian critics of liberalism.[53] However, aside from the question of ideological placing or contemporary appeal, there is, I believe, enough self-sustaining merit in Thomasius's thought to warrant an appraisal of it in its own right.

In addition to the distinction between two ethics of mutuality, not the least remarkable of Thomasius's contributions to political theorizing is his juxtaposition of two contrasting types of "purpose," or, more precisely, two contrasting sets of purposive strivings. While he allowed for overlaps, he nevertheless insisted on keeping analytically separate those

---

52 See on this point. Werner Schneiders, *Die wahre Aufklärung: Zum Selbstverständnis der deutschen Aufklärung* (Freiburg and Munich: K. Alber, 1974). Indeed, Thomasius could rightly be credited with having given significant direction to what Jürgen Habermas has called a "new notion of legitimation." "Popular Sovereignty as Procedure," in Bohman and Rehg, eds., *Deliberative Democracy* (Cambridge: MIT Press, 1997), 39. On the relation of legality to legitimacy, see David Dyzenhaus, *Legality and Legitimacy* (Oxford: Clarendon Press, 1997).

53 I touch on this issue in *Democratic Legitimacy*, chs. 3 and 9.

viewed as ultimate ends (*Endzweck in sich selbst*), whose purpose wholly lies in themselves; they typically are the goals of a religious community and contain their own justification, calling for no purposive reasons beyond themselves. The other set of purposes consists of extrinsic objectives (*Absehen*) and is characterized by ends within political society. While the ends of a particular community are *constitutive* – in that a community would not be what it is without them – the ends of society at large merely *confront* its members as objects of choice, as so many alternatives seeking support. Being open to debate and requiring processes of reaching agreement, they are neither self-justificatory nor self-explanatory. Unlike the consensual community, political society therefore calls for recurrent efforts to be directed toward the bridging of differences.

Of course, Thomasius remarks, if consensus could invariably be taken for granted, the need to forge special institutional ways for producing some common ground would be altogether dispensable. All that would be needed are rulers who, like philosopher-kings, know how to govern correctly. And, since their decisions could then be regarded as definitionally unassailable, any questioning or demand for rendering account – let alone any form of dissent – might be viewed as inexplicably weird, if not as a brazen act of wilful intransigence.[54]

THE MEDIATION OF CITIZENSHIP:
CONCLUDING REMARKS

It appears that Thomasius's sharp distinction between community and society had its major source in a deep-seated suspicion that beneath an unmediated societal oneness there could be covertly lurking an inarticulated plurality of values, views, and interests, raising the danger of a highly problematic kind of unity; problematic because, in order to subsist, it may demand potentially repressive forms of political homogenization of the kind that Rousseau adduced, as we shall note. Thomasius certainly made no secret of his preference for less absolute and less final resolutions of conflicting claims, feeling as he did that open disagreement courted fewer problems than a doctrinally imposed consensus based on professedly universal truths that, once discovered, are forever

---

54 ES, 358, 360. There is not a little irony in Thomasius's remark, because he considers Plato's notion of philosopher-kings a "nonsensical idea." He refuses to believe that philosophers have any privileged knowledge of practical politics, and fears that they are likely to do more harm than good. See also Thomasius's *Kurtzer Entwurff*, 169–70, and *Erinnerung Zweyer Collegiorum*, 34.

held to be irrefutable. Politics, in short, exists because of a *lack* of consensus. And this is so not only because people differ about values, or about their priority as objects of public policy, but also because they themselves are at times torn by conflicting assessments of a situation and undecided about what courses of action deserve maximal support. Bridging, therefore, may involve an internal process as much as an external process; and public deliberation and discourse may assist in clarifying the former as in mediating the latter.

Thomasius by no means questions the desirable existence of broad agreements within a political society (of however plural opinions) on certain core *principles* such as truthfulness, the keeping of promises, or helping those in distress. What he questions, however, is that any such general understandings necessarily entail specific agreements about the choice or urgency of public ends, or about who should govern and how, over what range of concerns, and such like. And the danger that he sensed was that the public could be made to think that these kinds of agreement coincided or, worse still, that they *ought* to coincide; and that any political society that cannot embrace the whole possible gamut of plural values is therefore courting its demise.[55]

Among the bold steps that Thomasius was taking to promote an ethic of civility in political efforts coming to terms with credal differences, he particularly stressed the need for tolerance and equity so as to augment a climate of public mutuality. And despite his inner tensions' causing him to doubt the effectiveness of purely secular remedies, he could not entirely suppress a comparable uncertainty about the secular effectiveness of religious intervention. All the same, this did not stop him from hoping for "sparks" of disinterested spiritual love to ignite a secular

---

55 Thomasius does not *advocate* dissensus or "adversary politics" for its own sake – the sort of thing that critics of "adversary democracy" such as Jane J. Mansbridge have been lamenting in America; nor is he blind to hazards of deep cleavages or ruthless antagonism, but, on balance, he prefers open disagreement to its suppression or to a dualistic public consciousness that sees all issues in terms of a sharp either/or, so that those who cannot wholly agree are of necessity implacable enemies. See, for example, EV, 229 and AV, 95–9, 267–9, 293–4. Just as there can be shades of agreement on basic values of conduct and the degree of equity, so there can be shades of disagreement on questions of their political implementation; and Thomasius is anxious to rid people of the mistaken idea that the former entails the latter, that credal consensus on generalities *means* political consensus on particularities, without denying that there *can* be also *fundamental* disagreements on values themselves.

ethic of civility, just as his loss of confidence in purely secular remedies did not stop him from shouting from the rooftops what he wished others to hear. "Enlightenment" – although he did not use the term himself – therefore characterized not only the content of his teachings, but also their method and the manner and means of their dissemination. And it was the method as much as the content that moved men and women into aspiring to a degree of civic consciousness, of which they hitherto were generally held to be totally unfit – and of which they themselves had thought themselves totally unfit.

Taken together, therefore, in terms of content and in terms of method, this surely is no mean achievement. Opinion may quite properly differ about what originality Thomasius may justly claim in this or that direction, but on the question of "rightful decorum," as a civic ethic *sui generis* within an autonomous politics marked by plurality, he impressively transcended the doctrinal heritage on which he had drawn.[56] In their broader ramifications, his ideas also remarkably touch on issues raised in contemporary discussions on liberal and communitarian theory, as they also strikingly foreshadow, in their emphasis on open debate and unfalsified modes of consciousness, contemporary preoccupations with "ideal speech situations." Concerning both issues, Thomasius's central aim seems to have been to infuse into the discourse of public life a degree of vibrancy that was altogether novel, and into political action a degree of mutuality and integrity that it is still struggling to acquire. While he denied that communitarian modes of thinking could be transplanted into political society, he did encourage the hope that public objectives could assume patterns of shared acceptance in the course of free and open debate. Yet, although he expressed the belief that agreement might be attained in this manner, sufficient to carry through the

---

56 Among foreign influences, that of Locke was undoubtedly the most dominant in Thomasius's theory of reason – as, we noted earlier, he himself fully acknowledged. The emphasis on thinking for oneself, on being one's own master, and on disregarding authorities most strikingly echoes themes in Locke's *Essay concerning Human Understanding*. Similarly, the emphasis on prudential reasons as a sanction for the principle of reciprocity may well have had its source in Thomasius's reading of Locke. In this connection it is perhaps not without interest that Thomasius's prudential grounding of reciprocity – as the paramount principle of civic relations – markedly contrasts with Rawls's comparable emphasis upon it, in that Rawls derives it from expressly *moral* sanctions. See his "The Idea of Public Reason Revisited," *University of Chicago Law Review* (64), 1997, 766, 769–71.

work of legislation within a climate of reciprocal civility, he was less sanguine than contemporary theorists of the "ideal speech situation" about the extent to which political consensus would imply unanimity on whatever was good, right, or true, in universal terms. For, jut as he consistently affirmed that the mediated and contingent oneness of societal citizenship was radically different from the unmediated and implicit oneness of communal fellowship, he no less consistently denied that the very texture and perception of "agreement" in these two contexts was one and the same or even comparable. Neither, he urged, should therefore be confused with the other; while each has its place and reasons for being, each draws on quite dissimilar sources of human association, and each is sustained by quite dissimilar forms of cohesive sanctions and reciprocal understandings. Were this not so, Thomasius argued, were they identical, the domain of politics and citizenship would have long been pre-empted, for there would literally be no point in its existence.

If he had said nothing else, making this issue so abundantly clear merits in itself, I should think, Thomasius's urgent resuscitation from oblivion. And, whether or not he is in some ways justly overshadowed by others can hardly in the slightest belittle his work in this direction. Here, as in his attempt to combine plurality with reciprocity, Thomasius disclosed an intensity of personal commitment that was little short of total, and which, for want of a better way of describing it, could perhaps be said to qualify for the epithet "religious," centred though it was on the concerns of secular society, and rooted as it was in foundations that were prudential rather than strictly moral. That he opted to derive the norms of public life from prudential reasons had, we noted, a good deal to do with his determination to uphold the intrinsic autonomy of the political as such, as well as with his conviction that this autonomy was more firmly anchored in a shared consciousness of citizenship in and through public discourse than in the rulership of secluded philosopher-kings. For, like Hannah Arendt was to do, Thomasius repudiated the vision of a governance devised by superior lawgivers in favour of a "politics of life," warts and all, because he could not bring himself to believe that philosophers have any privileged knowledge of practical politics. Instead, he preferred standards of reciprocity to evolve in the course of people's day-to-day business within civil society, just as he liked to think that those entrusted with government will themselves come to recognize the value of decorum in their use of power.

Whether or not Thomasius's preferred vision of civic mutuality and the decorum of power is the more desirable or more sustainable one, it undeniably seems closer to the professed ethos of contemporary mainstream democracy. And, while I would hesitate to say that this is what Thomasius wishfully anticipated, his preference did set off a line of thinking about public self-enactment which, in its combined emphasis on autonomy and interdependence has not ceased to engage debate and which, in several particulars, still is as refreshingly daring as it was at its inception.[57]

57 For example, David Braybrooke, Professor of Government and Philosophy, University of Texas at Austin, a distinguished scholar on Natural Law, refers to Thomasius as "a writer who speaks to our own age about the problem of giving due place to the distinctive demands of community and citizenship."

6

Public Reason and Political Self-Mastery: Jean-Jacques Rousseau

AS ROUSSEAU TELLS US in his *Confessions,* he was first stirred into serious study by Voltaire, in the late 1730s, in particular by Voltaire's correspondence with the Crown Prince of Prussia, who ascended the throne as Frederick II in 1740. The correspondence had recently been published and, as Rousseau records, was causing quite a flurry.[1] It is apparent from the letters that Frederick was quite taken with Thomasius, whose demand for rational accountability by rulers was a central theme in the king's throne speech.[2] Although Rousseau mentions his interest in Leibniz and Spinoza (among others) during this period, it is not clear how much he directly knew about Thomasius – whose paternity of the German Enlightenment is in a way comparable to Voltaire's paternity of the French Enlightenment. A number of striking parallels in their thought seem evident, however, notably as regards the notion of accountability in the civic realm, the transformation of reason in the service of reciprocity, and the negative interpretation of enlightenment and autonomy, in terms of the removal of sources of false consciousness and undue dependence as well as a profound disdain of gross inequalities. In what follows I shall draw attention to these parallels, without at all wishing to imply that they in any way detract from Rousseau's own originality or furnish proof of Thomasius's influence in these concerns, since, clearly, Rousseau was not infrequently drawing on ideas which Thomasius himself had drawn on.

1 Jean-Jacques Rousseau, *The Confessions* (1781), trans. J.M. Cohen (Harmondsworth: Penguin Books, 1953, 1971), 205.

2 For fuller details see my "Rightful Decorum and Rational Accountability," in *Christian Thomasius,* ed., Werner Schneiders (Hamburg: Felix Meiner, 1989), 187–98).

SOCIAL MULTIPLICITY
AND POLITICAL COMMITMENT

Like Thomasius, Rousseau was well aware of the plurality of human interests, and of whatever sets people apart in their different roles – as fa-
thers, friends, employers, magistrates, physicians, and so on – and he
knew equally well that some interests might not be compatible with others. "For every two men whose interests may coincide," he remarked in
the Preface to *Narcissus,* "there are a hundred thousand, perhaps, whose
interests are totally opposite."[3] And in a note to the third chapter of
Book II of the *Social Contract* Rousseau observed: "If there were no different interests, one would scarcely be aware of the common interest
since it would never encounter any obstacles; everything would go
smoothly of its own accord, and politics would cease to be an art."[4]

Citizenship, in other words, the coming together of any agreement
about what people have in common in the way of shared interests, purposes, or opinions, is not the feat of "natural" dispositions or intuitive
feelings among individuals, but the laborious work of reasoned judgment. This, for Rousseau, is precisely what distinguishes the "citizen"
from the "patriot." People do not naturally think of themselves as citizens because they do not instinctively identify with others. Rather,
Rousseau believed, as did Kant after him, that *instinctively* they distrusted, if not disliked, one another, since *naturally* they are not sociable. Unlike patriots who, in response to the love they directly feel for
their native soil, do what they cannot help doing, citizens are the product of mediating forms of processes – argument, deliberation, negotiation, and the "cancelling out of pluses and minuses."[5] For, although
not by nature sociable, neither are they combative, for combativeness
– and here Rousseau markedly departs from Hobbes – does not arise
in nature, but only in society, where everything conspires to make humans combative and fragmented.[6]

3 Rousseau, Preface to *Narcissus, The Miscellaneous Works of Mr. J.J. Rousseau*
(New York: Burt Franklin, 1767, reprint 1972) II, 138.

4 Rousseau, *Social Contract,* bk. II, ch. 3, note 7.

5 Ibid., bk. II, ch. 3.

6 Rousseau, *Discourse on the Origin of Inequality* (1755), trans. G.D.H. Cole,
The Social Contract and Discourses (London: Dent, 1946), 188–91 (72–5).
Subsequently referred to as *Inequality.* (Page references in brackets are to the
revised edition of Cole's translation by J.H. Brumfitt and J.C. Hall, London:
Dent, 1973.)

Without disputing, therefore, that "society" puts obstacles into the path of civic mediation, thereby making agreement only contingently possible, he nonetheless wished to maintain that *persistent* disagreement was avoidable, given the absence of clashing selfish interests. Accordingly, lingering plural positions on what was good for everybody on *general*, as distinct from purely *private*, grounds, were evidently ruled out by definition.[7] At the same time, Rousseau must have suspected that individuals *could* have different views, regardless of their private interests; for he would otherwise hardly have sanctioned censorship and other repressive measures (in Book IV of the *Social Contract*) which strike liberal readers as so highly unpalatable.

Surely, had he harboured no suspicions at all about people's ability to form divergent views of the common good – mistaken though he may have held them to be – without being selfish or criminally perverse in one form or another, he would not have recommended such radical measures. In other words, he must have realized that "opinions" and "interests" are not one and the same thing, when he fully granted, for example, that individuals could cherish opinions for religious reasons, and do so with utmost sincerity, and that such convictions, therefore, could conceivably have nothing to do with egoistic ends. Indeed, he went so far as to concede their right and freedom to hold such views, provided they did not propagate them publicly. For, only in the latter event were they to be banned, because only then did they threaten *political* accord on the public good.[8]

Rousseau clearly went out of his way *not* to impute questionable motives to people or to deny them the right to *have* opinions. Still, he *was* inclined to attribute dissident views to misconceived "universalism" among only a minority of citizens (such as "philosophers") as he also somehow did believe that there was only one correct way of thinking about the common good and that, however sincerely people desire to bring certain things about, there are always cogent and justifiable grounds for restraining them from translating their beliefs into action, or from inciting others to do so.[9] Sincerity of motives is no doubt desirable, but it does not in itself *define* citizenship. Rousseau might agree with liberals that it is no business of the state to inquire into a citizen's personal motives or private beliefs; what he would not accept, however,

7 Rousseau, *Discourse on Political Economy* (1755), trans. G.D.H. Cole, *The Social Contract and Discourses*, 236–7, 244 (120–1, 128).

8 Rousseau, *Social Contract*, bk. IV, ch. 8.

9 Rousseau, Preface to *Narcissus*, 138.

is that citizens should *act* as though they did not feel committed to honour principles they publicly avowed, since this would undermine the state itself, and the general will on which it was founded.[10] For, once an association had been founded, the overriding consideration had to be to preserve it, even if this demanded the expulsion of dissenters. Although Rousseau wished to uphold citizenship as a commitment based on publicly discussible and publicly defensible grounds, he was tormented by doubts as to whether individual commitments would be strong enough to withstand the pressures of changing moods and interests; and, ceasing to be binding, they would cease to be *commitments*.

These doubts had their principal source in his uncertainty about most people's grasp of the nature of specifically *bounded* commitment. For, unlike a professed pledge to humanity in general, such a commitment is highly circumscribed and totally inconceivable outside the confines of statehood. Especially to the philosopher, Rousseau adds with not a little scorn, such boundaries have no meaning; theirs is a world in which far-away Tartars are loved above their neighbours.[11] Despite the fact that "the term *human race* suggests a purely collective idea, in which a real union among individuals simply does not figure," they prefer this image to reality.[12]

And just as a social union, to be real, must be bounded, so must the meaning of citizenship itself. Otherwise, a *patrie* cannot be a home to those associating with other individuals anxious to form a civic union. On this view, citizenship demands a degree of *ex*clusiveness as well as *in*clusiveness, by virtue of which people experience a sense of belonging and affinity, when "neither the stealthy machinations of vice nor the modesty of rectitude can escape public notice and public judgment."[13] Rousseau points here to an obvious yet important fact; namely, that space creates differences of relative proximity and relative distance. Underscoring this fact, and driving home the lesson to be learned from it, Rousseau sets boundaries to civic commitments. Limits, Rousseau tells the Poles, are clearly called for; Poland is far too large as a single state to

10 Rousseau, *Social Contract*, bk IV, ch. 8. See also *Political Economy*, 244 (128): "The worst of all abuses is to pay apparent obedience to the laws, only in order to break them with security in reality."

11 Rousseau, *Political Economy*, 246 (130); see also Rousseau, *Emile* (1762), trans. A. Bloom (New York: Basic Books, 1979), 39, and Preface to *Narcissus*, 136.

12 Rousseau, *Geneva Manuscript*, in R.D. Masters, ed., *On the Social Contract* (New York: St Martin's Press, 1978), 159.

13 Rousseau, *Inequality*, 144 (28).

yield any scope for civic consciousness or a sense of belonging; it would do well, therefore, to convert into a confederation of multiple autonomous entities, on the pattern of the Swiss Confederation.[14] Ideally, it is within the city-state that the authorization in and through rationally mediated processes, which definies citizenship, can potentially be suffused with the spontaneous sentiments that animate patriotism.[15] Contrary to the message of the philosopher of unlimited humanity, reality informs us that the more extended a state is, the greater is the plurality of interests and the weaker are the civic bonds of commitment linking and binding its inhabitants. Whatever sentiments are conjoined with reasons of utility then become more and more vapid, if they do not altogether evaporate. A *world*-citizen simply is no *citizen*.[16]

To be sure, plurality of interests and opinions did not cease to constitute a political reality for Rousseau: citizenship *was* a mutuality different from patriotism, in a way that recalls Thomasius's distinction between "society" and "community." There *are* occasions in which citizenship and patriotism *could* coincide, but any conditions that might engender this coincidence must be viewed as something quite separate from the ingredients that definitionally constitute each. Thus, whereas in patriotism being *implies* commitment without any further explanation, citizenship demands distinct mediation resting on *extrinsic* reasons. Unlike patriotism – one of the "greatest miracles" of all political virtues, through which human action achieves feats of lasting glory that "dazzle our feeble eyes" – citizenship does not originate in spontaneous will and intrinsic sentiment, but rather is the product of deliberative will, in which instrumental reasoning plays by far the greatest role.[17] For, whereas in acts of patriotism purpose and end coincide – since what is done is done for its own sake – in acts of citizenship the end of action lies beyond it. As in the union of association itself, instrumental reasons form the bedrock and the justification for membership within a state. Without such rationally mediated agreement, there can be no legitimate compact and no binding commitment. The authorization of a social union is *not* like a miracle; neither forming a social

14 Rousseau, *Considerations on the Government of Poland* (1772), trans. F. Watkins, *Rousseau: Political Writings* (Edinburgh: Nelson, 1953), 181–2, 201–2. For much the same reasons Rousseau predicted the demise of the great monarchies of Europe (*Emile*, 194).

15 Rousseau, *Inequality*, 144 (28).

16 Rousseau, *Political Economy*, 246 (130).

17 Ibid.

compact, nor entering into a political commitment (symbolized by the general will) is an event comparable to meteors dropping out of the sky. Humans do not magically agree, from irresistible instincts, or because they like each other, share the same colour if skin or the same religion or language; none of these elements by themselves impel them to form a *political* association.[18]

Admittedly, there can be no nation in the absence of cultural affinities of one sort or another to build on; yet, for the creation of a distinctly *political* culture, in which binding obligations are embedded, so to speak, people must see a point in sharing it, and for reasons that, while embodying objectively valid *im*personal grounds, at the same time contain shared *personal* reasons.[19] A civic culture is fully accessible only if those partaking in it also have a personal stake in it. Only then do individuals become *citizens*, living and working together as free partners in a climate of reciprocity, *experiencing* the difference between what they derive from being citizens and what they would derive from being purely on their own.[20]

Much of what Rousseau has to say on coming to agreement and forming a union is redolent with remarkable realism, and with no beating about the bush as to what it means to submit to common laws. By sheer inclination, he observes, people will have nothing to do even with the best laws; for even these they view as "constant privations," as a "yoke" imposed on them. The true mark of the Legislator, therefore, is not merely to propose laws that are good in themselves, but to make people see that these laws are of advantage to them and that they have the crucial relevance to their joint ethos and well-being that renders them capable of being sustained and upheld.[21] Rousseau knows that there is nothing in individual wills to incline them to accept general rules, *unless* such general rules promise to establish *reciprocal* relations, in and through which individuals gain more than they surrender, so that by working with and for others they truly work for themselves. Here, as in Thomasius's conception of reciprocity, prudential reasons loom paramount. For the Legislator to *persuade* individuals to transform themselves from independent into interdependent beings, he must induce them to consult their prudential reasons and not appeal

18 Rousseau, *Geneva Manuscript*, 159.
19 Rousseau, *Political Economy*, 235, 240, (119, 124).
20 Ibid., 249 (133): see also *Emile*, 39, 85, and Preface to *Narcissus*, 138.
21 Rousseau, *Social Contract*, bk. I, ch. 8; bk. II, chs. 1, 7; *Emile*, 464.

solely to their emotions, since only then are they likely to gain the conviction that as isolated persons they can do very little to promote and
protect their own vital interests.[22]

PURITY OF SENTIMENTS
AND REASONED RECIPROCITY

Clearly, on this argument, citizenship, and the commitment it implies,
does not *derive* from the love of one's native soil commonly associated
with patriotism. Whatever *patrie* means for the patriot, in other words, is
not the same as what it means for the citizen. Citizenship, like statehood
itself, is nothing natural, instinctive, or spontaneous. One as much as
the other is an artificial *creation*, the outcome of rational choice. In contrast to patriotism, sentiments are secondary; their purity is far less important than the force of reciprocal obligations that they generate. In
acting as citizens we are not called upon to disclose or justify our personal motives or even the intensity of our dedication. All we are expected to do – yet this is by no means negligible for Rousseau – is to
honour the ends we publicly avow. Citizens, unlike patriots (or lovers)
may hold all sorts of private beliefs, or entertain whatever feelings are
most dear to them. What principally matters is the *will* entailed in a
commitment publicly made, and the coherence between such a will and
its execution. For, without matching public utterance with public deed,
the meaning of "commitment," we noted, is lost. Public lying is blame-
worthy, not on account of the private motives that prompt it but on account of its inconsistency with publicly assumed commitments. For such
inconsistency threatens the very basis of citizenship, the reasoned foundation of mediated reciprocity. A legitimately grounded state simply
cannot afford to incur this risk if, in order to survive, it seeks to maintain
a credible continuity between public avowal and public deed. Consequently, in order to go on being what it was meant to be, Rousseau insists, a state cannot but punish the transgressor.[23]

Putting it slightly differently, in order to amount to an obligation,
citizenship requires *im*personal defensibility, a form of justification imper-
vious to feelings of affection or hostility. It is because of this requirement
that Rousseau puts so much weight on *public* reasons, on the shared intelligibility of reasons employed in public discourse. And he does so, again

22 Rousseau, *Social Contract*, bk. II, chs. 4, 7.
23 Ibid., bk. II, ch. 4; bk. IV, ch. 8.

not unlike Thomasius, in order to lend substance to the idea of accountability. If people, not once or twice, but routinely, say one thing in public but, in truth, do quite another, reasons cease to *count* as reasons, and accounting for action in terms of reasons becomes an absurdity. A patriot, not unlike a father, has only to consult his heart; a citizen, however, must be able to give (and demand) reasons that can serve as explanations or justifications. Unlike feelings and passions, which are neither explicable nor discussable, reasons *are*, provided they are intelligible and, being so, potentially defensible or challengeable. Love is not a matter of discussion or argument; we love or we don't love, but no amount of reasoning will *make* us love. Will, as rational choice, by contrast, *demands* deliberation, the weighing of pros and cons, and the discussion of alternatives, in order to direct its purposive thrust. In short, to be accounted for, will must rest on judgment and intelligible reasons. Hence a magistrate who listens solely to his heart when rendering a verdict fails in his duty – if he is not on the way to becoming a traitor.[24]

That something close to a trade-off is an integral part of reasoning and acting as a citizen is perhaps best demonstrated in Rousseau's account of what undoubtedly is the most severe test: a citizen's willingness to die in defence of the homeland. Without detriment to selfless acts of altruism, Rousseau demands that public reasons be given for why *citizens* should sacrifice their lives for the good of their country. And, all the more so, because otherwise there is a real danger that a government might arbitrarily demand such a sacrifice. It may invoke the safety of the state, speak of "reasons of national security," and so on; but, unless such reasons withstand the challenge of discursive scrutiny as *public* reasons, they are mere assertions and, as such, simply will not do. Not publicly explained – or openly challenged – a phrase like "national security" constitutes one of the most "execrable maxims" ever invented by tyrannical powers, "the most false that might be proposed, the most dangerous that might be accepted, and the most directly opposed to the fundamental compact of association. For a government may demand the ultimate sacrifice not to protect the state but only itself."[25]

24 Rousseau, *Political Economy*, 235 (119). A recent writer, also anxious to rehabilitate the notion of patriotism, seeks, unlike Rousseau, to run together what Rousseau was determined to keep apart, namely, the sentiment of patriotism from the rationality of citizenship. See Maurizio Viroli, *For Love of Country* (Oxford: Clarendon Press, 1995.)

25 Rousseau, *Political Economy*, 248 (132).

The principle of reasoned justification that Rousseau invokes here is the principle of reciprocity. Unless citizens are convinced that the devotion or respect that the state demands of them is in turn bestowed on them by the state, unless they feel assured that the protection of the humblest of them is as much the concern of the state as it is expected to be theirs, no one can extract from them the duty to die for their country; for nothing is as sacred as the life of the ordinary citizen.[26] Hence, to die in combat for the state is a civic duty only if it rests on a shared understanding of mutuality: citizens fight for a country if and when in doing so they protect those of their fellows who in turn are willing to protect them. And the basis for such a shared understanding is not sentimental love but reciprocal *interest*; reasons of reciprocity must tell citizens that to protect their lives they have to protect their country. Indeed, such reasons should persuade them that the danger of losing their lives *as* citizens, that is, as members of a state, is infinitely smaller than the danger of having no *patrie* to call their own.[27] As long as the Jews, for example, are fragmented, deprived of a land of their own, Rousseau remarks, so long will they remain unable to escape the tyranny exercised against them.[28] Not only are humans assured of greater safety as members of a state of their own, they are also more likely to be truly *themselves*. And only then are they genuinely free and capable of moral willing. Freedom and morality are thus equally bound up with a sense of being at home in one's world.[29]

To be sure, such a shared ethos of reciprocal inclusiveness, together with a sense of civic duty, draws on sources that are not confined to purely prudential reasons. Not unlike *amour de soi*, the noblest sentiment that, by Rousseau's account, humans can have, the combination of reciprocal inclusiveness and self-obligated civic mutuality involves an amalgam of reason and feelings. Indeed, for Rousseau, this inner fusion of rationality and love confers its abiding strength upon the bond between oneself and others, in terms of both a consciousness of citizenship and the consciousness of lawful reciprocity it demands.

A rationally grounded sentiment seems to Rousseau, therefore, the surest warrant for the emergence of a societal ethos of *lawfulness*, which for

26 Ibid., 249 (133).

27 Ibid., 247–8 (131–2); Social Contract, bk. II, ch. 4.

28 Rousseau, *Emile*, 304.

29 *Political Economy*, 247–9 (131–3); *Letters from the Mountain* (1764), *Oeuvres Complètes* (Paris: Gallimard, 1959–69), III, 841 (hereafter referred to as *Letters*).

him, as subsequently for Kant, is an essential condition of civic reciprocity. To corroborate his stand, he draws a parallel between life in civil society and life in pre-political nature. Its idea is to demonstrate that for laws in society to have the quality of impartiality, they must mirror the generality of natural laws.[30] Yielding to them must, accordingly, presuppose a recognizable basis of reciprocal applicability, so that whatever dependence arises is *equal* dependence, when "no one depends on the other to a greater extent than the other depends on him."[31] The law, thus viewed, unlike any other master, has no favourites; and only the law, therefore, is truly *general*, brooking by its rational objectivity no exceptions whatsoever. It alone is thereby able to create an *overall* lawfulness and, with it, a reinforced sentiment of inclusive citizenship.[32]

But, to bring about equality before law, social conditions in general are not merely peripheral. Of this Rousseau was as conscious as was Thomasius. A state that fails to generate suitable social conditions, or even fails to see the need for them, might indeed disclose little of the "rationality" of law, its objectivity or impartiality. For Rousseau such a state is a purely fabricated compact, a fraudulent state, that protects – if it does not promote – inequality, instead of preventing it. And, what is worst about such a state is that, in feigning generality, it ensnares people into mistaking the appearance of legitimacy for genuine legitimacy.[33] Clearly, if the rationality of law means anything for Rousseau, it means impartiality, a characteristic he attributes to the governance that exists in nature, and a characteristic he deems essential for a *patrie* to be a *juste patrie*. As outspoken as Thomasius, and far more outspoken than Kant ever dared to be, Rousseau tells the Corsicans: "The fundamental law of your Constitution must be equality. Everything must be related to it, including authority, which is established only to defend it."[34] The first and greatest public interest, he declares

30 Rousseau, *Emile*, 85; *Letters*, III, 842–3.

31 Rousseau, *Emile*, 85. Rousseau attempts to recreate the basic conditions that nature imposes on humans: (i) dependence on only impersonal or objective laws; (ii) absence of personal subjection implicit in people's isolation and independence of each other; and (iii) a fundamental equality of conditions for all, since all are equally subject to the forces of nature.

32 Rousseau, *Emile*, 85; *Letters*, III, 842–3; *Geneva Manuscript*, 161.

33 Rousseau, *Emile*, 85–9; *Letters*, III, 841; *Geneva Manuscript*, 161.

34 Rousseau, *Constitutional Project for Corsica* (1765), trans. F. Watkins, *Rousseau: Political Writings*, 289 (subsequently *Corsica*).

elsewhere, is always justice, based on reciprocity. And justice is necessarily a form of equality: "He who fears exceptions loves the law."[35]

There can, accordingly, be no rational order without the impartiality and reciprocity of law, but neither can there be a just or lawful state
that fails to establish, by way of ground rules, basic understandings
able to forestall the fraudulent state in which "the rich keep the law in
their pockets and the poor prefer bread to liberty."[36] Unless, therefore, enforceable rules exist about the admissible extent of inequality,
and unless such rules form an integral part of a social ethos, no political union or civic mutuality can survive. Property may be "sacred," as
Rousseau never ceased proclaiming, but this does not elevate it above
law.[37] For, once it rises above law, property endangers the public good.
He therefore urges the Corsicans to confine private property "within
the narrowest possible limits; to give it a measure, a rule, and a rein,
which will check, direct, and contain it, and keep it always subordinate
to the public good."[38] Once wealth succeeds in usurping justice, a
state is no longer worth having. If esteem and authority can be bought
and sold like commodities in the market, they are empty of meaning.
No citizen, therefore, "should be rich enough to buy another, and
none so poor as to be forced to sell himself."[39] In his advice to the
Corsicans, Rousseau is even more explicit; "Everyone should make a
living and no one should grow rich; that is the fundamental principle
of the prosperity of the nation."[40] He elaborates this principle by explaining that excesses in wealth, causing obesity on the one hand and
servility on the other, run counter to the very concept of citizenship.
For citizenship is incompatible with gross inequality, its inclusiveness
being fatally impaired.[41]

It follows that an undue imbalance of wealth and income militates
against the emergence of a rightful state, for such inequity lacks the reasoned sentiment of civic mutuality and civic inclusiveness. There is no
ambiguity about this thesis. Rousseau makes it crystal clear that a state in
which inequality is nurtured rather than curbed is a state in peril. The

35 Rousseau, *Letters*, III, 891; see also *Inequality*, 202–6 (87–91).
36 *Letters*, III, 890.
37 Rousseau, *Political Economy*, 254–5 (138–9).
38 Rousseau, *Corsica*; Watkins, *Rousseau: Political Writings*, 317.
39 Rousseau, *Social Contract*, bk. II, ch. 11.
40 Rousseau, *Corsica*; Watkins, *Rousseau*, 308.
41 Ibid., 316–17.

rationality of lawfulness is flawed if it is bereft of a passion for reciprocal fairness. Hence, he considers "strange and fatal" any constitutionality in which the "accumulation of riches always facilitates the means of further accumulation, and in which it is impossible for him who has nothing to acquire anything." Under such a constitution "an honest man has no means to extricate himself from poverty ... and must necessarily renounce all virtue to become a respectable person," for it is an order in which "knaves are the most honoured."[42] Clearly, once the means of acquiring wealth and the means of acquiring authority are one and the same, Rousseau observes in *Corsica*, nominal power may still be in the hands of magistrates, while real power is in those of the rich. "Under conditions such as these, the goal of ambition becomes twofold: some aspire to authority in order to sell the use thereof to the rich and thus themselves grow rich; the rest, the majority, go directly after wealth, with which they are sure one day of having power, either by buying authority for themselves, or by buying those who are its depositaries."[43]

A rightful state, therefore, is one build on the bedrock of reciprocity and fortified by impartial law, in which, because of its pervasive sense of social justice, reason and sentiment become one.

INTEREST, OPINION, AND DEMOCRACY

The emergence of reasons of the heart requires, according to this argument, a social fabric of civic reciprocity in and through which humans have a sense of membership within a state and a feeling that it pays to observe its laws. It "pays" because rationality *and* sentiment tell them that it is in their joint interest to preserve and protect a union in which property can be treasured without denying it to others, just as freedom can be enjoyed for oneself without depriving others of it. In short, the point of civic reciprocity is to realize that individuals *are* able to live with others without harming them or being harmed by them. It is to see oneself as a being whose existence is bound up with the existence of a greater whole; so that, being part of it, one can in a tangible way feel and identify with others as a *member*.[44]

42 Rousseau, Preface to *Narcissus*, 139.

43 Rousseau, *Corsica*; Watkins, *Rousseau*, 327–8.

44 Rousseau, *Emile*, 79, 104, 460; *Political Economy*, 251, 254 (135, 138).

A common interest, therefore, is not simply the aggregate or coincidence of interests that individuals have in common. For even identical interests, Rousseau well knew, are capable of producing strife and competition, rather than mutual understandings, agreement, or unity. Nor is it a natural or spontaneous desire directly derivable from "interest" alone. No one would deny, for example, that people waiting for a bus have everywhere a transparently identical interest: to get from here to there. Yet, not everywhere do they form an orderly line. Why? Because, as Rousseau stresses, any such regulated conduct is the result of a reasoning process, associated with the formation of a mediating *judgment* concerning what is fair, not merely for selves as selves, but as selves being an integral part of a context of ordering rules that they consciously share with others.[45] Which, perhaps, is not far from saying that the interest of all, like the will of all, would not, without such reasoned understandings, naturally or necessarily coincide with the common interest as the "general will."[46] For, not unlike the formation of the general will, it embodies the *simultaneous* engagement of purpose and deliberation, in which, as Kant would put it, an enlarged mentality comes into its own.

So conceived, a general interest, or general will, emerges from concerted modes of public thinking and, once formed, assumes, as it were, a life of its own that is qualitatively distinct from whatever motives or interests originally prompted the opinion-forming process. As in our example, resolving to wait in line is not directly deducible from one's interest in getting what one immediately wants, but rather is the outcome of mediating reasoning about boarding a bus with a minimum of strife and bother. Such an agreed-upon order is comparable in essence to a shared *ethos*, which for Rousseau is the core of a *public* opinion, properly so called. Without such a thing as a degree of shared consciousness of what is done or not done within the context of common interests, there can be no general will to form a union, and any state coming into being devoid of it is in truth no advance at all.[47] The point to note here is that laws or rule making and what Rousseau understands by public opinion are not things apart; and that, if they are, states have no real, and certainly no legitimate, existence.

45 Rousseau, *Social Contract*, bk. I, chs. 1, 2, 7; *Emile*, 464. On this point see also Collingwood, "Political Action," 162.

46 Rousseau, *Social Contract*, bk. II, ch. 3.

47 Ibid., bk. I, ch. 8; bk. II, ch. 12; bk. IV, ch. 7; *Political Economy*, 235, 240 (119, 124); Preface to *Narcissus*, 138.

Rousseau expresses utmost astonishment that political theorists fail to recognize that it is not constitutions that make or break a state, but the nature and quality of public opinion. For, what sound health is to the human body, the presence of public opinion is to the body politic.[48] Therefore, in saying that, once formed, rules regarding a common interest or a general will have a life of their own, Rousseau presumably has in mind a certain continuity of understandings that are widely shared, and, for practical purposes, provide a fundamental direction for what could be said to be fair with respect to everybody.

Thus, there would be no need to re-establish the terms of reciprocity each time citizens are confronted with the duty to fight for their country, provided that there is shared trust within a society, in its civic institutions as well as in ongoing procedures designed to guard and protect them. Under these conditions – and the existence of a vigilant citizenry periodically making sure that they continue – individuals do not have to work out each time what they give up to the state in return for what they receive from it. It follows that, given that national governments are trusted to use their constitutional powers legitimately, by observing principles of reciprocity as validating bases of their authority, the question of the particular force of civic commitments in particular cases does not need to constantly be reopened.[49]

Still, it is one thing to establish public opinion as the critical source of legality and civic trust, as well as the effective grounding of generality and reciprocity; it is another thing, however, as I have indicated, to take for granted that governments actually honour the trust accorded to them by observing its validating principles. About this Rousseau had no illusions whatsoever. And whether or not he was downright pessimistic about governments' paying respect to the constitutionality of the authority that the citizenry had entrusted to them, he felt it advisable to advocate safeguards against two dangers: that governments might usurp the sovereignty of the people; and that the people themselves might fail to guard it. Interestingly, as we shall note, of the two dangers it was the second that most worried Rousseau.

Although no advocate of direct democracy, Rousseau did insist on popular sovereignty. The actual *administration* of government he was perfectly happy to leave to professional magistrates, provided their political authority was conditional, that is, subject to the scrutiny and sanction of the legislative assembly, in which all who qualified for

48 Rousseau, *Social Contract*, bk. ii, chs. 6, 12; bk. i, chs. 7, 8.

49 Rousseau, *Political Economy*, 247–8 (131–2); *Social Contract*, bk. ii, ch. 4.

citizenship were to ensure that "the people" had the last word. And, to make certain that this would happen, Rousseau fastidiously detailed rules of procedure designed to preserve the founding principles of the union. It should be kept in mind, however, that the citizenship he associated with popular sovereignty was *not* based on a universal franchise; it excluded all women and all men not owning *some* property of their own.[50] Only remotely, therefore, can Rousseau's understanding of civic inclusiveness be assimilated to contemporary ideas of "strong democracy."

In point of fact, the participating citizenry that Rousseau envisioned differs little from what most eighteenth-century liberals, including Kant, envisioned; and few of these viewed themselves as democrats. Indeed, the main procedural measures that Rousseau proposed were intended as a check *on* government and not as an instrument for participation *in* government – the idea being to keep government and sovereignty recognizably apart, in order to assert the authority of the citizenry as the supreme legislative body. Principally, they were to act as reminders of two distinct jurisdictions: their extent and their limits. Thus, magistrates should, on the one hand, know how to use their powers fully, and, on the other, respect the limits of their powers. Likewise, while citizens should grand magistrates a discretionary space in which to act, they should at the same time closely watch their activities. Implicit is Rousseau's conviction that the only democracy that is politically workable is an indirect democracy in which a separation between the executive and the legislature is indispensable. By the same token, to be held accountable, an executive must be given a space in which to *do* something;

50 In the *Project for Corsica* Rousseau makes an explicit distinction between "patriotism" and "citizenship," in order to define their respective legal status. There are three kinds of membership within the state. Anyone born within it is an "aspirant"; every legally married aspirant who has some property of his own, apart from his wife's dowry, is to be enrolled in the class of patriots. Every patriot, married or widowed, who has two living children, a house of his own, and land enough to live on, is to be enrolled in the class of citizens. (*Oeuvres*, III, 919; Watkins, *Rousseau*, 302.) Hence, in contrast to present-day understandings, not everyone born in a country or naturalized by law is a "citizen" who is entitled to vote in the assembly. Thomasius has offered no definition of citizenship or the right to vote, as far as I have been able to establish. Kant's definition of voting citizenship, we shall note, was possibly even narrower than Rousseau's, although he did make clear that every (male) person, regardless of his property, counted as only one vote and, unlike Rousseau, specified no class of aspirants or patriots.

otherwise there is nothing for which it can be expected to account to the legislature, nothing for which it can be blamed or praised.

In short, democracy ought to be an *accountable* system in which administration is separate from legislation, with governmental power being bounded by the constitution. Citizens grant this power to the government, which, in turn, owes to the citizens-in-assembly an account of what it has been authorized to do. And it is by means of these reciprocal understandings that democracy, while guarding the maintenance of popular sovereignty, is to keep sight of the difference between legislation and administration, that is, between the *validation* of its authority and its *exercise.*

Since, in these reciprocal understandings, political accountability assumes so central a role, and since, moreover, the theme of accountability *per se* forms such a vital conceptual bridge between Rousseau's thinking on autonomous agency and normative self-legislation and that of Kant, I want to trace its philosophic-anthropological background in Rousseau's writings, albeit within austere limits, in the next section.

Summing up the present section, it might not be wrong to say that, precisely because of his uncertain faith in national self-mastery and the reality of the rule of law – a problem he equated to squaring the circle – [51] Rousseau wavered between two alternatives. One alternative was to treat people like children who are compelled by threats of dire consequences to do what they would not do for themselves, even though it was good for them. Manipulatively, they would thus be *made* to act in ways that would prevent them from harming themselves and each other.[52]

The other, and more attractive, alternative was to encourage citizens by means of a suitable institutional environment to see the advantage of internalizing the principle of reciprocity in processes of self-enactment. In effect, institutions were to generate habitual acts of reciprocal reasoning on the part of individual selves, by virtue of which reason and sentiment were eventually to converge, and impersonal laws were to beget personal commitments.

THE BIRTH OF ACCOUNTABILITY

In his discourse on inequality and in his letter to the Archbishop of Paris, Rousseau attempts an essentially historical and psychological

51 See Rousseau's letter to Mirabeau, in C.E. Vaughan, *Rousseau's Political Writings* (Cambridge: Cambridge University Press, 1915), II, 160–1.
52 Rousseau, *Social Contract*, bk. I, ch. 7.

approach to accountability. At heart he treats accountability as an emergent phenomenon within what Kant described as conditions of asocial sociability.

In Rousseau's thinking (as in Kant's), a consciousness of accountability could emerge only within the context of social life. In the solitary state of nature, as portrayed by Rousseau, persons do not see themselves in relation to others. There is neither a sense of mutual proximity and mutual distance, nor any comparative judgment of being superior or inferior to others. "Only knowing himself, an individual does not see his own well-being related to others, positively or negatively."[53] Not being consciously aware of others, a person sees no need to consider them, to take them into account. Only with the growing recognition of the existence of others do people begin to reflect and speculate upon the effect of their actions on others; and only then do they start anticipating the possibility of having to explain and justify them. Social conscience arises at that point; but not until this happens do considerations of right and wrong enter human minds, retrospectively or prospectively.

The change does not take place all at once, however; there is a process of transition at work, and it is in the course of this transition that consciousness of selfness gives birth to a disposition of viewing oneself as part of something other than oneself – the beginning of what might be described as a feeling of extended selfhood. And, Rousseau stipulates, with this feeling there arises the need for communicative language and some standards of mutuality, in order to relate to, or distinguish oneself from, others, by way of identification, comparison, and evaluation.[54] In the wake of these evolutionary changes, human action assumes an entirely new complexion. Language – and, through it, the mediation of thought and concepts – creates a certain space between humans themselves as also between humans and nature. Experience is no longer direct, and the mediation itself, paradoxically perhaps, drives a wedge between reasons and emotions, as it does between selves as subjects and selves as objects. Indeed, the latter separation can go as far as to induce people to view themselves as others view them, or as they wish to appear to others. As a result, people are inclined to act on the basis of this quasi-objectified self-understanding, so that their being and appearing follow different paths, and they often do not themselves know who they

53 Rousseau, Letter to the Archbishop of Paris (*Oeuvres*, IV, 935–6). See also *Inequality*, 180, 190–8 (64, 74–82); and *Emile*, 235, 289–90.

54 Rousseau, Letter to the Archbishop, *Oeuvres*, IV, 936–7; *Inequality*, 202–5 (86–90).

really are and what they really want. This development occasions two distinct and altogether dissimilar outcomes. On the one hand, it encourages deception to make deep inroads into human relations; while, on the other, it renders possible a measure of impartiality and detachment. Yet, whether it generates deceit or detachment, the self is no longer what it was, the solitary subjective self.[55]

Significantly, despite these changes, Rousseau is anxious to maintain or recreate the *balance* that he associates with the state of nature, a balance essentially between a person's needs and a person's power to meet them and thereby derive from this balance a sense of self-sufficiency, if not independence. Having moved away from being solitary to a stage in which we have become conscious of the existence of others, we do not cease to view ourselves as persons who can make things happen in the external world. Only now, with the new knowledge of a world including others, do we begin to realize that, in order to make things happen, we can no longer ignore the interests of others, not simply for their sakes, but also, if not chiefly, for our own. And this means that we have to blend our own subjectivity with the subjectivity of others within the new objectivity of a life with others.[56]

Rousseau makes two important points here. One is that, seeing ourselves in this new context, we not merely act upon a world of others but are also acted upon by this world. Moreover, any wrong done to a person is now perceived not merely as a personal injury but as evidence of public contempt, as an infringement of a person's *public* rights. And this infringement is now viewed as a far greater outrage than the harm itself. The other point is that agency as such is transformed by this twofold perspective, in that it is now seen not only from the subjective standpoint of the actor but *simultaneously* from the objective standpoint of the law or a hypothetical observer. And it is in this circumstance that Rousseau saw the germ of a new *public* consciousness and the source of *moral* reciprocity, as well as the problems issuing from either. For now concepts of right and wrong, just and unjust, make their appearance; and these concepts intrude upon public conduct by calling for generally binding *standards*. And whether or not we readily apply them to our own conduct, as we do to that of others (as Rousseau caustically observes), we can no longer do without them; the new public consciousness simply *demands* them.[57]

55 Rousseau, *Emile*, 275; *Social Contract*, bk. I, ch. 8.
56 Ibid.
57 Ibid., bk. II, ch. 12.

By bringing in standards, however, Rousseau clearly wants to do more than restore the balance between means and ends, or the equilibrium between wants and the power to satisfy them, which he associates with the state of nature. And this "more" takes the form of combining law with freedom, in order to usher in the idea of *normative* freedom, an idea that was to be the fulcrum of Kant's theory of moral autonomy and, by approximation, of political right and legal justice. Rousseau no doubt recognized that restoring the balance of nature in *society* demanded that objective and external standards enter the very texture of thinking and willing, as much as of acting. Despite being sceptical about our readiness to apply normative standards as subjective principles to *ourselves*, he did not rule out the possibility that, if we so *will*, we *can* act in accordance with general laws as subjective maxims, once we publicly accept standards as reasons that are objectively valid. In other words, having the capacity to blend objectivity and subjectivity, humans make moral willing and autonomous acting within society *conceivable*. We merge our subjective will with the recognition of and submission to an objective rule of right-acting; and it is by means of this fusion of personal volition and impersonal rationality that, in Rousseau's view, we create the necessary, if not sufficient, condition for the working of accountability.

The idea of merging the subjective and the objective dimensions of acting in society is a persistent theme in Rousseau's political speculations. In his optimistic moods he goes so far as to imagine that, given a context of reciprocal public thinking not warped by a corrupting influence of one sort or another, a union could emerge in which individuals could live without being in conflict with each other and the world at large. It would, alas, have to be a situation characterized by such a complete merger between the subjective and objective that principles of right acting would reside as much *within* individual selves as in the world into which they are placed. For, thus internalized, these principles would no longer face humans as things alien; they would be graven in their hearts, and not on tablets of stone.[58]

To be sure, so perfect a merger would render politics virtually dispensable. Rousseau is not unaware of this or, conversely, of the limits of the politically attainable. All the same, he (rightly) maintains that, without at least some degree of interpenetration of the objective and subjective, there can be no forms of joint undertaking. A wholly subjective self, unable to grasp idea of a joint commitment, simply cannot at all envision what it is to be a *member* of anything.

58 Ibid.

In effect, Rousseau traces here, together with the birth of account-ability, the genesis of thinking in terms of membership within a political entity. Without a consciousness of such membership, he says, a political union is a mere aggregate, held together by brute force, in which peo-ple are compelled, but not committed, to comply.[59] This is not to say, however, that "consciousness" is enough; for, in order for it to translate into political commitments, *will* must intervene. But this is not the end of the matter, either; since, for will to intervene appropriately, it must it-self undergo a mediating process. "Every free act," Rousseau elaborates, "is produced by the concurrence of two causes, one mental, namely that which determines the act, and the other physical, namely the force that executes it."[60] Just as consciousness is not sufficient, will, as sheer *power*, is not enough. I have to be consciously wanting to walk to an object if I want to reach it.[61] Just wanting, however, will not get me there either, if I am unable to walk. "A paralytic who wills to run gets no further than an able-bodied who wills *not* to run."[62]

Evidently, neither consciousness, as mental determination, nor will, as physical determination, issues in actual commitments. Consciousness and will have to coincide, although Rousseau does not profess to know how this comes about.[63] All he is certain about is that "willing" is not blind im-pulse in such an event. "I will as I judge, and I judge as I will; and it is by acting itself that will combined with judgment manifests itself as well."[64] This, for Rousseau, constitutes the "first principle" of action within society.

Once again, however, Rousseau insists, this is not all there is to it if ac-tion is to be *accountable* action. For it to be so, *choice* is essential. Will is important, but it is not synonymous with choice. While usually more than mere impulse in humans, will, even if it is never entirely divorced from reason, is not tantamount to choice issuing in action. Indeed, it is precisely the contingency of choice, in and through the conceptual *formation* of the will – as distinct from its sheer physical *power* – that distinguishes human *enactment* from an animal's *determination*. "Nature commands all animals, and animals obey. Man feels the same impulse, but he knows he is free to acquiesce or resist."[65]

59 Rousseau, *Emile*, 79, 104, 460; *Political Economy*, 251, 254; *Social Contract*, bk. i, ch. 3.

60 Rousseau, *Social Contract*, bk. iii, ch. 1.

61 Ibid.

62 Ibid.

63 *Emile*, 237, 280.

64 Ibid., 273–4.

65 Rousseau, *Inequality*, 170 (54).

In other words, human will, although it usually combines impulse with the causality of reasoning, does not necessarily issue in overt action, however intensely it serves as a source of motivation. For, in order to bring about human self-enactment as a rationally accountable deed, motive has to combine with *choice*. And this requires the mediation of purposive ends, since they alone contain the directional reasons that provide the basis for the twofold process of deliberate choosing and accountable acting.

In addition to serving as a basis for rational accounting, purposive ends are for Rousseau signposts toward a particular social order – a view that (we noted) Collingwood strikingly echoes. Humans, Rousseau argues, may know little about divine or cosmic purposes, but this does not stop them from enacting purposes of their own in the creation of an order in which to live with others.[66] And, being concerned with the genesis of accounting within such a self-created order, he puts maximum emphasis on directionally purposive reasons that are *public* reasons.[67]

PUBLIC REASONS AND POLITICAL ACCOUNTING

Yet, for all his emphasis on intelligibly rational accounting in the public realm, Rousseau was not blind to the possibility that reasons could be used to deceive no less than to authentically account. Often enough he deplores such cover-ups in the *Discourses* and in his observations on history in *Emile*.[68] Reasons, then, he charges, are employed as mere pretexts, intended at times to disguise abominations of the vilest kind as fully justifiable reasons of state.[69] If we bear in mind, moreover, that in modernity reasons are generally demanded or expected – thereby adding fuel to the proliferation of such fabrications – Rousseau's trenchant indictment of the use of blatantly sham "public reasons" is hardly melodramatic or in the least exaggerated. If anything, it only too realistically portrays what has become known as "ideology" in its most pejorative sense.

Modern man, Rousseau argues, feeds on make-believe – especially when actual reasons appear less credible than spurious ones – and incessantly indulges in wishful thinking and flights of self-deception which, to an alarming degree, are worse than fraud and trickery. For, while in lying the truth is still known, in reveries and illusory fancies it

66 *Emile*, 275.
67 Rousseau, *Political Economy*, 235, 236, 240.
68 Rousseau, *Emile*, 237–43.
69 Rousseau, *Political Economy*, 235, 237, 239, 244–5, 248, 250.

no longer is. Now people see what they want to see, not what stares them in the face; they sooner see what they believe than believe what they see.[70] The chains that bind them in fanciful disguises bind them much more effectively than the unadorned chains of the most despotic of tyrants; they neither notice nor care how their wills are bent, their freedom sapped, and their vision clouded. Totally adrift, as though at sea, they are exposed to powers they can neither anticipate nor control; and, no longer knowing where they are going or what they are about, their only escape is fancy and self-delusion.[71] Self-deception, in short, has become the only route to sheer survival.

Underlying these strictures is Rousseau's fear that, once people realize that they are routinely fed with fibs, they cease to believe anything. And, once this happens, reasons, as well as public reasons, fail, like inflated currency, to make any purchases. Accounting for actions, in the private or the public realm, then clearly becomes absurdly pointless. This fear appears to have haunted Rousseau from the *First Discourse* to the *Reveries of the Solitary Walker*. And yet its spell of utter gloom occasionally gives way to a more hopeful stance or, at any rate, to a more qualified pessimism, as, for example, in the *Social Contract*. For here Rousseau has some positive proposals to make that might assist in the recovery of civic life and the public domain in general. Admittedly, these proposals, he tells us, are intended to be pressed into service only in his native Geneva; but, regardless of Rousseau's professed intentions, these proposals undeniably launched upon the world a message that was anything but parochial. The gist of that message is that institutions *can* make a difference to a society by producing a "remarkable change" in humans. More specifically, the message contains the hope that institutions can engender an invigorated commitment to constitutionality and the strict observance of its norms, and thereby create a public climate in which accountability could be made to work.[72]

On this hopeful note Rousseau seeks to encourage the belief that, if only reasons for action would combine with a will based on reflective judgment, accounting could be made not only credible but *authentic*. For then it could generate a twofold consciousness among people: that of truly *choosing*, and that of acting upon reasons that not merely

70 Rousseau, *Discourse on the Arts and Sciences* (1751), trans. G.D.H. Cole, *The Social Contract and Discourses*, 120–1, (4–5).

71 Ibid., 122–3 (6–7).

72 Rousseau, *Social Contract*, bk. I, ch. 8; see also *Letters from the Mountain*, *Oeuvres*, III, 809–10.

serve as discursive *instruments* but are truly *constitutive* of what is said and done. Moreover, the production of this twofold consciousness signals for Rousseau not only the substitution of true reasons for mere rationalizations but also that of moral freedom – that is, a freedom that takes into account the existence of others and *their* freedom – for natural freedom.[73] And, whether or not replacing natural independence by social *inter*-dependence establishes indisputable morality as regards individual conduct, it is meant to provide essential foundations of *public* conduct within a new and distinctly *political* morality. Also, by involving forms of *conceptual* mediation – engaging directional reasons and reflective judgment – actions in society assume a radically different complexion. For actions now result from processes of will-*formation* rather than from those of sheer will-*power*, thereby comprising indirect and contingent causes instead of direct and necessary causes. And the difference is not less than that between unaccountable *doing* and accountable *choosing*.

For Rousseau, three constituents enter into such conscious and accountable forms of human agency in the political domain: answerability, intelligibility, and third, though not least important, justifiability. The first refers to authorship, to owning up; the second to explaining and making plausible whatever has been done; and the third to defending conduct as appropriate and timely. Although it is undoubtedly the third constituent, the legitimation of action, that preoccupied Rousseau, he insisted that all three constituents ought to be brought into play as separate issues, in order to obtain from the executive clearly specific answers to the legislature.[74] More basically still, Rousseau wanted to make sure that in such questioning two crucial conditions were met: One is that a sovereign exist who is *above* government; the other, that in accounting to the citizens a government observe standards of generality of a kind that ensures that whatever reasons are given are genuinely *public* reasons.[75] Formally, therefore, the rendering of rightful political accounting implies that governments recognize the assembled citizenry as their masters. And, operationally, it implies the existence of regular meetings of the citizens-in-assembly, in strict adherence to procedural safeguards set by the constitution. The *how* of politics is clearly as important for Rousseau as the *what*.

73 Rousseau, *Emile*, 280–1.

74 *Social Contract*, bk. III, ch. 18.

75 Rousseau, *Political Economy*, 235–6, 240; *Social Contract*, bk. III, ch. 18; bk. IV, ch. 1.

That this is the case emerges impressively from all of Rousseau's writings on politics. Instructions about how to conduct proceedings in assembly so that they accord with the principle of popular sovereignty assume centrality in his *Political Economy*, his *Social Contract*, his advice to the Poles and the Corsicans, and in his masterpiece, *Emile*: "Under whatever name the executive is elected, the chiefs of the people can never, without violating the social compact, be anything but the officers of the people. It is they whom the people direct to execute the laws and it is they who owe the people an account of their administration."[76]

Nothing could be clearer or more straightforward. Kant, as we shall note, speaks of "masters" rather than "officers" of the people, but somehow never succeeded in being as clear or straightforward about what precisely he had in mind by upholding the principle of popular sovereignty. Rousseau, on the other hand, is determined to make sure that civic trust in the executive is not taken for granted, as he leaves us in no doubt that the best constitution is of no avail if it fails to act as a constant reminder of the fact that civic trust needs ongoing endorsement. And this demands that governments render regular evidence of acting in accordance with the spirit and letter of the constitution, whose observance they have been charged with. For only thus can they palpably demonstrate their respect for the public good as society's supreme arbiter.[77] Hence, to keep alive the supremacy of the public good, each assembly must invoke the general will as a reminder that what has been done or was to be done conformed wholly with it, and that whatever reasons were given by the executive were intelligibly *public* reasons.[78]

Procedures of this kind, Rousseau explains, need the strictest application; not so much because of pervasive vice and malice as because of pervasive fickleness and fallibility on the part of magistrates and citizens alike; for both are human, and, being human, they do err, they do forget, and, most of all, they love to delude themselves, in that many think quite sincerely that they act in conformity with the public good and in accordance with public law when, in fact, they follow their private inclinations.[79] Rousseau's concern with procedures may appear somewhat pedantic; and some may go even further, dismissing procedural rules as mere rituals, devoid of deeper meaning. Questioning the general will so that it should always reply could thus be thought no different from

76 Rousseau, *Emile*, 463.
77 *Social Contract*, bk. III, chs. 11–14.
78 Ibid., bk. IV, ch. 1.
79 *Geneva Manuscript*, 161.

asking questions during the catechism or the Passover meal. Yet, surely, if to ask such questions is viewed as an empty ritual, the defect is not in the ritual itself but in those using it, for emptiness does not *define* a ritual. Indeed, Rousseau makes it apparent that not infrequently a ritual alone can recover what is in danger of becoming faded or jaded, and thus serve as a warning against gross neglect, furtive abuse, or vapid complacency. Principally, therefore, questioning the general will in assembly is intended to call into mind time and again the act of union; the idea, that is, that to will in society is not simply to will for oneself, but to will for oneself as part of a whole.[80]

Nor is it pedantic to keep reiterating that procedural rules are designed to preserve fidelity to the constitution as the operative ethic of a people, for this ethic is hardly peripheral to the integrity of its civic life if, as Rousseau holds, its observance can make all the difference between tyranny and freedom and, thereby, between the demise and the survival of a rightful union. Whether and how procedural rules are observed can decide if citizens are able to speak, express opinions, raise questions, and breathe freely, or are intimidated and silenced under one pretext or another, be it the "national interest," "public security," or "law and order." In a word, a procedural ethic, properly applied, is to guard against the use of rules and reasons to undermine rather than to protect political freedom.[81] For, once the perversion of rules and reasons occurs, it causes utter disarray within a political order by bringing all law into disrepute.[82] Public language itself may then be brought into jeopardy, eroding the very basis of civic trust, and, by thus threatening the union itself, lead it to the brink of ruin.[83]

SELF-MASTERY AND POLITICAL WILL: CONCLUDING REMARKS

It might perhaps be objected that if governments are so rigorously held in check, their capacity to function at all is virtually paralysed. For, is their effectiveness to act not altogether stifled if they constantly have to

80 Rousseau, *Political Economy*, 251; *Social Contract*, bk. I, chs. 7, 8.

81 Ibid., bk. III, ch. 18.

82 *Political Economy*, 240–1, 244. The perversion of rules or commands Collingwood attributes to a lack of understanding of what makes an order a *political* order and an interest a *public* interest rather than a partial interest. ("Political Action," 165–7).

83 *Social Contract*, bk. IV, ch. 1; *Political Economy*, 244–5, 247–8.

look over their shoulders? Not so, Rousseau replies. It is not strong government that causes concern; to urge citizens to keep a watchful eye on their magistrates is not to plead for feeble executives. To interpret control in this way is to misconstrue the nature and purpose of political accountability. Magistrates, Rousseau argues, should never be afraid to use their powers to the full as long as they use them legitimately, in line with the constitution. Emphasis on procedural integrity is not meant to curb administrative authority. On the contrary, it is meant to strengthen it, to make it recognizably the instrument, if not the exemplar, of public reason and the public good itself.[84]

On closer reading, however, it is evident that Rousseau's main worry was not so much the danger of excessive zeal on the part of the executive to usurp the supreme authority of the citizenry, or excessive attempts by the citizens to keep their government in check. Rather, what he appears to have agonized over most intensely was the danger that citizens themselves would devote neither the time nor the energy to attend assemblies, to vote, to ask questions of the executive, or indeed to bother with politics altogether. Thinking that public business was not really their private business – that it did not, as far as they could see, directly concern them – a good many, Rousseau feared, might prefer to delegate their civic duties to others, perhaps even pay them to do what they themselves felt were unwelcome chores.

Increasingly, if this were to go on, governments would in reality have little to worry about; so that if popular self-mastery were threatened, it would be so, not because the executive ruthlessly disregarded the supremacy of the legislature, but rather because the latter cared little about guarding it. "Soon the inconvenience of everyone deciding on everything forces the sovereign people to charge a few of its members with the execution of its wishes … Imperceptibly, a body grows up which acts the whole time. A body which acts the whole time cannot give an account of every action; it only gives an account of the main ones; soon it ends up by giving an account of none."[85]

Accordingly, once citizens abandoned their constitutional obligations and left sovereignty to their governments, Rousseau's stipulated condition of political accountability would no longer obtain. Under these circumstances, procedural norms designed to ensure the posing of questions in the legislative assembly would lose their point through disuse. Rights and obligations one does not care to have are rights and obligations one cannot be deprived of.

84 *Political Economy*, 245; *Inequality*, 212 (96).
85 Rousseau, *Letters. Oeuvres*, III, 814–15.

Rousseau's fears that citizens might neglect the exercise of their most sacred rights and duties *as* citizens seem to have induced him to superimpose on procedural constitutionality a form of governance that is virtually disconnected from it. Clearly, it is one thing to grant governments discretionary powers, or to discourage incessant meddling with the way the general will is administered or interpreted – since this might fuel distrust unduly – but it is quite another thing to give governments a totally free hand. Devices of the kind described in Book IV of the *Social Contract* were no doubt intended as last-ditch efforts to stave off utter disaster: All the same, they smack of a degree of paternalism that could not but erode the idea of national self-mastery as the supreme sanction of a rightful politics, as well as fatally undermine the principle of self-legislation that Kant so eagerly took over from Rousseau. Hence, despite the clarity of his proposals for political legitimacy, Rousseau does not escape the kind of ambivalence that, we shall find, marks Kant's political thought.

For Rousseau, despite giving much attention to procedural details in order to lend credibility to the idea of popular sovereignty, notably by insisting on regular accounting by the executive to the legislature, leaves us somewhat in the dark about his key concept, the general will. Thus, there is an endemic lack of clarity about its strictly political interpretation and application, as contrasted with its postulated moral and psychological content, in the form of trans-egoistic properties. In particular, once the general will is pressed into service to cope with plurality, we find Rousseau advancing at least two very different conceptions. In one conception, the general will is meant to emerge from unimpeded civic deliberation in the creation of a rightful political order. In the other conception, however, it evidently contains its self-validation antecedently, regardless of numbers and opinions. Here it rests on a rightness to which the citizenry must defer, since what is intrinsically right must be unconditionally valid for everyone. Any disagreement, therefore, can only amount to a defect in those who are unable to recognize the general will for what it indisputably is.

Whereas in the first conception the general will only contingently *follows* acts of self-legislation, in the second "a priori" (transcendent) conception it *precedes* these. And while under conditions of the former, dissent is a real possibility, under those of the latter it is inhibited, if not altogether mute. To be sure, Rousseau does insist on voting. But what is the use of voting, if outcomes are predetermined, and numbers of little or no relevance. A general will that validates itself antecedently needs no further sanction, and any government invoking it has *prima facie* rightness on its side. Clearly, once rightness is a built-in given within governmental claims made by those entrusted with power, the question relentlessly arises as to how such claims are to be countered. Merely to pose this question is to disclose the problem lurking in its answer. Under these conditions, voting seems a purely symbolic exercise alarmingly indistinguishable from tokenism. For, once discourse is inhibited, deliberation becomes contrived, and opting for alternatives is virtually foreclosed.

Speaking as the proponent of popular sovereignty, Rousseau demands both utmost autonomy and utmost vigilance on the part of the citizenry and full and truthful accounting by the magistrates. Yet, speaking as the proponent of a general will as a morally transcendent causality, he favours a political process in whose engagement the sovereign people has little or no say. Just as the former puts emphasis on "opinion" and the "people's will," both expressed in open debate, the latter distrusts "discussion" for fear that it may turn into "lengthy debate" and "divisiveness," and thus foreshadow the ruin of the commonwealth.[86] Admittedly, Rousseau was sincerely disposed to believe that, given proper institutions, procedural and transcendent expressions of the general will would coincide. In this belief, a city-state like Geneva nurtured for most of his life the hope that it might effectively avert a situation in which citizens voted with their pocketbooks, bought and sold positions of authority, and mistook sham accounting for genuine accounting. And it was in this belief and in this hope that Rousseau projected the image of a republican freedom that by its boldness and eloquence aroused Kant's profound admiration and prompted his persistent resolve to build his own moral and political edifice upon it.

Yet, for all that, Rousseau's faith in national self-mastery as the pillar of a rightful polity, although it was a true faith, was nevertheless a highly guarded faith. He could never altogether suppress a painful uncertainty that "Geneva," as a symbol of potentiality, would ever become a political reality in the actual world, and that things as they might be would ever become continuous with things as they are. The promise of creating a civic order in which individual selfhood and public selfhood, subjectivity and objectivity, self-choosing and right-acting would increasingly tend to converge might thus never find fulfilment. Rousseau himself had few illusions that the breach would ever be healed; for, in the main, he could not help wondering whether the future could be viewed as anything

---

86 *Social Contract*, bk. IV, ch. 2.

other than a harbinger of evil, an ever-threatening seducer whose corrosive work could at best merely be held back.[87]

Much of this pessimism, as well as a number of apparent perplexities in Rousseau's position on political self-mastery, is virtually implicit within the peculiar circularity of his nature-versus-culture argument. For, the transformation it suggests from a stage in which people are scarcely human to a stage in which they are scarcely able to halt their degradation leaves little scope for buoyant expectations regarding the ultimate triumph of good over evil.[88] Thus, while he liked to believe that the limits of moral growth were "less narrow than we think," and persistently maintained that creating improved institutions would engender trans-egoistic, civic-republican, dispositions, eventually capable of bringing about the disappearance of Europe's great monarchies, he also cautioned against illusory expectations.[89] Distressingly aware, as he increasingly was, of disruptive sources within human nature itself, and not merely within social institutions, he seems, in the final analysis, to have been even less confident than Kant – who shared most of Rousseau's gloomy moods – that the passing of time would carry within itself the dawn of better things to come.

It is a moot point, therefore, whether Rousseau's political thinking can rightly be looked upon as the birth of a revolutionary consciousness. Widespread though this view may be, it seems to rest largely on the

87 Rousseau's less than optimistic expectations of human progress are evident throughout his writings. Most expressly his pessimism comes through in *Emile*. 268–75 (*Oeuvres*, IV, 567–79) and in his letters to Deschamps of 8 May 1761 (*Correspondance complète*, ed. R.A. Leigh, Geneva and Oxford: Voltaire Foundation. 1965–86), VIII, 320, and to Mirabeau of 26 July 1767 (Vaughan, *Rousseau's Political Writings*, II, 159); see also note 51 above.

88 For a fuller treatment of Rousseau's nature-culture doctrine, see my *Self-Direction and Political Legitimacy: Rousseau and Herder* (Oxford: Clarendon Press, 1988), esp. 9–12, and chs. 6 and 13.

89 *Social Contract*, bk. III, ch. 12, and note 14 above; see also my *Herder on Nationality, Humanity, and History*, ch. 7, and *passim*, my "Patriotism and Citizenship in Rousseau," *Review of Politics*, 46 (1984) 255–65; "Will and Political Rationality in Rousseau," *Political Studies*, 32 (1984), 369–84; and "Rousseau's Agonizing over Political Accountability," *Studies in Political Thought*, 1 (1992), 3–17. For a perceptive overview of the (rather voluminous) literature on Rousseau's concept of the general will, see J.M. Porter, "Rousseau: Will and Politics," in J.M. Porter and Richard Vernon, eds., *Unity, Plurality and Politics* (London: Croom Helm, 1986), 52–74.

fallacy of *post hoc ergo propter hoc*: that is, on the confusion between sequence and consequence. Rousseau himself would most likely have
been astonished by Robespierre's interpretation of his political vision almost as much as by the attribution of its paternity. Either way, he would
have been inclined to entertain only the slenderest hopes in his alleged
offspring's chances of success.

But, then, there appears to be a strange discrepancy between the appeal or effect of Rousseau's public writings and the prevailing pessimism
characterizing the contents of his private correspondence. The former
therefore managed to arouse a degree of confidence in civic virtue and
national self-mastery that the latter conspicuously lacked. Possibly, Rousseau also *seems* more hopeful than Kant because he put so much emphasis on education as a means of changing human attitudes, in contrast to
Kant who, we shall note, seriously questioned any way of eradicating humanity's basic defects.

All the same, Kant did disclose considerable faith in the possibility of
creating an ethos of lawfulness in the wake of piecemeal juridical constructivism, even in the absence of any sign of *moral* progress – a faith
and a method which hardly recall Rousseau. Thus, while I have no wish
to overdraw the contrast, a good deal does point to almost a reversal of
prevalent views about the respective optimism of two of the most influential thinkers of modernity.

7

Rational Principles
and Civic Self-Legislation:
Immanuel Kant

THE SELF-PROFESSED IMPACT of Rousseau's thinking on Kant's *re*-thinking is well known and well documented. The oft-quoted statement by Kant, made in the early 1760s, gives vivid expression to this crucial impact, which, as Ernst Cassirer correctly observed, assigns credit to Rousseau not so much for any particular theory of his own as for the influence Kant claimed he had on his general attitude and his general mode of philosophizing. "Rousseau has set me right ... I learned to respect human nature, and I should consider myself more useless than a common labourer if I did not believe that this alone gives added merit to establishing the rights of man."[1]

There are indeed striking similarities, especially in regard to our central theme, besides equally remarkable differences of content and nuances of emphasis, together with a mixture of liberal and not so liberal overstones. Most pervasive, however, is a shared mood of gloom about the reality of *moral* progress, although Kant discloses a measure of optimism about *legal* advances, by way of gradual steps toward public right.

Yet, while settling for slow progress and a narrow scope of the politically achievable, Kant at the same time vastly extended its operative space beyond the confines of Rousseau's republic. Thus, although not indifferent to rightness *within* states,[2] he usually thought of humanity at

1 Cited in Ernst Cassirer, *Rousseau, Kant and Goethe* (New York: Harper, 1963), 2; my translation of Kant's *Works* (Berlin: Prussian Academy ed., 1902–), XX, 44.

2 See especially Kant, *Anthropologie in pragmatischer Hinsicht*, 2nd ed. (Königsberg: F. Nicolovius, 1800), 326–8. See also *Perpetual Peace* (1795/6). Appendix I, "On the Disagreement between Morals and Politics in Relation to Perpetual Peace," in Hans Reiss, ed., *Kant's Political Writings*, trans. H.B. Nisbet (Cambridge: Cambridge University Press, 1970, 1991), 116–25 (hereafter cited as *Reiss*).

large when speaking of "society," just as he thought of "universal history" when speaking of the past – a manner of theorizing that Rousseau commonly viewed as irritatingly vacuous.[3] But then, here, as in his general quest, Kant might well have been applying, no less than searching for, a sense of "enlarged mentality."

SELF-ENACTMENT

Kant's essay "What is Enlightenment?" (1784) discloses perhaps most forcibly the tragic note in his thinking on enlightenment as well as the mixture of overtones I have been alluding to.[4] To the latter I shall return subsequently. As for the disclosure of a tragic note running through Kant's speculations on *Mündigkeit*, the reaching of the age of reason, this will not entirely come as a surprise to those familiar with the *Aufklärung*, the German Enlightenment. Most of its originators (including Thomasius) were anything but sanguine optimists unaware of the complexity of life in society; and, evidently, much the same is true of the French *lumières*.[5] It appears, at any rate, that if "coming of age" is viewed as definitionally symptomatic of modernity's "humanism," then *Mündigkeit* – which Kant characterized as the capacity to speak and think for oneself – reveals difficulties at least as puzzling and potentially disturbing as those of earlier ages in which human self-enactment was not considered at the centre of things.[6]

The inner tensions that beset the *Aufklärung* were not unknown to Kant. Nor was he at all confident that the *capacity* to think and speak for oneself would entrain *popular* enlightenment or the emergence of a new humanity. Nonetheless, despite all his reservations, in his later works, self-thinking (*Selbstdenken*) was for him the *sine qua non* of political self-enactment as much as of moral self-direction. In the essay on enlightenment, however, the content of self-enactment at the personal level is not

3 See Jean-Jacques Rousseau, *Geneva Manuscript*, in R.D. Masters, ed., *On the Social Contract* (New York: St Martin's Press, 1978), 161–2; see also Rousseau, *Emile*, ed. Allan Bloom (New York: Basic Books, 1979), 473; and *Social Contract*, bk. II, ch. 12.

4 Thus Kant felt that enlightenment and reform could only come from above, through elitist guidance, if not autocratic direction.

5 On the sense of tragic resignation in French Enlightenment thought, see Peter Gay, *The Party of Humanity* (New York; Norton, 1971), 288–90.

6 I have touched on this point in "Self-Direction: Thomasius, Kant, and Herder," *Political Theory*, 11 (1983), 343–68.

thus predetermined: anyone reaching the age of reason is able, if not entitled, to be his or her own judge of what to do, without being committed to act morally. Individuals then simply use their *Mündigkeit* in order to pursue goals that are decided *by* them, not *for* them. Self-enactment, thus understood, is adequately grounded, provided that actions involve the mediation of will, judgment, and one's own purposive reasons, regardless of their motivation or outcome. If actions are "morally free" in the sense that Rousseau uses the term, they are so in contrast to being "naturally free" in that they entail a system of laws within the context of civil society. In other words, actions are freely chosen within the limits of reciprocal *rights*.

Unlike Kant's later position in the *Critique of Practical Reason* (1788), in which self-enactment is closely linked with *moral* autonomy, in the essay on enlightenment it seems chiefly related to combining reason and choice in the attainment of *any* performative end. As *Mündigkeit*, the coming of age, it first and foremost affirms the capacity of acting upon reasons of one's own. And although this rational causality, *qua* self-chosen goals, implies for Kant, as it does for Thomasius and Rousseau, the ability to render account for one's deeds, it does not carry the further implication of possessing a recognizably moral quality.[7] What it does, nevertheless, is to widen the meaning of reason in two significant directions. In one direction, broadened reason could now serve as a practical causality in both the private and the public realm. In the second, and more specific direction, it could be potentially relevant in the assertion of civic rights. Either way, Kant could draw not only on Rousseau but also on his German predecessors such as Leibniz, Christian Wolff, and Thomasius – as, in fact, he did.

It was precisely this twofold dimension of widened reason which enabled it to serve as a self-sustaining principle of explanation and validation of whatever was done or left undone.[8] Politically, it could therefore perform a central role in public discourse, in that reason could now be expected to explain why people should obey a will other than their own.

7 Although "accountability" implies an ethic of its own, rational accountability is not synonymous with moral responsibility.

8 The self-sustaining quality of reason is implicit in Kant's conception of autonomy. On the precritical Kant in this connection, see John H. Zammito, *Rousseau, Kant, and Herder and the Problem of Aufklärung in the 1760s* (Amherst, New York: Humanity Books, 2001), 201–23. See also Alexander Kaufman, "Conceptions of Freedom in Rousseau and Kant," *Review of Politics*, 59 (1997), 25–52.

The plausibility of such an expectation was, as we noted, publicly recognized by Frederick the Great, and there can be little doubt that this recognition had its bearing upon Kant's advocacy of constitutional liberalism during Frederick's reign, as it likewise had something to do with a certain back-sliding during the illiberal regime of Frederick's successor. But, equivocations aside, the link between Kant's interpretation of *Mündigkeit* and the concept of public accountability succeeded in transforming not merely the conceptual status of reason but also its effective part in civic life.

The point to reiterate, then, is that while reaching the age of reason and *moral* self-enactment are distinct notions for both Rousseau and Kant, the idea of individual self-enactment and the idea of civic self-government *are* conceptually related, and are so in both a logical and a psychological sense. They are related logically in that they involve, in comparable ways, the principle of "self-legislation" – itself and unmistakably political metaphor. Just as political organs are able to issue rules and laws governing their particular area of valid jurisdiction, so individual selves are in a position to issue rules and precepts to govern their own conduct. By extension, analogously, *mündige* individuals could demand to be treated as *mündige* citizens. At least so Kant appears to have presumed in his vision of the liberal republic, in which citizens are deemed to have the right to speak for themselves as members of a shared public realm.[9]

Psychologically, the ideas are related, in that each involves deliberate choosing and, with it, consciousness of authorship, as well as the potential obligation to render account. This is so even if accountability need not substantively imply *moral* expressions of responsibility, since maturity (in Kant's essay on enlightenment) does not require acting on a precept or maxim that is universally applicable as a moral principle.

All the same, it could be argued that in both its logical and its psychological relatedness, *Mündigkeit* is rightly considered the indispensable condition of *moral* self-enactment, as, in fact, it is in the *Second Critique*. What is nevertheless perplexing, however, is that in his earlier work on reaching the age of reason Kant does not rule out that individuals use their *Mündigkeit*, their ability to act "on reason and understanding without the guidance of another," to opt for *Unmündigkeit*, for the continuation of *im*maturity.[10] Indeed, Kant insists that the perpetuation of immaturity is not something forced on people by external circumstances;

---

9 See, for example, Kant, *Perpetual Peace* (*Reiss*, 100–2); and *Theory of Right* (1797), (*Reiss*, 138–42).

10 Kant, "An Answer to the Question: 'What is Enlightenment?'" (*Reiss*, 54).

on the contrary, he puts the blame squarely on human nature itself. If, however, *Unmündigkeit* is the actual choice of most people, Kant must have considered the prospects of significant *popular* enlightenment and, through it, of civic recovery, as exceedingly slim, quite unlike Thomasius, who invested so much of his political faith in it.

SELF-CHOSEN IMMATURITY

According to Kant's argument in his essay on enlightenment, then, a proportion of humanity quite happily and knowingly wants to remain *unmündig* for life, even when nature has long emancipated humans from alien guidance. Why? Not because they are uneducated, under-privileged, or lack reason or understanding but simply because it suits them; out of sheer laziness, intertia, or want of courage, they do not wish it any other way.[11] Possibly fearing *any* change, they turn a deaf ear to *sapere aude*, the motto of the Enlightenment. If others want to set themselves up as guardians, let them; that would not disturb their peace of mind; certainly they would do nothing to make it difficult for others to assume the task of guiding them. Even if a revolution were to put an end to autocracy, to the rule of a tyrant, this would not change their mentality. Hence, the new regime would be confronted by the same un-thinking mass, unfit for any reform in the direction of freedom and the wish for self-enactment – in substance, things would go on as before.[12]

This view, empirically well-founded or not, hardly suggests that there has been the kind of radical conversion that Kant attributed to Rousseau's influence in such moving terms during the 1760s. At any rate, Kant's opinion on the scope of popular enlightenment yields lit-tle evidence of such a conversion, or of his having abandoned the low estimate of the majority of his fellows. For, clearly, he thought it most unlikely that ordinary people would wish to choose self-enactment in *public* life. Oddly or not, however, this is not so much at variance with Rousseau as might be supposed. Certainly, Rousseau did not go so far as to deny external factors any causality in his finding that so few of his contemporaries took part in public pursuits. Nor did he assert that humans would deliberately choose to stay *unmündig*, to the extent of legislating themselves into slavery. On the other hand, he recognized just as clearly as Kant that being able to look after one's private affairs was in itself no warrant at all for wanting to engage in public affairs as

11 Ibid.
12 Ibid., 55.

a *citizen*. Granted, all persons, of average mental and physical capacities, whether male or female, are able, as soon as they reach the age of
reason, to choose the means of preserving and asserting themselves, as
best they can, and, in this regard, are therefore deemed to be their
own judges – their own masters, in a sense.[13] However, seeking self-
mastery in *civic* life, in order to attain *political* freedom, requires, Rousseau makes clear, more than choosing for oneself, in that the context
of choosing involves goals that transcend private interests and exclusively personal freedom.[14]

On this score, Kant's position on self-direction in "What is Enlightenment?" or his conception of freedom in society as a freedom *sui generis*, is
not far from Rousseau's position, although he later takes up the idea of
Mündigkeit as a sort of regulative principle of *moral* self-direction which,
arguably, goes beyond Rousseau's idea of "moral freedom." But, then, it is
not clear whether Kant already thought in these terms in 1784. In the
event that he did not, what he had to say on *Mündigkeit* must stand by itself, and bear, if at all, only most tenuously, on what he had to say on reason and moral autonomy in the *Second Critique* (1788) or, for that matter,
in the *Critique of Judgement* (1790), the essay *Theory and Practice* (1793), or
in still later works, at any rate in the sense he employed it in *Enlightenment*.

This hypothesis seems to me the most likely, especially in view of the emphasis Kant put after 1784 on the distinction between acting *in accordance
with* a precept of duty and acting *for the sake* of it, identifying the former
with complying with law, and the latter with wholly enshrining it. Rousseau,
less precisely, used the term "moral freedom" not only in conjunction with
life in civil society, *qua* "extended selfhood," involving the consideration of
others, but also *qua* obeying a law one has prescribed for oneself, which
closely prefigures Kant's principle of "self-legislation," within the moral
realm in particular. Unhappily, the term suggests all kinds of worthwhile
ends with which *freedom* is at best only very indirectly connected. We may
grant that, in principle, only what is done freely and upon reasoned judgment can qualify as moral, without implying that freedom in itself instructs
us what we should do. Hence, by stating that something was done freely, albeit by enlisting reasoned judgment, we are merely describing in what particular manner it was done; we are not thereby assessing it as having been
the *right* thing to do or to have brought about.

In essence, however, in introducing the concept of moral freedom,
Rousseau wished to distinguish it from natural freedom, as Kant

13 Rousseau, *Social Contract*, bk. i, ch. 2.
14 Ibid., bk. i, ch. 8.

subsequently did when speaking of freedom *in society*. And, on closer reading it emerges that they were both not so much concerned with two kinds of *freedom* as they were with two kinds of *will*; that is, with a will based on reasoned judgment as opposed to a will merely based on impulse or sheer fancy. For only will as judgment was for them capable of bringing about not only "self-mastery" but also a societal order of *public* right, in which "freedom" implies the freedom of others. Apparently, however, neither of them feared that, despite engaging will together with reason, self-mastery, *qua* "man ruling over himself," would induce "man to legislate himself into a beast, *without* ceasing to be his own sovereign," as J.G. Herder maintained in the *Ideen*, his philosophy of history.[15]

Although Kant came close to thinking along these lines in his negative interpretation of *Mündigkeit*, he nevertheless followed Thomasius and Rousseau in seeing in such an option the abandonment of self-directing agency, if not its total perversion. At the same time, though, Kant did not expressly link reasoned willing with *accountable* agency, since he seems to have been less preoccupied with the latter, focusing instead on *rightful* agency, on actions' being right, first and foremost, in either a strictly moral sense or a constitutionally juridical sense. Also, as time went on, Kant increasingly felt that if any advance in rightness could be expected, it was most likely to occur in the legal sphere.[16] Therefore, if he thought of "accountability" *per se*, it was essentially in connection with *legal* responsibility, while, as regards *political* accountability (we shall note), he was both less precise and less consistent than Rousseau or Thomasius.

Thus, although Kant unquestionably thought of accountability as the logical entailment of moral autonomy, it is possible that he was little inclined to advance it beyond Rousseau because his expectations of any progress in *moral* rightness were exceedingly low. Two fears accounted for this despondency: the fear of servility and the fear of wilfulness. Both – submissiveness to others, and the impulsiveness of anarchic willing – conspired (he felt) against true moral emancipation.[17] Whatever progress,

15 Herder, *Works*, ed. B. Suphan (Berlin: Weidmann, 1877–1913), XIII, 147.

16 Kant, *Perpetual Peace* (*Reiss*, 126).

17 Kant, *Anthropology*, 191. For a penetrating analysis of the distinction between "wilfulness" and "will" in "Kant's theory of autonomy, see Lewis White Beck, "Kant's Two Conceptions of the Will in their Political Context," in *Studies in the Philosophy of Kant* (Indianapolis: Bobbs-Merrill, 1965), ch. 13. Of particular interest is Beck's linking Kant's "true will" with Rousseau's general will, while identifying "arbitrary will" (*Willkür*) with Rousseau's will of all (226).

seemed at all likely to him was therefore confined to the legal sphere, because this sphere *was* compatible with coercion in a way in which the moral realm by definition was not. Even if people themselves were free to enact their own laws, Kant doubted (again not unlike Rousseau) that they would freely do what those laws enjoined them to do.

Hence, lacking confidence in self-legislation alone, Kant by and by recognized that coercive legal sanctions could not be dispensed with in society; people as they are would simply always try to get around the law.[18] He referred to people as they are actually found in society as phenomenal beings, in contrast to those (hypothetically) mature and fully rational beings in whom subjective (actual) will coincided with their objective (rational) will. That he was deeply troubled by the former's servile and anarchic propensities is grimly evident from a number of his later works, such as his treatise on religion (1793) and his lectures on anthropology (1798). Unlike Rousseau, therefore, Kant was rather reluctant to believe in transforming human dispositions in a truly moral direction in and through the creation of a framework of laws in civil society. Immaturity seemed to him so widespread that no early cure appeared at all in sight.[19]

THE RATIONAL AND THE ACTUAL

The ontological distinction between the phenomenal and the noumenal self nonetheless was for Kant the most crucially important device by which he sought to affirm that *ex hypothesi* there was a supreme principle of morals capable of providing an *a priori* foundation, a core axiom that was not derived from what we empirically claim to know about human nature, but was independently viable, on the assumption that man was a rational being as such. This was not because he held human reason to be incapable of error, but rather because, like Thomasius, he believed it

18 Kant, "On the Common Saying: 'This May be True in Theory, but does not Apply in Practice'" (1793), subsequently cited as *Theory and Practice* (*Reiss*, 82–5). I return to the question of coercion below. Carl J. Friedrich, in his Introduction to *The Philosophy of Kant* (New York: Random House, 1949, 1977), xlii–xliii, captures it well in saying that "freedom and law are the two axes of civil legislation" for Kant. And he adds, wholly in the spirit of Kant's *Anthropology*, that these two axes must be combined with force, if they are to achieve a constitutional order. For, while law and force without freedom make for despotism, force without freedom and law constitutes barbarism.

19 Kant, *The Contest of Faculties* (1798), (*Reiss*, 187–8).

capable of self-purging. Hence, without being a dyed-in-the-wool rationalist, Kant thought he could uphold reason as the supreme faculty of
the mind and, therefore, as the source through which universalizable
precepts could be discovered.[20]

To be sure, despite the supremacy of reason, Kant did not intend it to
serve as an unfailing guide for actual decisions in particular cases, but
merely as a basis for establishing what *kind* of grounds could qualify as admissible criteria for justifying any particular choice. Yet, despite this caveat, it is by no means easy to see how a purely formal principle could
help decide between *competing* moral claims, such as those which demand
the telling of the truth and those which demand protecting deserving persons form being harmed, for example, although Kant believed that, given
true reflection, reason *could* discern the superior duty.[21]

However, it may be open to question whether the concept of a perfectly rational being is able to carry the weight that Kant appears to put
on it. Clearly, it is one thing to see in reasoned choice a formal requirement to act morally, but it is quite another to *identify* it with morality.
Running together moral volition with rational cognition, moreover, not
only involves a rather precarious reductionism but it also deceptively
suggests that not to act consciously upon rational norms is to disqualify
action as moral action. And, to thereby exclude sympathy as a *moral* sentiment seems to me therefore just as misleading as loading rationality
with moral meanings that it simply need not possess.

Admittedly, the "critical" Kant, the Kant who had read and profoundly admired Rousseau's writings, no longer had his initial faith in
cognitive reason, in particular with regard to the empirical world. For,
in this regard, he had begun to feel acutely the limits of the knowable,
as he also somewhat startlingly began to realize that "reason" (*Ver-
nunft*) drove humans – needy (*bedürftige*) creatures as they are – *beyond*
the knowable, in the contemplation of God, freedom, and the immor-
tality of the soul – to cite Kant's own examples. All the same, even the
critical Kant held on to the belief that it was *reason* that enabled humans, as possessors of it, to "think into" the world a space beyond the
empirically knowable, in which they could understand themselves as
moral beings. And, in holding to this belief, he resolutely remained
faithful to the Age of Reason to an extent that neither Thomasius and

20 Kant, *Theory and Practice* (*Reiss*, 63–5). This is the principal argument in
Kant's *Groundwork of the Metaphysic of Morals* (1785).

21 Kant, *Theory and Practice* (*Reiss*, 72; see also 64–5; and Kant, "What is
Orientation in Thinking," Ibid., 242–3).

Rousseau nor Herder were able to be.[22] For all his qualifications about the empirical-cognitive range of reason, there seems little support for the view that Kant was prepared to dethrone reason in the domain of moral conduct, or, indeed, to seriously questions the unassailability of its supremacy.[23]

In the final analysis, therefore, rationality continued to serve as the paramount instrument of right acting, although in the realm of law and politics it was combined with coercive instruments, in order to ensure its constitutional force as well as its practical applicability. Nevertheless, Kant, as Thomasius and Rousseau before him, insisted that whatever co-ercion seemed necessary had to be in conformity with law. And, because of it, in making the leap from theoretical to practical reason, Kant de-manded that law take on the former's implied objectivity. For only then could a legal order constitute a *rational* order. Evidently, objectivity, *qua* impartiality, was for Kant the dominant characteristic of rationality. In-deed, his postulate of an "enlarged mentality" crucially rested on this strategy of operatively linking rationality as a practical causality with the idea of impartiality – a linkage Hannah Arendt self-professedly adopted in her own concept of representative thinking.

22 Thus, in *Perpetual Peace*, Kant declares that "reason at all times shows us clearly enough what we have to do" (*Reiss*, 116). And in *The Metaphysics of Morals* (1797/98) Kant flatly denies that there ever could be a collision of duties, because, if there were conflicting obligations, the stronger obligation could always be discerned by reason and, consequently, would always prevail (*Reiss*, 131). S. Körner characterizes Kant's understanding of reason as a "creative power" which has the "capacity to impose order and system" on human perception and human thought ... and thereby enables it "to reach the unknown and even unknowable." See his *Kant* (Harmondsworth: Penguin Books, 1955), 217. James Booth in *Interpreting the World: Kant's Philosophy of History and Politics* (Toronto: University of Toronto Press, 1986) echoes this view, by viewing Kant's emphasis on the autonomy of (delimited) reason as an attempt to open up spheres that, strictly, appear unknowable, as well as to provide a sustainable grounding of a rightful politics. Regarding the risk that Kant's emphasis on reason could have the effect of excluding non-rational or "sense" elements from moral conduct, see Lewis White Beck, ed., *Kant, Critique of Practical Reason and Other Writings in Moral Philosophy* (Chicago: University of Chicago Press, 1949), 23–9, 41–5.

23 On this point, see Beck, "Kant's Strategy," *Journal of the History of Ideas*, 28 (1967), 224–36. For a comparative discussion of Kant and Herder on this theme, see Susan Shell, *The Embodiment of Reason* (Chicago: University of Chicago Press, 1996), 183–9).

Kant's symbiosis of rationality with impartiality and public law also came to be invoked by subsequent democratic and revolutionary leaders in their propagation of change, as well as by those who felt betrayed by electoral or revolutionary pledges. Using "rationality" as a battle cry, they proclaimed that governments must not use methods appropriate to a kindergarten, since, as citizens, people do possess sufficient practical reason to speak and think for themselves. This being so, they had every right to choose the institutions they wanted or replace those they did not want. Recovering republican or democratic forms of governance thus became a matter of recovering rational purpose, and bringing about its political enactment in the public realm.[24]

That rational-constitutional principles have kept surfacing as the foundation of rightful government throughout modernity's darkest moments bears witness, I believe, to their remarkable resilience. In association with Thomasius's idea of civic reciprocity as the "decorum of power," Rousseau's emphasis on the rule of law, and Kant's doctrine of "public right" within a *Rechtsstaat*, these principles of "public reason" have come to serve as political sanctions of liberalism, participatory democracy, and the kind of representative republicanism that Kant himself favoured.

It is essentially against the backdrop of the anti-paternalistic dynamism which Kant projected into his republicanism – as an "approximation" (as he put it) to his moral precept of self-legislation – that the remaining part of this chapter reflects upon his idea of *political* self-legislation. In particular, it inquires more closely into the degree of continuity traceable between his strictly moral or "noumenal" vision and his political proposals for its "phenomenal" translation within a republican *Rechtsstaat* that combined legalism with liberalism.

In contrast to Rousseau, however, who in his optimistic moods believed that appropriate institutions could make a crucial difference not only to relations in civic life but also to individual human dispositions, Kant, we noted, was at best sceptical. Resignedly summing up his principal ground for such scepticism in the essay on universal history, he did

24 I should point out perhaps that "practical" did not mean for Kant what it usually meant for Thomasius, namely "useful," although both linked "practical reason" with moral action. The political extension of practical reason in the direction of civic self-consciousness has, rather poignantly, figured prominently in critiques of "Stalinism" by dismayed Communists. I have attempted to bring this out in *Pluralism, Socialism, and Political Legitimacy: Reflections on "Opening Up" Communism* (Cambridge: Cambridge University Press, 1991).

not mince his words: "Out of timber so crooked as that from which humanity is made nothing straight can ever be crafted."[25] This statement indirectly leads us to ask why his designedly political writings should yield a more hopeful, or minimally, less bleak, outlook. Posing this question in so bland a manner is not to suggest, however, that Kant himself was unaware of its inherent complexity. He certainly made every effort not to conceal the uphill struggle toward political rightness or the giant chasm that separated it from *moral* rightness. If he therefore considered gradual improvements in legality and political conduct possible, he by no means expected them to be the outcome or "product" of *moral* advances. Indeed, it is precisely in his *lack* of faith in the attainment of overall morality that he remarkably echoes Thomasius's parallelism of *two* ethics, of an intrinsic ethic of moral and religious convictions, and an extrinsic ethic of civic relations.

NORMATIVE SELF-PRESCRIPTION

The first sentence or the first section of the *Groundwork of the Metaphysic of Morals* (1785) consists of Kant's oft-quoted declaration that "nothing can possibly be conceived in the world, or even out of it, which can be seen as good without qualification, except a *good will*."[26] But, Kant hastens to add, what makes a will good is its volition, *per se*, and not its intended objective. And by "volition" he has in mind a particular quality of will that has nothing in common with the intensity of desire or any other form of craving. Instead, what makes a will *moral* in the true sense is that its operation so directs action that what is done is undertaken for its own intrinsic sake, and not merely in order to conform with an external duty. An action, therefore, is only validly moral if it involves a will, whose very existence implies a prior conception of lawfulness within actions, in and for itself (*allgemeine Gesetzmässigkeit der Handlungen überhaupt*).[27] Only then does a maxim become an internally prescribed

25 Kant, *Idea for a Universal History with Cosmopolitan Intent* (1784) (*Reiss*, 46). The translation is my own, based on *Works*, VIII, 23.

26 Kant, *Groundwork of the Metaphysic of Morals (1785)*, *Works*, IV, 393; trans. Carl J. Friedrich, ed., *The Philosophy of Kant* (New York: Random House, 1949, 1977), 140, (hereafter referred to as *Friedrich*).

27 Kant, *Works*, IV, 402. Kurt Borries, though he is highly critical of Kant's political thinking, approvingly singles out the idea of lawfulness as the central concern of his theory of the state. See his *Kant als Politiker* (Leipzig: Meiner, 1928), 202.

principle of duty, and a deed done for its own sake qualify as action in conformity with an objective, universal law; also, only under these conditions can individuals become law-making "members of a universal kingdom of ends, in which their fellow-humans are "always ends and never means only."[28]

Two points are worth nothing as particularly relevant to our focal theme. One is that every normative self-prescription implies for Kant a context of others, together with the idea that maxims or rules must form an integral part of a "system" of laws, in being generally valid, and hence *universal* in their application, brooking no exceptions. And the second point is that the individual selves prescribing them are participants in bringing them about as "law-making members," that is, as co-authors in the creation of overall lawfulness, whose *a priori* value they knowingly and willingly share. A *system* of laws, therefore, derives its obligating force from (i) a shared ethos that acknowledges the value of lawfulness in and for itself, and (ii) a common awareness that its source lies in acts of self-creation. The similarity between Kant's foundational ethic of rightfulness in society and that of Rousseau is impressively transparent.

At the same time, the shared ethos and the common consciousness of self-legislation have in each case a different locale – the context of "membership" is simply not the same. Although Rousseau refers to the body politic as a moral being, it includes only those who, as citizens, reside in a particular state. For Kant, on the other hand, the kingdom of ends includes every member of humanity, at any rate in the noumenal sense – a not insignificant proviso!

Yet, whatever the difference, there is for Kant, as for Rousseau, a common hypothesis: laws draw both their internal validity and their external obligating force from having been freely enacted by those intended to observe them. And, consequently, the hypothesis entails the twofold postulate that law-making must be joined with liberty, and that law-observing in society necessarily involves reciprocal constraints. If anything, Kant went still further than Rousseau in viewing the fusion of liberty with law as the indispensable condition of juridical *right*. Indeed, the idea of mutual constraints dominates much of the thrust of his *Theory of Right*. Clearly, the liberal Kant was no more squeamish than the allegedly illiberal Rousseau about speaking of "freedom under the law" and no less explicit about identifying law with *enforceable*

28 Kant, *Works*, IV, 428–9, 437–8.

law. Members of the phenomenal domain, "men as they are," need
constant reminding that the freedom of all demands the protection of
a law that has the backing of coercive force.

Evidently, once the assumption is made, as it was made by Kant as
much as by Rousseau, that there is an authentic will, or a reasoned will
or a common will, as distinct from an arbitrary will based on individual
impulse, fancy, or self-interest, forms of constraint by way of persuasion
or, if necessary, by force, are no longer ruled out. They are to serve as
aids to our putative will, making us seek to attain what we would wish to
attain, were we possessed of an unclouded judgment or of that degree
of rational maturity that would consider and respect the rights and freedoms of our fellows – an "enlarged mentality" to wit, which Hannah
Arendt particularly celebrates in Kant's political thinking.[29] From some
such measures, employing educational or legal means, both Kant and
Rousseau expected an enhanced civic consciousness to ensue, a consciousness conducive to the kind of merging of freedom and law that
both variously called for. In and through it, politics was to attain a pla-
teau of conduct that, constitutively, was *principled* conduct. And its governing principle was to be the maxim of reciprocity, according to which
selves act with other selves without harming them.[30] It was what self-
enactment *among others* was to *mean*.

Merging law with freedom in order to create a consciousness of self-
legislation is undoubtedly necessary, as it may well be in keeping with a
putative will directed toward right-acting. But, in highlighting the latter,
it only hypothetically promotes *free*-acting, that is choosing whatever
seems appropriate to individuals in their own actual judgment. And,
while loading individual choice with rational-moral imperatives may
effectively help to augment social reciprocity, it may nevertheless blur the
distinction between spontaneity and conformity or, for that matter,
between truly self-directed choosing and other-directed choosing – or, in
Kant's terminology, the difference between acting *for the sake* of duty from
a self-induced sense of obligation and acting by simply complying with
law *in accordance with* duty. Clearly, if coercive pressures are over-moral-
ized, they may only succeed in deceptively promoting autonomy and accountable self-governing, when in truth they mar or forestall both. It is

29 Kant, *Critique of Judgement* (1793), *Works*, v, 294. See also *Hannah Arendt,
Lectures on Kant's Political Philosophy* (Chicago: University of Chicago Press, 1982,
ed., Ronald Beiner), 42, 70.

30 Kant, *Theory of Right* (*Reiss*, 134–5).

evident that Kant, as Rousseau before him, had more than an inkling of this. For both try to get around this vexing problem by joining liberty with law through a fundamental contract, which takes the form of a collective act of self-legislation by a common will – in principle, at any rate.

I say "in principle" because neither Kant nor Rousseau was all that clear or confident about its working out in practice: the former merely postulated it as an *a priori* idea, an "as if" test of constitutional rightfulness, suggesting that it would coincide with what a hypothetical "united will" of the people as a whole would legislate for itself; while the latter frankly viewed such an attempt to be as implausible as the squaring of a circle.[31] And yet, the reasoning underlying the attempted fusion of freedom with law in order to promote a sense of reciprocal civic relations is not at all an unrealistic move. For one thing it calls attention to the fact that "self-legislation" within civic society consists essentially of law-making being directed at relations and interactions that involve *public* right, rather than at the realm of individual morality, in which the self-regulation of conduct is essentially governed by forms of internal self-prescription, and where any kind of external physical coercion would wholly invalidate the moral quality of action. For another thing, since rightful choices in this morally autonomous purity cannot generally be relied upon, it acknowledges the need for enforceable legal sanctions to act as safeguards against the encroachment of some individuals upon the rights of other individuals. After all, self-choosing frequently affects others, as it is itself affected by others. People act within a context of others, whose salutary and corruptive influences leave their mark on the *kind* of law civic society requires in order to cope with situations in which rights and freedoms clash, and in which individuals, therefore, cannot always be their own best judges.

Kant was not, as I indicated earlier, blind to the problems that confront the reconciliation of freedom with law, particularly in his late writings on politics, in which he increasingly admitted that constraints cannot be dispensed with. While he continued to insist that self-legislation characterized autonomous action *tout court*, he recognized and emphasized that, although "self-legislation" was a political metaphor, it would be deceptive if parallels between individual and collective self-prescription were too closely drawn. He warned accordingly against beguilingly obscuring the distinction between genuinely moral

31 Ibid., 139. See also *Theory and Practice* (*Reiss*, 79). Regarding Rousseau see C.E. Vaughan, *Rousseau's Political Writing* (Cambridge: Cambridge University Press, 1915), II, 160–1.

politicians and bogus political moralists who employed moral concepts to conceal their opportunistic schemes.[32]

Idealistic interpretations notwithstanding, the older Kant clearly was realistic enough to recognize that it simply does not follow that acting on maxims that individuals accept for themselves as ethical necessarily satisfies the essential requirements of civic life. Whatever importance he therefore attached to the universalizing principle as a criterion of rightful autonomous action did not stop him from acknowledging that the self-imposition of obligations by some may not constitute sufficient rational or moral grounds for others to consider these obligations as equally binding upon themselves. External legal constraints, in short, Kant agreed, cannot be escaped in civic society if it is to counteract "anarchic egoism" and the "servility of submission" (*Unterwürfigkeit*).[33]

At the same time it should be pointed out that while consensual self-legislation through the united will of a people may arguably prove an effective normative prescription for legitimizing coercion, as wells as for enhancing civic compliance, it is hardly going to do much for the elevation of freedom, or its moral quality. For, to make coercive laws rightful and submission to them generally obligatory *because* one has shared in the process of their enactment may or may not be a way to consecrate republican institutions of legality and civic mutuality. But to imply that this strategy simultaneously consecrates the idea of liberty in itself, as both Kant and Rousseau wished to maintain, may rightly be thought to be an unwarranted extension of the normative scope of collective self-prescription no less than of language *per se*.[34]

---

32 Kant, *Perpetual Peace* (*Reiss*, 121). A little earlier Kant writes: "These wordly-wise politicians, instead of applying the correct practice they boast of, resort to despicable tricks, since they are only out to exploit (and if possible the whole world) ... for their own private advantage" (*Reiss*, 119). Moreover, the real trouble with political moralists is not simply their mendacity but their inability to distinguish between *moral tasks* and *technical tasks* (*Reiss*, 122; Kant's emphasis).

33 Kant, *Anthropology*, 190–1. See also his *Metaphysical Elements of Justice* (1797) (Indianapolis: Bobbs-Merril, 1965), 112–13. Precisely because of their servility and egoism, Kant writes, some, if not most, act like animals, and hence need a master who sees to it that they do not except themselves from the laws. *Universal History, Works*, VIII, 22–3. (*Reiss*, 46–7).

34 I have touched on this risk of reductionism in *Democratic Legitimacy: Plural Values and Political Power* (Montreal: McGill-Queen's University Press, 2001), 52, 55–6. The ambiguity clearly lies in "freedom."

KANT'S REPUBLICAN ETHOS:
DIRECTIONS AND AMBIGUITIES

On the issue of collective self-legislation, as on that of politics in general, Kant exhorted his readers to bear in mind the difference between external form and inner substance; that is, between the nominal description of regimes and their actual workings. Accordingly, a constitutional monarchy, he argued, may be closer to the lawfulness of true republican constitutions – to the degree of political freedom they yield or governmental integrity they realize – than a formally republican system.[35] Misreadings of the intended thrust or meaning of several of Kant's political writings are undoubtedly squarely attributable to ambiguities in his use of political terminology – as I shall have occasion to observe myself –, but misinterpretations may arise (and have arisen) because his own urgings to differentiate between intrinsic substance and external form are not adequately being heeded.

Republicanism is, however, sharply distinguished from democratism. With republicanism Kant associated representative institutions, the separation of legislative, executive, and judiciary powers, and the free unfolding of diverse talents, propensities, and ideas; but, above all, he associated it with a liberal policy in respect of communicative publicity. Constitutionally, Kant regarded the establishment of a national legislature as the cornerstone of a *Rechtsstaat*, its supreme authority and the sole source of its law-making. Without such an institutional source of lawfulness, there can be no rule of law that is unconditionally valid for all. The executive organ of the republican state must therefore confine itself to the administration of law, in conformity with the letter and spirit of the law as enacted by the legislature.[36]

Democratism, by contrast, harbours for Kant the danger of despotism, and of a despotism of the worst kind; the three powers of governance being not separate but totally interwoven, the "general will" itself, as the highest democratic authority, "can assume a despotic expression"

---

35 Kant, *Perpetual Peace* (*Reiss*, 100–2).

36 Kant, *Theory of Right* (*Reiss*, 138–9). On this point see S. Shell's careful argument in *The Rights of Reason: A Study of Kant's Philosophy and Politics* (Toronto: University of Toronto Press, 1980). As Leonard Krieger sums it up: "An ethic of duty, and a politics of rights," in *The German Idea of Freedom* (Boston: Beacon Press, 1957), 86.

blocking every attempt to replace it. For any such move would mean that the united people revolted against itself.[37]

It should be borne in mind that, at the time Kant was writing, there were no political parties in existence in Germany and the possibility of *parliamentary* democracy was therefore totally out of the question. Yet, for all that, Kant was by no means mistaken in fearing despotic or dictatorial regimes under democracy. Manifestly, even in modern party-structured parliamentary democracies, the executive government, if backed by a substantial majority in parliament, can effectively negate the operation of governmental accountability or the exercise of any real check by the legislature upon the administration, not to mention "democratic centralism" under Communism.

Moreover, in keeping with conditions throughout eighteenth-century Europe, neither Kant nor Rousseau envisioned a universal franchise of voting. No women, no employees other than public servants (*Beamte*), and no persons who, even if self-employed (such as barbers), qualified as voters unless they could establish themselves to be "their own masters." Kant conceded, however that this "formula" bristled with difficulties;[38] and, although he had similar reservations about the distinction between active and passive citizenship – the alternative chosen by the French revolutionary regime – finding it to run counter to the very idea of citizenship, he nonetheless suggested it as an interim measure until "all members of the people" would work their way up to active citizenship.[39]

Still, however he finally envisaged citizenship, Kant's concept of "the people" seems a highly fictitious concept – or, at any rate, a problematically abstract one. At best, its actual meaning may be rendered in (formally) negative terms: the people are not so much what they are as what they are not, namely members of the nobility. Yet, even thus narrowed down, the people, identified with a country's adult members, are not really in their totality taken into account, and hence are in no position to bestow or withhold consent, let alone to partake in making the laws under

37 Kant, *Perpetual Peace* (*Reiss*, 101; see also *Theory and Practice* (*Reiss*, 81–2)).

38 Kant, *Theory and Practice* (*Reiss*, 75–7). "There was plenty of fiction in the notion of the people as a constituent of power," Peter Russell observes, writing about the Canadian Confederation, since here as in Britain and the United States, ample use was made of the "popular foundation myth," despite the fact that their systems of voting "excluded large elements of the population." In "Can the Canadians Be a Sovereign People?" *Canadian Journal of Political Science*, 24 (1991), 691–709, here 694.

39 Kant, *Theory of Right* (*Reiss*, 140).

which they are to live. Kant is therefore speaking almost figuratively when he says that "the legislative power can belong only to the united will of the people."[40] He appears to have been aware of this, for he seeks to clarify his use of the concept of the "people" by distinguishing between the "scattered mass of the people," who are "mere subjects," and the people as symbolizing those qualified to form a "united will" and, thereby, to represent the "universal sovereign," the supreme legislator, to whom the (executive) "ruler" is "beholden," and to whose laws "the ruler is subject."[41] He also says, however, that while the people "have jurisdiction over themselves," they cannot revolt against the ruler or lawfully punish him, if indeed they happen to succeed in deposing him, for all that the people can rightfully do is to "lodge their complaints."[42]

Granted, therefore, that Kant rightly draws attention to the possibility of democratic despotism, it is nevertheless hard to see how, in view of what he says about the scope of democratic self-assertion, there is any channel through which "the people" can in practice do anything, in the face of executive domination, other than revolt. For, in sharp contrast to Rousseau's emphasis on administrative accountability, there is no provision in Kant's republican constitutionalism for the regular rendering of account by the executive to the legislature. On the contrary, Kant goes out of his way to insulate the executive by denying that the citizens have any business "to judge how the constitution should be administered," regardless of abuses of power.[43] And it hardly helps matters when he speaks of the people as "*co*-legislators," or of the "head of state" as a "sovereign" whose authority "no one in the commonwealth can have a right to contest."[44]

What can equally give rise to confusion is the way Kant uses the term "legislator" in the singular form. For the sense in which he refers to it has nothing in common with Rousseau's understanding. For Rousseau thinks of the Legislator as an "outsider" invited by a particular nation to advise on constitutional matters, and presents him as a person who has no institutional power within a political order, and therefore has no means to enforce his legal proposals, or to *make* a nation accept them or submit to them. His role, in short, is purely advisory, whereas in Kant's

40 Ibid., 139.

41 Ibid., 141–2.

42 Ibid., 143.

43 Kant, *Theory and Practice* (*Reiss*, 80; see also 81–2).

44 Kant, *The Contest of Faculties* (*Reiss*, 182); see also *Theory and Practice* (*Reiss*, 81, 83, 85); and *Perpetual Peace* (*Reiss*, 127); and *Theory of Right* (*Reiss*, 161).

understanding of the term the legislator *is* possessed of coercive power. Thus, while Rousseau's Legislator is powerless to prevent the people from preferring bad laws to good laws, in Kant's version it depends on the "moral attitude of the legislator" whether or not, after "the disorderly mass has been united into a people, he will leave the people to create a lawful constitution by their own common will."[45] Kant, it is true, seeks to qualify the extent of the legislator's coercive power by stipulating that a "legislator cannot impose a law which a people cannot impose upon itself," but he gives no indication how this test could be applied in practice.[46] Although Kant's conception of the legislator possibly explains his speaking of the people as *co*-legislators, it sheds no light on who, precisely, the legislator is in his scheme of things, as it leaves wide open how and where the people as the "universal sovereign" come into the picture.

Despite these ambiguities, one thing emerges clearly enough, and all the more so because Kant himself is most explicit on it; the "it" here refers to *coercion*. A legislator is evidently required to employ "lawful coercion," which "every just political constitution in the truest sense demands."[47] And it does so, Kant argues, not chiefly for empirical reasons, such as the occurrence of violent clashes among individuals, but rather because coercion is made necessary by the *a priori* rational idea that, even if "men were benevolent" they would have to be made conscious through coercion that they no longer live in the state of nature "in which everyone follows his own desires." For only thus made conscious would they fully realize that they have agreed to abandon their previous mode of life in order "to submit to external, public, and lawful coercion" and to accept the pronouncement of a judge as the competent authority to decide upon disputes over rights.[48]

But, if the state of civic society cannot dispense with a central source of coercion in order to make *reciprocal* rights and freedoms possible, such coercion must be a "construction of right."[49] That much Kant makes abundantly clear throughout his political writings and his theory of right. We must, accordingly, "consider it absolutely necessary to couple the concept

45 Kant, *Perpetual Peace*, (*Reiss*, 117).

46 Kant, *Theory and Practice* (*Reiss*, 85); see also *Perpetual Peace* (*Reiss*, 118); and *Theory of Right* (*Reiss*, 138).

47 Kant, *Theory of Right* (*Reiss*, 135, 163); see also *Theory and Practice*, (*Reiss*, 73, 85).

48 Kant, *Theory of Right* (*Reiss*, 137).

49 Ibid., 134–5.

of right with politics, and virtually take politics as an applied branch of right, or, at any rate, make it a limiting condition of politics." If we do, we shall find that "the two are not at all incompatible."[50]

The idea of using juridical right as a limiting condition of political power principally underlies Kant's distinction between the external form of a regime and its inner working – a distinction that clearly echoes Montesquieu's between laws as such and their operative ethos.[51] Obviously thinking of Frederick II of Prussia, Kant maintains that even if a constitution formally "provides for an absolutist ruling power," it may in reality enable a regime to "govern itself in a republican way," and thus prepare the ground for "the people themselves being able to *create for themselves* a legislation ultimately founded on right."[52] Since, however, no individual, *per se*, can create a *common* will, what is required first "is an additional unifying force," designed to inaugurate a state of right *by force*."[53] On this coercive authority of the common will "public right is subsequently to be based," and, through it, "each is to decide the same for all and all are to decide the same for each."[54] Only then can a state be a rightful body, for only then will its laws exercise reciprocal coercion, which alone "is of necessity consonant with the freedom of everyone," and which procures for the members of a state institutions enabling them "to enjoy their rights within a *status civilis*." The best constitution of a state, therefore, Kant echoes Rousseau, "is one in which power rests with laws instead of with men," and the rule of law prevails.[55] Coercion, as much as freedom, must be under law, for coercion to be endured and freedom to be shared. This, in essence, is Kant's line of

50 Kant, *Perpetual Peace* (*Reiss*, 118, 124).

51 Montesquieu, *The Spirit of the Laws*, II, 4, 5.

52 Kant, *Perpetual Peace* (*Reiss*, 118). John Rawls's interpretation of Kant's principle of autonomy, as politically applied, is of interest. See his *A Theory of Justice*, (Cambridge: Harvard University Press, 1971), 251–7. See further, more specifically, his "Kantian Constructivism in Moral Theory," in *Journal of Philosophy* 77 (1980), 554–72. It suggests a "procedure of construction," in the course of which autonomously thinking people will increasingly agree for reasons of their own to public principles of justice. (554, 564). I believe Rawls's interpretation and elaboration to be fully in keeping with what Kant had in mind about the eventual emergence of a republican constitution through piecemeal legal construction.

53 Kant, *Perpetual Peace* (*Reiss*, 117) (Kant's emphasis).

54 Kant, *Theory of Right* (*Reiss*, 139).

55 Ibid., 174.

thought about the approximation of political lawfulness to moral lawfulness and about a politics that is republican without being utopian.

POLITICAL SELF-LEGISLATION: ADVANCE OR IMPASSE?

If, then, there are ambiguities, or even perplexities, in Kant's exposition
of his political theory, there is nonetheless no lack of down-to-earth realism. This sense of realism also characterizes his tracing of the past and his
plotting of the future. Coupled with it is a sort of tragicomic urbanity, if
not resignation, which comes through rather poignantly in a story Kant
tells with some relish about a doctor who believes in healing through as-
siduous comforting. It forms the conclusion of one of Kant's latest works,
The Contest of Faculties (1798). He offers it as a "speedy cure" of the understandable despair which, in view of countless political evils, many experience in reviewing the welfare and progress of mankind.

This is the story: "A doctor who used to console his patients from day
to day with hopes of imminent recovery, telling one that his pulse was
better, and others that their stools or perspiration heralded an improvement, etc., received a visit from one of his friends. 'How are you, my
friend, and how is your aliment?' was the first question. 'How do you
think,' was the reply. '*I am dying of sheer recovery*!'"[56] In a more serious
vein, Kant offers principally two remedies, by means of which "the human race, for all its frailty" may reasonably hope for recovery. One is
that "every people give itself a civil constitution of the kind that it sees
fit," and the other that there be a growing realization that "the only intrinsically *rightful* and morally good constitution which a people can
have is by its very nature disposed to avoid wars of aggression," and
which, therefore, must be a republican constitution, "at least in its conception."[57] Kant saw "the source of all evils and moral corruption" in
war; its prevention, accordingly, provided a "negative guarantee" that
the health of nations might progressively improve, "or, at least, would
not be disturbed in its progress."[58]

As to the progressive improvement of morality in the strict sense, Kant
was a good deal less confident. Indeed, he made a point of stressing the
lack of symmetry between a probable increase of legality and a rather
doubtful growth of actual morality. Thus, while we may expect to see less

56 Kant, *The Contest of Faculties* (*Reiss*, 189).
57 Ibid., 182.
58 Ibid., 183.

violence on the part of those in power and greater observance of public regulations as a result of advances in legality, we should not infer from such outward improvements of conduct within civic society even "the slightest increase in the basic moral capacity of mankind."[59] We simply "must not expect too much of humans," Kant says, and warns philosophers not to play into the hands of politicians who would be only too happy to exploit expectations of continuous moral progress for their own self-serving ends, knowing full well that they are delusions springing from "the fantasies of overheated minds."[60]

In light of Kant's remarks on the prospects of *Mündigkeit* in itself resulting in popular enlightenment (noted earlier), it hardly comes as a surprise to find that he had little or no faith in reforms that originate from below. Whatever advances were to occur in legality could not therefore be the work of popular *self*-legislation; rather, to bring about such self-legislation, a stimulus was needed "not *from the bottom upwards*, but *from the top downwards*."[61] Unlike his erstwhile student, J.G. Herder, who fiercely argued against Kant in favour of reform from below, Kant consistently upheld his belief in elitist direction, preferably from enlightened autocrats such as Frederick II of Prussia, whom Kant genuinely and profoundly admired as a model reformer. Only in this manner, he felt, could it lawfully as well as authoritatively be demonstrated that a process of reform *was* possible within actual history, and that, moreover, unlike revolutions, it would prove an eminently predictable way of getting somewhere.

All the same, Kant's direction of thinking was not at all historical. As he himself conceded, his concern was not to build upon the experience gained in the past. It was not a history of the past but a history of the future – what he called "predictive or *a priori* history" – that fascinated him. Kant mentions in this connection the self-fulfilling prophecies of the Hebrew prophets who were "themselves the architects" of the events they were foretelling. Our politicians, Kant caustically adds, "behave in exactly the same way, so far as their influence extends, and are just as successful in their prophecies."[62] On Kant's argument of predictive history, people's confidence in self-legislation will be enhanced

59 Ibid., 187–8.
60 Ibid., 188.
61 Ibid., 188 (Kant's emphasis). As was noted in ch. 1, note 35, Kant took a poor view of reform from below, dismissing it as too idealistic, tantamount to "putting the cart before the horse." *Works*, VIII, 366–7.
62 Kant, *The Contest of Faculties* (*Reiss*, 177–8).

once they gain the perception that laws can be *just* laws and that their operative supremacy has the backing of *lawful* power, that is, of public authorities that are themselves subject to the law of the land, to public *right.*[63] The trouble is that confidence building as regards the impartiality, accessibility, and integrity of legal and political institutions is no simple or easily achievable matter. Patience is much called for; to be at all successful, reforms must, above all, be undertaken at the right time. Indeed, timing, Kant agrees with Rousseau, is of the essence. Premature reforms, instead of producing improvements, may in truth give rise to anarchy, and, like revolutions, involve attempts to bring about reforms "by unlawful means."[64]

Timing alone, however, is not enough; advancing toward political self-legislation in the right manner makes considerable demands on human nature itself. Unfortunately, because of the immaturity, servility, and egoism in some if not most individuals, humankind on the whole behaves in the public realm not very differently from animals, unless there is a master who sees to it that people do not except themselves from the laws.[65] In the absence of a master, they "misuse their freedom with regard to others of their kind, and even though as rational beings they desire a law which would provide limits for the freedom of all, their egoistic animal inclinations misguide them into excluding themselves whenever they can."[66] A master is needed, therefore, "who can break man's will and compel him to obey a *general* will, under which every man could be free."[67] But, Kant asks, where is one to get such a master from? And he replies: "From nowhere else but from mankind." The result is an infinite regress, because "this master is in turn an animal who needs a master."[68] Sadly, Kant concludes, a complete solution is impossible, and this absurd impasse therefore threatens to transform the pursuit of self-legislation into a mirage.

Nevertheless, despite these seemingly unsurmountable roadblocks, Kant suggests a way out by invoking the idea of a teleological force in history comparable to that in nature. While he is not denying that

63 Kant, *Perpetual Peace* (*Reiss*, 118). In a note Kant adds that *any* legal constitution, "even if it is only minimally *lawful,* is better than none at all" (Kant's emphasis).

64 Ibid.

65 Kant, *Universal History* (*Reiss*, 46).

66 Ibid.

67 Ibid.

68 Ibid.

history as a whole appears to be an enigma, bereft of any plan or purpose and devoid of even instinctive drives identifiable with nature, he nonetheless feels that humans, endowed with rationality, will, and freedom, cannot resist investing history with some plan or purpose, however hidden. This, at any rate, is his argument in the Second and Third Principle of his *Idea for a Universal History* (1784). To this argument he adds another discovery of his, the "asocial sociability of man."[69] Kant attributes to this peculiar mix of antagonism and attraction, not only all development of culture but "the cause of lawful order in society," for which he gives thanks to nature for having bestowed on "man his quarrelsomeness, his enviously competitive vanity, and his insatiable desire to possess or to rule."[70]

Nature's boon does not alter the fact, however, that governing a people is a tremendously difficult task which requires, in addition to a constitution, "great experience in many activities and, above all, a *good will* ready to comply with the commands issued by the constitution." Hence, if any progress is to come about at all "it will only do so very late in history and only after many unsuccessful attempts."[71]

The core of Kant's "predictive" philosophy of history is contained in the Ninth Principle, in which he speaks of a "*justification* of nature – or rather perhaps of *providence*" – and its hidden plan or purpose to achieve "a perfect civic association of mankind."[72] Toward this end "the rights of man must be held sacred, however great a sacrifice the ruling power may have to make ... for all politics must bend the knee before right"; that is, the right which "can only come from justice," and the justice which transparently possesses the "formal attribute of publicness."[73]

An essential part of the "justification of nature or providence" consists for Kant of a growing self-understanding in humans that they possess "the quality or power of being the *cause* and the *author* of their own improvement."[74] However, such self-understandings are rendered possible only, Kant stipulates, if there is actual evidence that humans are endowed with freedom to enact their self-improvement. For only if they have such evidence to draw on is there a chance for them to tangibly *experience* the possibility of self-enactment, a chance to make a dent on occurrences

69 Ibid.; and in *Friedrich*, 118–21.
70 Ibid., 121.
71 Ibid., 123 (Kant's emphasis).
72 Ibid., 129 (Kant's emphasis).
73 *Perpetual Peace* (*Reiss*, 125).
74 Kant, *The Contest of Faculties*, (*Reiss*, 181).

that impinge on their lives. "We must search, therefore, for an event that would indicate whether or not such a cause exists and whether or not such a causality is active within the human race, showing a *tendency of improvement.*"[75]

For Kant the French Revolution was such an event *par excellence*; it provided massive evidence for the possibility of human self-enactment and civic self-legislation. Admittedly, Kant, like other contemporaries, witnessed this "drama of great political changes" as "onlooker, rather than as participant," but this did not detract, in his view, from its momentous importance as a world event. Without condoning "the atrocities and the misery" that it involved – a price "no right-thinking man" would wish to pay – he shared "deep moral sympathies" for the ends of the Revolution as goals for all humanity.[76]

What principally matters, then, is that humans, whether as participants or as spectators, learn that they *can* make a difference to the course of history, that they can have a share in implementing the plan of nature or providence which Kant invoked in his teleological theory of human progress. In invoking supra-human forces, therefore, he does not appear to have encouraged passivity or inaction but, instead, to have sought to make people feel more confident in the outcome of their efforts, whatever their scale or significance. Indeed, in the third section of "Theory and Practice" he expressly emphasizes that an invigorated belief in the teleology of nature, history, or providence could not but promote the human pursuit of ends promising the improvement of conditions – a view he also put forward in *Religion within the Limits of Reason (1793)*. To be sure, he did not go so far as to suggest that humans could create a truly *ethical* community without the aid of divine agency; what he did do, however, is to make clear that the working out of the divine plan *did* depend on human effort or, at any rate, on humans' acting *as if* it did.[77]

75 Kant, *Universal History*, (*Reiss*, 50–1, *Friedrich*, 127); and *The Contest of Faculties* (*Reiss*, 181–2) (Kant's emphasis).

76 Kant, *The Contest of Faculties* (*Reiss*, 182–3). Hannah Arendt was profoundly impressed by Kant's observation that, while the French Revolution had global ramifications, most contemporaries were merely "external public onlookers, without the slightest intention of actively participating" (ibid., 183). It endorsed her own view that politics was essentially a drama in which the bulk of humanity played the role of spectators.

77 Kant, *Theory and Practice* (*Reiss*, 87–90) and *Religion within the Limits of Reason* (*Works*, VI, 100–1). Bernard Williams, in *Problems of Self: Philosophical Papers* (Cambridge: Cambridge University Press, 1973), refers to Kant's teleological

It was precisely because Kant wanted people to believe in their own self-enacting powers that he came out so strongly against any attempt to obstruct individuals in "seeking their welfare in any way they chose as long as it would be compatible with the freedom of others." He therefore condemned all forms of state interference which treated citizens like children, fearing that such paternalism could be the harbinger of despotism, "which hampers the vitality of industry and saps the strength of the whole state."[78] Like Wilhelm von Humboldt after him, Kant pleaded for a thoroughgoing limitation of governmental agency in directions that could weaken the self-reliance of persons or in any way restrict their fullest development or their capacity for self-expression. Interestingly, though perhaps not surprisingly, Kant's theory of *Mündigkeit* – advanced to encourage self-enactment and acting responsibly – has been pressed into service in two opposite directions. In one direction it has served to justify the exclusion of the state from social and economic life and, thereby, the depoliticization of society; while, in the other, it has been invoked to buttress demands for participatory democracy and, thereby, the broader politicization of society.

And yet, Kant was no more of a laissez-faire liberal than he was a proponent of participatory democracy. The latter is generally known; less known, however, is that Kant would hardly have favoured the privatization of public services, and would have fiercely opposed the draining of educational budgets in order to finance aggressive wars. "Our rulers," he openly declared, "have no money to spare for public education, nor for anything

thinking about nature as "a kind of secular analogue of the Christian conception," having in mind also Kant's idea of respect being owed to all men "as equally children of God," (235), not unlike Nietzsche, who referred to Kant as an "underhand Christian" (cited in Patrick Riley, *Will and Political Legitimacy* [Cambridge: Harvard University Press, 1982], 139). Riley contrasts Rousseau and Kant regarding the basic source of morality, by means of a close analysis of reason, will, and sympathy (134–44). See also his monograph on *Kant's Political Philosophy* (Totowa, New Jersey: Rowman and Littlefield, 1983), which is a highly original teleological reading of Kant's political thought. And, unlike commentators who *derive* Kant's political thought from his moral philosophy, Riley speaks of politics and morality as *sharing* a realm of overlapping ends and purposes – notably peacefulness and civility (168).

78 Kant, *Universal History* (*Reiss*, 50) and *Theory and Practice* (*Reiss*, 74). Kant made clear that if governments try to *impose* moral incentives for legal observance, they will generate despotism and not republicanism – one of several Kantian jabs at state manipulations of religion.

else that concerns the best interests of the human world, because all the
money has in advance been allocated to the demands of making war."[79]

Thus, whatever we make of Kant's liberalism, he never ceased to uphold education and other public goods, just as he never ceased to de-
nounce warfare, tyranny, and abject egoism. Clearly, his was a nuanced
liberalism which, while it opposed governmental paternalism in matters
of individual conviction and individual creativity, fully endorsed the
need for public constraint to ensure that the liberty of some did not deprive others of theirs. And, contrary to some interpretations, Kant took
considerable pains in his political thought *not* to suggest a facile continuity between legality and morality, or to give the impression that politics was a direct or logical "outgrowth" of ethics, rejecting any such talk
as nothing but illusory humbug.

KANT'S POLITICAL LEGACY: ANTI-HUMBUGISM

Integrity was, without a doubt, the supreme quality that Kant cherished
above everything else in humans and their creations. Conversely, though
with the same intensity, he abhorred bogusness. Thus, while he valued
both reason and constitutionality, he was suspicious of claims in support
of a constitution that professed to be wholly the work of pure reason. "It is
certainly *agreeable* to think up political constitutions which meet the requirements of reason (particularly in matters of justice). But it is *foolhardy*
to put them forward seriously."[80] So wrote Kant in one of his last writings
to be published during his life, *The Contest of Faculties*. Similarly, as we
noted, he sharply distinguished between moral politicians – persons who
adhered to principles of honesty and honour – and political moralists –
persons who used moral concepts for self-serving ends and deluded
others by dwelling on fanciful policies.[81] Similarly, too, Kant knew how to

79 Kant, *Universal History* (*Reiss*, 51) (my own translation).

80 Kant, *The Contest of Faculties* (*Reiss*, 188). Kant adds in a note examples of
utopias, and comments: "It is a pleasant dream to hope that a political product
of the sort envisaged will one day be brought to perfection, at however remote
a date."

81 Kant, *Perpetual Peace* (*Reiss*, 121). Thus, the British people are deliberately
deceived by their politicians, Kant states (in *The Contest of Faculties*), in being
made to believe that they live under a constitutionally *limited* monarchy when, in
fact, they live "under an *absolute* monarchy," notwithstanding the two houses of
parliament, intended "to furnish ostensible proof of parliamentary freedom,"
Kant cites this "insidious approach" as an example of a most despicably
"mendacious form of publicity" (*Reiss*, 186–7) (Kant's emphasis).

keep legality and morality separate, and carefully refrained from expecting lawful citizens to be morally perfect. Indeed, he went so far as to allow for the possibility of "a nation of devils" as long as its members had enough common sense to realize that lawlessness is not good for them or any of their problems.[82] For citizens need to act only according to law, and not for its own sake, even though they have to know the difference between acting according to *law* and acting according to their own inclinations or considerations of utility.[83] In *Theory and Practice* Kant illustrates this distinction by citing the example of an executor of wills.[84]

Legality, for Kant, however, did not mean sheer legal positivism. What he had in mind was lawfulness as *Rechtsgesinnung* in itself; that is to say, the possession of a shared ethos of legality that, as an intrinsic good, resides in the conviction of most, if not all, individuals, making them feel that law is essential for the coherence of a societal *order*. Collingwood, it seems, argues along similar lines about the meaning of rule-governed conduct. A promise is binding "even though neither I nor anyone else can be proved to gain by keeping it ... for a promise has something of the nature of a self-imposed law." To be sure, Kant fully realized, this does not make a legal order moral, just as conversely, moral self-legislation does not create in itself an overall legal order, since the latter demands a constitutional framework that, for Kant, implies lawful coercion.[85]

But, for coercion to *be lawful,* judicious "masters" are required. Preferably, he would have liked them to be blessed with the wisdom and integrity of Rousseau's Legislator, so that they could guide rather than coerce people to act lawfully. Alas, he sadly doubted that the masters would be appreciably different from the rest of humanity, being made of timber scarcely less warped. And since Kant, unlike Burke, had only minimal faith in the power of hallowed beliefs to render liberty and governance more gentle

---

82 Kant, *Works,* VIII, 366. Hans Saner, *Kant's Political Thought: The Origins and Development,* trans. E.B. Ashton (Chicago: University of Chicago Press, 1973) presents Kant's political thinking as an "organic outgrowth" of his moral philosophy. While I am not clear about what this is supposed to mean, I do feel that Kant is remarkably consistent in setting apart *civic* requirements from strictly *moral* requirements. And I believe, too, that in this respect Kant shared more with Hobbes than he himself liked to think or a number of commentators (including Saner) are prepared to concede.

83 Kant, *Theory of Right (Reiss,* 133).

84 Kant, *Theory and Practice (Reiss,* 70–1).

85 Kant, *Theory of Right (Reiss,* 135); for R.G. Collingwood's argument, parallelling Kant's emphasis on the creation of a legal-political order, see Collingwood, Political Action," *Proceedings of the Aristotelian Society,* 29, (1929), 162–3.

in their interpersonal workings, he put almost exclusive emphasis on the reciprocal force of a legal system that originated from a "republican constitution" in whose creation the people (however defined precisely) had a share (however indirectly), by dint of which they were, in appropriating it, obligated to observe it. It alone, rather than any appeal to "ancient opinions and rules of life," held out for Kant the promise of ensuring liberty as much as of legitimizing governmental power. Fearing that few people would respect the freedom of others or assume the burdens of truly moral self-enactment, he opted for effective laws as the arbiter in a *Rechtsstaat*, laws before which all are the same, regardless of rank or disposition. They, alone, for practical purposes, are the highest authority. It is not the person of the prince, accordingly, that deserves to be ultimately revered, but law itself; *it* is the foundation of all right.[86]

And yet, it was not law *per se* but freedom that was Kant's principal concern. However, he felt convinced that there could be no freedom in society without law; no freedom, that is, which could be equally enjoyed by all. Much of his apprehension about revolutions was in truth due to his fear that, in abrogating legality, they would invite arbitrariness rather than freedom. The high-sounding and quasi-utopian claims of redemption made by revolutionaries only helped to deepen his mistrust. He could not help wondering whether the slogans of liberty, equality, and fraternity would not merely serve to mask inhumanities but would also raise unrealizable expectations and thereby generate wholesale disenchantment. Kant, it is true, did not deny the morality of claims in support of the creation of universal human rights. But even they did not allay his suspicion that, sooner or later, disillusionment would set in, and those who had hoped for a drastic improvement in their lot, anticipating the removal of injustices of all kinds, would experience profound disappointment.

All in all, he judged revolutions too illegal, too unpredictable in their planning, and too messy in their outcome, to constitute a real basis for reform. Instead, he preferred gradual improvements which, though much less dramatic for participants and spectators alike, were also much less irrational and violent, and yet far more likely to succeed.[87]

86 Burke, *Reflections on the Revolution in France*, 94. Echoing Rousseau, Kant made the rule of law the central principle of his *Theory of Right* and the quintessential contention of his political thought.

87 "Planning," as the vital component of his gradualism, Kant principally associated with choosing the right moment for putting reforms into practice. As Claudia Langer observes, Kant feared premature reforms because he suspected that, arousing fierce opposition, they would invite civil strife, illegality, and disorder, if not complete chaos. See her *Reform nach Prinzipien* (Stuttgart: Klett, 1986), 14–18.

Unfortunately, apart from his political gradualism, Kant suggested no procedural mechanism that could try to come to grips with the old problem of *qui custodiet ipsos custodes*, – of how to ensure constitutional control over governments through ongoing processes of parliamentary scrutiny. Aside from his insistence on the separation of governmental functions as a check to monolithic power, there is, as far as I can ascertain, barely a hint of the importance that Rousseau attached to regular accounting by the executive to the legislature. This is rather startling because, not unlike Thomasius and Rousseau, Kant did view accountability as conceptually related to both autonomy and reciprocity. It is surprising also because of his recurrent urgings in support of openness and publicity as hallmarks of a republican order, together with his loathing of secret societies (such as the freemasons), lest these make the hidden still more hidden or stealthily fan rebellious agitation.[88]

On the other hand, Kant, like Rousseau, was wary of too much public debate or political discussion, for fear of popular divisiveness; his reticence on governmental accountability may therefore not have been entirely accidental. Bold though he was in demanding the free expression of ideas, he was simultaneously worried that public criticism might provoke revolutionary thinking rather than promote constitutional reforms through "legality." As a result, he seems to have been wavering between encouraging publicity and counselling against it, lest it impair gradualism. And it was this wavering that chiefly laid Kant open to charges of political backsliding, if not of actual indifference to legitimate grievances.[89]

This said, there can be little doubt about the seriousness of Kant's resolve the challenge whatever was accepted merely because it was the "done thing" conventionally, and to challenge it in terms that involved the fullest engagement of reflective reason in a way that transcended all tradition. In J.W. Goethe's words, Kant succeeded in "penetrating the

---

88 Kant, *Perpetual Peace* (*Reiss*, 125–7); see also *The Contest of Faculties* (*Reiss*, 186–7). F.C. Beiser recounts in *Enlightenment, Revolution, and Romanticism* (Cambridge: Harvard University Press, 1992) that Kant was by temperament suspicious of popular movements, fearing unrest and in-fighting, because he doubted that people could ever agree among themselves (54). See also Kant, *Works*, VIII, 310.

89 As Howard Williams puts it in *Kant's Political Philosophy* (Oxford: Blackwell, 1983): "Kant has no advice to give to the protesting citizen who is faced by a tyrant or dictator" (156). In his remarkably lucid and well-balanced study, Williams questions Kant's consistent liberalism, seeing him more as a "pragmatic conservative" (179).

armour of all rigid ways of thinking that had befogged the century."[90] In his anti-traditionalism Kant fearlessly exposed every form of tutelage, utopian make-believe, and high-handed dogmatism, determined to strip the world of its old signposts and its comforting homilies. It may therefore not be wrong to conclude that it is first and foremost Kant's intellectual boldness that constitutes his paramount contribution to modernity. Arguably, too, it was this surge into a terrain with no "banisters" to lean on which had so powerful an impact on Hannah Arendt's own musings on thought and action, as she herself acknowledged fulsomely, not only in her writings and lectures but also in private correspondence. Like Kant, she too felt that political philosophy should be challenging if it was to justify its existence. Whether her own interpretation of Kant's challenging philosophy is itself beyond challenge is admittedly another matter altogether.[91]

90 Cited in Cassirer, *Rousseau, Kant and Goethe*, 71.

91 See Ronald Beiner, ed., *Hannah Arendt, Lectures on Kant's Political Philosophy* (Chicago: University of Chicago Press, 1982), 142, where he remarks that Arendt was "very free in the handling of Kant's work, making use of his writings in accordance with her own purpose." If so, she was not a bad disciple of Kant. For it was not beyond himself to jump to rather blanket generalizations to make his (theoretical) point. Note 81 (above) demonstrates this rather poignantly. It cites Kant saying (in *The Contest of Faculties*) that British politics is making use of a "mendacious form of publicity," deceiving "the people with the illusion that their monarchy is limited," when in fact "it is *absolute.*" Kant's basis for this allegation is the "fact" that "the monarch of Great Britain has waged numerous wars without asking the people's consent." The king can get away with this, since the representatives of the people always "agree with him, for he has the authority to award all offices and dignities." Kant denounces all this as a thoroughly "insidious approach" of a "corrupt system" (*Reiss*, 186–7). This statement could be said to verge on a serious misrepresentation of British governance since the execution of Charles I, unless Kant did not know that "the Crown" in reality referred to H.M.'s *government*, and not to the monarch alone – which I doubt. What is more likely is that Kant arrived at this (rather sweeping) verdict in view of George III's determination to rule personally (1760–1820), with the help of an acquiescent minister (Lord North), who appears to have held that it was a minister's duty to execute the monarch's orders rather than to devise a policy of his own. (I am indebted for this information to my long-standing friend and correspondent Peter Greaves, an Oxford scholar of British history.) Clearly, Kant went too far; but, judging what went on in Britain (and America) during his own lifetime experience, his allegations were not entirely groundless.

But then it is, in the final analysis, for the reader to judge what is or is not genuinely Kantian in Arendt's interpretation of culture, history, or politics. Few, however, would deny, I believe, that Arendt's profound distaste for utopian idolatry, no less than the prevalent flavour of her critical thinking, was strikingly Kantian in conception. Above all, what she unmistakably shared with Kant was an uncanny sensitivity to all that was bogus, and a passionate disdain for mendacity as the concomitant of the curse of phoniness, especially if it was overlaid with surface piety or glossed with surface consistency.

8

External Principles, but no Banisters:
Hannah Arendt

ALTHOUGH ARENDT ATTRIBUTED her line of political thinking chiefly to Kant, in her emphasis on an autonomous ethic of political action she discloses striking similarities with Christian Thomasius, whose ideas she probably learned about in the course of her reading of Lessing.[1] At the same time, her (selective) amalgam of sources includes writers who are almost as frequently mentioned as Kant, such as Aristotle, Machiavelli, Montesquieu, and Tocqueville. What she chiefly had in common with all of them is the celebration of the public domain, its distinctive freedom and plurality.

After tracing Arendt's conceptual distinctions, if not polarizations, together with attempts of conceptual blending – in particular between antiquity and existentialism,[2] I am suggesting that, apart from her contribution to political thought, Arendt demands serious attention as a critic of modernity and as an imaginative historian of ideas, who engaged in reinterpreting such core notions as reason, knowledge, thinking, judgment, action, and meaning, by resolutely going her own way, regardless of contemporary fads.

---

1 By her own admission, Arendt felt chiefly indebted to the leading thinkers in the German tradition of philosophy, notably Lessing and Kant, in addition to her mentors Martin Heidegger and Karl Jaspers, although, in important respects, she also departed from both.

2 On this attempted fusion, see L.P. Hinchman and S.K. Hinchman, "Existentialism Politicized: Arendt's Debt to Jaspers." *Review of Politics* 53 (1991), 435–68.

THE IMPAIRMENT OF CONTINUITY AND JUDGMENT

Using such allegories as the broken thread of Ariadne, or being left with an inheritance without a testament, Arendt conveys a depiction of modernity as an age without a past, marking a total break with any sense of continuity. "Without testament or, to resolve the metaphor, without tradition," she writes in *Between Past and Future*, "there seems to be no willed continuity." In truth, however, her statement suggests more than temporal discontinuity, for it betokens an even deeper malaise, namely, an era rendered unrecognizable as the abode of *humanitas* in both its beliefs and its exertions. For, as Arendt herself explains, thought and reality have "parted company," their inner bond has snapped. One no longer guides the other, nor makes it intelligible, and, all the more so because "old verities have lost all concrete relevance."[3] As a result, the past is no longer of assistance in coping with the present, let alone with the future. ·

To illustrate the extent of the drastic transformation of thinking and acting, Arendt cites Tocqueville's reaction to the changes that the American Revolution wrought. Overwhelmed by them, as events "incomparably greater than anything which has taken place in the world before," Tocqueville felt that we no longer could count on the past to throw its light on the future; "the spirit of man walks through the night" in utter darkness and obscurity.[4] To act now, Arendt concludes, is to act without any clear direction, without signposts or "banisters" to help us; enveloped in darkness we have, each of us, to generate our own light as we plunge into the future.

Never before, to my knowledge, has *self*-direction been urged in more uncompromising terms. Not even the most radical Enlightenment proponents of individual autonomy went quite that far. Nor do I recall anyone whose anguish over the predicament of action in modernity was so deeply personal. In both its range and its tone it surpasses even Thomasius's agonizing over the inability of human will to align itself with what reason and rightness command. At the same time, Arendt's dismay with the age in which she found herself went beyond expressions of disorientation and grief. Indeed, much that she wrote in "exile" took the form of a stirring appeal to humanity to turn inward, not merely, or chiefly,

3 Hannah Arendt, *Between Past and Future* (New York: Viking Press, 1961, 1968), 5–6, (hereafter BPF).

4 Alexis de Tocqueville, *Democracy in America*, (Garden City, New York: Doubleday, 1969), 703 (Ed. J.P. Mayer).

for a contemplative soul-searching, but rather for summoning up a determined effort to recover ways of regaining the public realm. Women and men, acting jointly, were to bring to light the meaning of self-governance by inserting themselves anew into the world. If this appeal was not applicable solely to tangibly political objectives, it was nonetheless an unmistakable clarion call to action in defiance of the perplexity of living in a universe in which traditions have worn thin or have faded altogether. And the degree of defiance that she brought to bear on her call for the recovery of the public world was such that it at the same time fanned her resolve to revive her own spirits and help her to renew faith in the possibility of human freedom as well as in the prospect of being once again a *citizen*.

It was above all the loss of her civic rights and freedoms in her own country that struck her like the opening of an abyss, of a bottomless pit that split her apart from the world and culture she had known. All of a sudden she had become a pariah, an outcast, in an order of things in which she had no place. And yet, among those to be obliterated in the New Order, Hannah Arendt saw herself as someone still frantically trying to fathom the well-nigh unfathomable. While this search for meaning on the surface focused on political events, she was in truth anxious to explore far deeper layers of human thinking and human acting. For, when she brooded over what had made Hitler possible, not as a clown, but as an all-powerful architect of an edifice of unprecedented organized brutality, she could not help recognizing that to come anywhere close to comprehension demanded the transcendence of the narrowly political. To Arendt, therefore, the quest for an answer (or answers) became the most pressing issue of her day-by-day thinking, first in France, then in America. In a real sense, *becoming* a refugee acted as the gadfly of her intellectual revolt.

Arendt's first major work, *The Origins of Totalitarianism*, should be seen, therefore, not so much as the expression of an academic engaged in her professional specialty, as that of a personal need to come to terms with an onslaught that threatened whatever belief she had in the possibility of a common humanity. This visceral threat Arendt traced to the fissure of two kinds of relationship: the relation with one's fellow-beings and the relation with the reality that enveloped her very existence. In both directions, the fissures exemplified for her the blurring of sensibilities, causing the loss of people's ability to perceive what is, ought to be, or deserved to be cherished. She felt that this blurring eroded the basis of thinking itself and, with it, the capacity to judge. Hence, it is not "the convinced Nazi or the convinced Communist," she argued, that caused the greatest worry, but rather the number of women and men "for whom the distinction between fact and fiction (i.e., the reality of experience) and the distinction between true and false (i.e., the standards of thought and judgment) no longer existed," so that "making sense" as such was in jeopardy.[5]

The root of this perverted consciousness Arendt diagnosed as the misperception of a fabricated world, a world of mere "making," for the authentic world of "acting," the world of creating together with others something that, unlike working to a blueprint, was a feat that stretched into an unknown distance and whose outcome or "product" was wholly incalculable. And what troubled Arendt was that the world, in mistaking the fake for the real, could not but obscure the image of *humanitas* beyond recognition, if not forever obstruct its recovery.[6]

Still, she did not altogether falter. Being the person she was, she *had* to struggle on; indeed, in momentary flashes she managed not only to overcome the gloom enveloping her but to start hoping anew that humanity might regain the capacity to view things as they are, to think, and to realize that the gods being worshipped are but leaden idols. The nagging question, however, remained: What was it that caused the crisis of modernity to be so deep-seated that its cure became so problematic? The answer, she feels, consisted mainly in the difficulty of detecting, amidst the general befuddlement of the age, the particular confusion between making and acting. This difficulty is compounded, she agrees with Thomasius and Kant, by the distortion of practical judgment. And, like them, she sees a possible remedy not in the accumulation of more *knowledge*, but rather in the cultivation of better *taste*. It is the atrophy of this quasi-aesthetic property which, together with a widespread blunting of reflective thinking, impedes recovery. Unless something can be done to prevent further deterioration, reality will remain cloaked; the veil will remain unlifted, and a remedy will defy unearthing.[7]

The distinction between making and acting is the cardinal theme of Arendt's most influential work, *The Human Condition*, and a subject to which she kept returning in subsequent writings. It is a distinction closely related to others she made, such as between the private and the public, between freedom and necessity, and between truth and opinion.

5 Arendt, *The Origins of Totalitarianism* (Cleveland: World Publishing, 1951; ed. used, 1966), 474.

6 Arendt, *The Human Condition* (Chicago: University of Chicago Press, 1958), 204–6, (hereafter HC).

7 Arendt, "The Crisis in Culture," BPF, 219.

In what follows I want to comment on these distinctions, their problematic polarization, and the bearing they are intended to have on the ills of modernity that she so acutely portrays.

Surveying her overall position, I shall suggest that there are two kinds of recovery postulates in her work: one is designedly aimed at politics, the other, more diffuse and broadly cultural, is bent on salvaging the link between thought and action in modernity. In my summing up, I hazard the guess that it is in the second recovery postulate, as an insightful critic of modernity, determined to preserve continuity and purpose, that Hannah Arendt will foremost be remembered.

INFINITY AND FINALITY

Modern theories of behaviourism may well be accurate, Arendt scathingly observes, in viewing contemporary life as typified by purely routinized behaviour.[8] This is so, she claims, because behaviour (associated with "making") has virtually replaced action. The daily routine of coping with what she calls life's necessities, which characterizes the private realm, so dominates people's outlook that it leaves them neither time nor inclination for pursuits lying outside this realm – pursuits that, unlike habitual behaviour and the making of objects of finality, venture into infinity. Identifying the private realm essentially with social, economic, and purely personal interests, she sharply contrasts it with the public domain, the domain of politics and supra-personal interests. And her persistent grief is that the social has relentlessly swallowed the political, just as the ordinary has devoured the extraordinary. The upshot of this "functionalization" has been that the drab, banal, and commonplace have ousted the memorably great and the totally uncharted, unanticipated, and thus intrinsically unpredictable.[9]

What is more, means and ends have come to be calamitously blurred, if not completely reversed. Economic matters, for example, which formerly belonged entirely to the private sphere and were viewed as means of sustaining individual households, are now a collective concern and the mainstay of the public realm. In the course of this blurring, action proper, and its autonomous integrity in entering the space of the unknown, has been lost sight of. Yet, in enveloping the public realm, the private realm has itself, at the same time, lost its distinctiveness. Gone, Arendt laments, is the privacy of family life, of friendship and fraternity, of "the intimacy of the

8 Arendt, HC, 295.
9 Ibid., 31, 38–9.

heart."[10] The transfer of the instrumental ethic of the household and of private business to the public domain, therefore, has in no way helped to enrich the content of the uniquely private. The loss of the public world has, in short, been no gain for the private world.

Arendt presents this transfer from one ethic to another as a reversal of existential meanings as such, if not as a drastic metamorphosis of reality itself. For, what originally was meant to be hidden – the domestic and the intimate – was now exposed, and what was meant to provide and augment light to illuminate human greatness was now condemned to darkness and obscurity.[11] And the realm where the reversal of meanings has in Arendt's view been most baneful, is politics, the public realm *par excellence*. It has caused freedom and speech, the defining ingredients of political life, to be utterly degraded. Instead of being located in the infinite, the sphere of bold leaps into the unknown, freedom has now been placed in the finite sphere, exactly the area outside of, and opposed to, politics.[12] Speech, which, according to Arendt, acquires its true purpose in politics, is now reduced to "idle talk," and, in its place, force or violence, originally held to be inimical to politics, is now looked upon as its universally defining characteristic.[13]

Precisely because humans of contemporary modernity feel incapable of facing the uncertainty in which freedom is shrouded, and unwilling as they are to accept the unpredictability of outcomes, they substitute making for acting. As a result, the process of stepping into an unknown future is assimilated to that of routine production, in which the nature of the end-product is known from the start. However, the trouble does not end there. As a corollary of this substitution, the operation of reason, too, undergoes a basic transformation, in that what originally served as an instrument of reflection is now a tool for calculation. Modern rationalism, therefore, is no more real than modern realism is rational.[14]

Following in the train of this change and the substitution of the unpredictable by things wholly calculable, there has been another reversal, no less fateful: the denigration of death and the exclusive adoration of health and welfare. Taking care of one's body and one's comfort now usurps the primacy of honourable deeds. Social needs, economic wants, and biological claims virtually absorb the totality of existence; the circle

10 Ibid., 36, 61, 200.
11 Ibid., 65.
12 Arendt, "What is Freedom," BPF, 148–50.
13 Arendt, HC, 4, 29, 186.
14 Ibid., 257, 274.

of reversals is consummated, finality replaces infinity. And nothing counts anymore but material or bodily demands, and whatever generates pleasure or profit.[15]

Coupled with the move from infinity to finality is an entirely new mode of confrontation between truth and politics. Whereas in Plato's frame of thinking the confrontation typically occurs at the high level of reasoned argument or reasoned agreement, in the world of modernity, marked by finality, truth clashes with the political on the lowest level of human exploits, its conflicting needs and interests – no contrast could be sharper or more extreme.[16]

Whether Arendt's portrayal of the modern world or, for that matter, of her ancient exemplar, the Greek *polis*, is a faithful portrayal is for the purpose of this discussion of lesser import. More to the point, I suggest, is the extent to which the diverse polarizations, and the meanings they are intended to carry, succeed in shedding light on Arendt's first kind of recovery postulate, her vision of a new way of interpreting political action. To get this objective into clearer focus, it seems desirable to have a closer look at what her distinction between making and acting entails in terms of the reasons and agents that are to assume centrality in her projected alternative.

THE PERVERSION AND THE REDEMPTION
OF POLITICS

Notwithstanding Arendt's admiration for components of the Platonic intellectual legacy, she accuses Plato of having been the first to rationalize the retreat from infinity to finality in politics, by recommending a switch from action to making.[17] In order to escape the haphazardness of a situation in which a plurality of humans enact something new, something whose outcome is that of infinite contingency, Arendt charges, Plato sought to create a predictable order that people could master and, therefore, control. Intending to put an end to the frailty and fickleness of democracy, Plato spelled the doom not only of democracy, but also,

---

15 Ibid., 286–92; see also Arendt, *On Revolution* (New York: Viking Press, 1965), 58.

16 Arendt, HC, 182; see also "What is Freedom?" BPF, 151–2, and "Truth and Politics," BPF, 263.

17 Arendt, HC, 197.

claims Arendt, of politics altogether.[18] In effect, therefore, he is taken to task for having *perverted* politics as the prime mover in the public realm by transmuting the nature of *action*, properly so called. Rather than seeing politics as causing things to happen out of the free initiative of free agents, Plato viewed it as the *result*, and not the *author*, of agency; for, political action being now defined as rulership, as the possession of knowledge about mastering events, consists of nothing more than the issuing of instructions, if not commands. Thus, in place of the idea of people acting in the plural, as equal citizens, Plato put the idea of monocracy, the monarchic notion of a philosopher-king.[19]

Not unlike Thomasius in his passionate rejection of this idea, Arendt indignantly dismisses it as typifying the *vitiation* of action in the civic realm, disclosing as it does an understanding of politics in which the paradigmatic actor is seen as the master-craftsman, the expert who knows exactly what is to be done, why, and how.[20] And "knowing" precisely *means* master-minding, being fully in control, in view of which it simultaneously identifies, rationalizes, and justifies *power*, thus making knowledge the source and the right of rulers to issue orders. Conversely, those lacking this knowledge are unable to *design* blueprints, the basis of action; their task, therefore, is to carry out orders in the *execution* of blueprints; indeed, it is their legal duty.[21] As such, any refusal to obey commands calls for punishment. Accordingly, Arendt concludes, enforceable sanctions are needed, to back up commands. Acting in the public domain, notably in politics, is therefore rendered unthinkable in the absence of legalized violence. Politics, turned into "making," simply *demands* it.[22]

Once acting is converted into making, and making implies having certain knowledge about outcomes, "knowledge" becomes a world that, for Arendt, is therefore altogether separate from thinking. Although she acknowledges that thinking is distinct from acting, she is nonetheless adamant in regarding thinking as an indispensable part of acting. Hence, while *knowing* and acting are wholly separable notions, *thinking* – as the activity of deliberation – and acting are not. The very moment thought

18 Ibid., 197–203.
19 Ibid., 157, 203.
20 Arendt, HC, 198; see also "What is Authority?," BPF, 112–14.
21 Arendt, HC, 201.
22 Ibid., 202–4.

and action part company, action ceases to have meaning.[23] The thesis of their distinctness *as well as* their connectedness is elaborated in one of Arendt's latest writings, *The Life of the Mind,* where thinking and acting are seen as inextricably joined within the dynamics of authentic human perception and human creativity. To think, she states, is to step back and ask yourself, "Why am I doing this?" or "What is the meaning of what I have done?" And, to engage in such thinking and reflecting (Arendt echoes Thomasius) requires no higher learning or special qualifications – it is something anybody can do. Thus understood, thinking has nothing in common with technical or scientific expertise, logical skill, or linguistic prowess; nor, for that matter, should it be confused with metaphysical speculations on divine essences or eternal substances. *Anyone*, in short, is free to dwell in thought upon beliefs, practices, events, and experiences.[24]

Unlike the know-how of making, thinking pertains to what is *not* fixed or certain. If knowledge relates to the tangibly attainable, thinking relates to the inherently incalculable. One is like a well-surveyed piece of real estate, the other like a terrain uncharted. In Arendt's exposition, therefore, thinking makes no knowledge claims. What instead is quintessentially involved is a sort of inner dialogue, in the course of which the self questions itself and the self also answers its own questions. Arendt credits this understanding of thinking to Socrates and Plato, for whom the thinking self is akin to two-in-one. It is not lack of *knowledge* that Arendt diagnoses as the source of the "banality of evil" in *Eichmann in Jerusalem,* but the absence of thinking, of stopping to reflect upon what is demanded of one as a human being. Eichmann simply carried out orders, but he did not act. By the standards of Nazi-Germany, Eichmann behaved correctly, in the manner of all those who do what they are told and do so because it saves them from trouble, and because it cannot but help their advancement. Evil is banal when it occurs in such pedestrian manner. Not too happy with this presentation of evil, particularly in Eichmann's case, I sought further elucidation from Arendt. She explained "banal" by contrasting it with the memorably great. Banal was simply ordinary – *gewöhnlich*, combining the meanings of pedestrian with those of vulgar and base. Furthermore, to go along mindlessly, to swim with the tide unthinkingly, is the hallmark of the conformist,

23 Ibid., 159, 202.

24 Ibid.; see also Arendt, *The Life of the Mind* (New York: Harcourt Brace Jovanovich, 1978, two vols. ed. Mary McCarthy), 1, 180.

a characteristic held in common with the routinely obedient bureaucrat, whether or not he is also an opportunist.[25]

Leaving aside the question as to whether evil could ever be banal, it is, I believe, important to take notice of Arendt's emphasis on *thinking* about what we do, have done, or are about to do, regardless of how much we know, can know, or should know in the pursuit of goals, values, or means-to-ends relations; and "know" in the way we know the outcome of following an instruction manual. Thus, although at first sight it appears that those engaged in acting should never dwell upon their undertaking, such an inference is not only overdrawn but quite mistaken, if it should be construed to signify that Arendt urges people to act thoughtlessly. Instead, what she seems to have had in mind is that the meaning of a public deed lies beyond what its author had intended. Accordingly, those who make their mark in history by acting in politics are never really in control of what they have started, and hence *masters* of their destiny, let alone the architects of the future of others. It is not surprising, therefore, that Arendt uses the metaphor of a "miracle" as the closest analogue to enactments in politics and history.[26]

From this perspective of viewing action, Arendt understandably censures Marx for applying Vico's formula of historical understanding. For, in it, history is intelligible to humans because it was *made* by humans. But this, says Arendt, implies that actions are viewed entirely from hindsight, as *completed* processes, and, therefore, as though they were no different from the mirror image of Plato's blueprint conception of action. From such an *ex post facto* stance, she is quite prepared to grant that occurrences are in principle knowable, as regards both their direction and their consequences, since process and outcome are from the outset routinely familiar. Hence Marx, as Vico before him, is blamed for having routinized human action, thereby causing no less than "the escape from action."[27]

---

25 Arendt, *The Life of the Mind*, I, 191; see also ch. 18 as a whole. Also *Eichmann in Jerusalem: A report on the Banality of Evil* (New York: Viking Press, 1963, 1965), 126. Elisabeth Young-Bruehl, Arendt's biographer, confirms this interpretation of banality in "From the Pariah's Point of View: Reflections on Hannah Arendt's Life and Work," in Melvyn A. Hill (ed.), *Hannah Arendt: The Recovery of the Public World* (New York: St Martin's Press, 1979), 3–26, esp. 16–17.

26 Arendt, "What is Freedom?," BPF, 169; see also HC, 209, 215–19, 222, 290.

27 Arendt, "The Concept of History," BPF, 79. This almost looks like a return to Christian doctrines, according to which it is inevitable that humans should act in the dark, not knowing what is to become of their actions – a position that Vico only partially challenged.

To be sure, action, like making or "fabrication," has a definite beginning; unlike fabrication, however, action has no definite end. Being a leap into the unknown, action stretches forth unendingly; it "reaches into infinity; it literally endures throughout time, until mankind itself has come to an end."[28] Logically enough, Arendt concludes that those acting in the public realm never really know what they are setting in motion, and are therefore liable to incur the burden of responsibility for consequences they neither foresaw nor intended. Such, however, is the cost of plunging into the future, a price that has to be paid if acting is to take the form of self-generated surging ahead, come what may. Precisely because "making" minimizes or entirely eliminates this cost, it disqualifies itself from counting as action. As a result, making stands to action in the way passivity stands to vital power; unlike power, making can therefore never start anything genuinely new.[29]

A further contrast that Arendt adduces lies in the free-floating character of authentic action. Action proper, she contends, is unconditional, in the sense of being unfettered by considerations of antecedents or outcomes. While making is governed by means-to-ends relations and is linked to material and biological needs, actions are utterly free, unbounded by wants, needs, or conditions of the moment. By the same token, actions are held to be independent of motives or goals, as well as of conventional norms; their defining criterion is a quasi-transcendent and inherently self-sustaining *principle* – a causal category that sparks off deeds without determining them. Whereas dispositions, states of mind, or intentions issue from "within the self," the uniqueness of a principle lies in its capacity to inspire "from without."[30] Removed from subjective willing in its source, it is, conversely, neither derivable from nor reducible to so-called objective necessity, in its goal. It is simply what it is, an uncaused causality, in, but not beyond, itself.

Arendt claims to be adapting here Montesquieu's concept of virtue, and she lists such features as honour, freedom, or glory, which inspire from without, totally detached from motives or promptings to produce this or that result or to conform to particular demands. To act on a principle, therefore, is to act for its own sake.[31]

Evidently, she is searching for an autonomous standard to justify action in and for itself. Like Kant's categorical imperative, public action,

28 Arendt, HC, 125–6, 209.
29 Ibid., 209–10.
30 Ibid., 125; "What is Freedom?," BPF, 151–2; *On Revolution*, 137.
31 Arendt, "What is Freedom?," BPF, 152–3.

self-grounded within its activating principle, carries its value and justification in itself. Unlike Kant's categorical imperative, however, Arendt's "principle" does not *demand* compliance; it is not so much the enunciation or token of a sense of duty as it is the expression of an unbidden recognition of appropriateness, comparable to manifestations of aesthetic taste, as in the appreciation of beauty in a painting or an artist's performance. Indeed, the idea of "performance" appeals to Arendt especially as an exemplar, by lending itself most eminently as a model of public action, in that those who engage in public action most closely resemble the virtuosi artists of this world.[32] Like them, men and women of action perform in order to establish a space in which self-sustaining principles can make an appearance, words can be heard, and deeds seen, talked about, remembered, and, most importantly for Arendt, turned into stories.[33]

POLITICAL MORALITY
AND HUMAN SELF-DISCLOSURE

Bringing about a deed in the public domain, then, has little to do with intentions or the computing of consequences. What matters, and matters alone, is the "performance" itself, the launching of a new beginning in the light of an external principle. Deeds so enacted are *sui generis*; they are feats that so "shine in their radiance as to be worthy of remembrance."[34]

This is undoubtedly an unusual and highly original portrayal of action within an equally unusual and highly original vision of politics. All the same, a number of troubling thoughts irresistibly arise which, in turn, urge closer enquiry into the central point of the diverse, and highly polarized, distinctions that (we found) Arendt adduces – between acting and making, thinking and knowing, principles and intentions – and, in particular, the question whether her real point is not a determined plea for, and a fierce dedication to, the extraordinary *per se*. If so, are mundane matters such as earning a livelihood or looking after one's welfare too trifling and commonplace to deserve public attention? I do not think so; I very much doubt that Arendt wished to brush aside such concerns and considerations. Nor was she inclined to underrate the responsibility that rested with those in the public realm who make decisions about health, welfare, social justice, or war and

32 Ibid., 153.
33 Ibid., 154–5.
34 Arendt, HC, 184–5.

peace. And while she had her dramatic moods, and a profound sense of the supra-ordinary in human life, her overall outlook was urbanely down-to-earth. Undoubtedly, she cherished the belief in a reconstituted political order, in which humans would seek to transcend issues confined to private material needs. Yet, whatever the issues were that entered the political domain, Arendt's dominant concern was almost indistinguishable from that of Kant: the existence of utmost integrity and the resolve to avoid using words intended to deceive or to incite violence and brutality.[35]

Unfortunately, Arendt does not let us in on the secret of how she expects glory and dirty hands to be kept apart. The only recognizably moral guide that she appears to offer is a highly personal code of honour: There are things one simply does not do if one is to be able to live with oneself. This is somewhat paradoxical, since the ethic she links with the *supra*-personal, public sphere, can thus hardly be described as *im*personal. Her suggested moral guide may or may not work in ordinary social relations or in strictly private conduct, but even if it did, would it be equally applicable to human agency in the wholly divergent public sphere?

There is undeniably room for clarification here, especially in view of Arendt's own emphasis on the distinctiveness of the two spheres, but I nevertheless doubt that her resistance to moral absolutism warrants the charge of "moral separatism" or that of sheer arbitrariness or "personal idiosyncracy."[36] Nor can I share the suggestion of an intimate friend of Arendt's that she generally was inclined to lean "a little too heavily on paradox."[37] By contrast, another commentator has argued that those who interpret her "amoral" conception of public action as indifference to morality, tend to over-emphasize "the expressive dimension at the expense of the communicative one." The reason he gives is that Arendt has changed her philosophical-anthropological position in the time between her *Human Condition* and her essay *On*

---

35 Ibid., 179.

36 See, for example, Martin Jay and Leon Botstein, "Hannah Arendt: Opposing Views," *Partisan Review* 45 (1978), 351–3; George Kateb, *Hannah Arendt: Politics, Conscience, Evil* (Oxford: Martin Robertson, 1984) 28–39; and Seyla Benhabib, "Judgment and the Moral Foundation of Politics in Arendt's Political Thought," *Political Theory* 16 (1988), 29–52.

37 Carol Brightman (ed.), *Between Friends: The Correspondence of Hannah Arendt and Mary McCarthy* (New York: Harcourt Brace, 1995), XXIII, 2; see also ibid., 296, where McCarthy instructs Arendt that it seems a "mistake to force a key word … to mean what it doesn't normally."

Revolution, without integrating her "expressive" stance with her "communicative" stance on participatory democracy.[38]

Be that as it may, I cannot help feeling that her distaste for a strict parallelism between individual and political morality – a distaste she shared with Kant – had its true root in opting, as Thomasius has done, for a political morality *sui generis*, in conformity with the general thrust of her thinking on agency in the public realm. If so, it was because she recognized that there could be principles of political morality that had no analogue in principles of individual morality; and that to hold otherwise could only get things mired in confusion. For example, one could hardly claim a parallel semblance between general moral principles *per se* and the specifically political injunction that no ruling party is to legislate its permanent entrenchment in order to prevent any electoral alternative to itself. If, therefore, she is guilty of a lack of clarity on this issue, the problem may be lying in her almost exclusive emphasis on principles embodying highly intangible ends, such as glory or infinity. For why, and in what way, could such principles serve as *justifying* principles? Just because ultimate consequences cannot be known, does it follow that reasoned policy objectives cease to be justifiable grounds for acting?

Arendt, to be fair, does acknowledge the distressingly problematic nature of acting in public, if only because of the difficulty of establishing appropriate standards in the form of fixed procedural rules. For, to establish these as necessary conditions, might, she fears, fatally undermine "plunging into the future," if, indeed, it would not amount to a flight, a downright retreat, from audacity, from the kind of courage true action demands.

This line of argument inescapably provokes, however, the most fundamental puzzle, the nagging perplexity, of why people should embark on action so pregnant with uncertainty, and defy all prudential considerations of its cost, its urgency, or, in turn, its very justifiability, with the possibility of getting nowhere. Why, that is to say, should people resist achieving results that are not so dubiously tangible? Why should they opt for greatness, if it means forever fumbling in the dark, reaching out after the infinite in a life so manifestly finite? Arendt's reply, seemingly simple enough, is in truth exceedingly complex. Not to create new space for the unfolding of the as yet unknown and unpredictable is, she says, tantamount to denying selves their chance for self-disclosure as

38 Maurizio Passerin D'Entrèves, *The Political Philosophy of Hannah Arendt* (London: Routledge, 1994), 90–2.

persons.[39] It is above all this virtually redemptive summons in Arendt's reply that invites further exploring notably as to the direction such action
and such self-disclosure is to take. Alas, this attempt, however way we
cast around, is anything but straightforward.

To begin with, it is not at all obvious from Arendt's account – despite
her arsenal of conceptual distinctions – why the personality of the per-
former need of necessity converge with the quality of the performance.
Things are not as cut and dried as she seems to suggest. Why, for example,
should the public pronouncements of a judge unfailingly reveal who he is
as a person? Presumably, her distinction between the "who" and the
"what" is intended to clarify this issue. The "what" in a person is supposed
to refer to the ordinary ways of coping with the "necessities of life," whatever this notion covers precisely, whereas those who act for the sake of a
"principle," in the special way Arendt defines it, acquire greatness
through their deeds and thereby typify the "who" in a person.[40]

Well and good, insofar as Arendt's distinction is concerned, at any
rate, despite its evident ambiguities. My main worry, however, is the relationship between the "whos" and the "whats" of this world. Are they necessarily different *persons*? For, could not the same person be perfectly
content to be a what most of the time, being timid, self-satisfied, or simply uninterested in public life, and yet perform feats that others happen
to consider bold and highly courageous? Paradoxically perhaps, Arendt
by no means rules out this possibility: an action is no less great if the
"hero" is in fact a coward.[41] But, then, in what revelatory manner do actions in public unveil the "personal qualities" of their authors, as Arendt
seeks to maintain?[42] Surely, all that her example shows is that human action is inherently unpredictable: the what can quite unexpectedly turn
into a who, whether the what is at all conscious of doing so. In that case,
however, does not the distinction between the who and the what lose
force in this sharply fragmented portrayal of humankind?

On closer reading, though, it emerges that Arendt is not so much setting apart the *qualities* of individual people as she is distinguishing between *types* or *statuses*. Thus, slaves and labourers are *born* "whats" and
hence, no matter what they do, they cannot qualify as "who" persons, at
any rate as long as they remain slaves or labourers; for as such, they are
subject to coercion by others, or are driven by the "necessities of life."

39 Arendt, "The Crisis of Culture," BPF, 223.
40 Arendt, "The Concept of History," BPF, 71.
41 Arendt, HC, 166.
42 Arendt, "The Crisis in Culture," BPF, 223.

Only the free, unburdened in this manner, are therefore eligible for citizenship, and it is they alone who potentially may achieve "who" status.[43] Accordingly, following closely the model of antiquity (perpetuated in political thinking for centuries), Arendt in effect stipulates two distinct categories of *selves*, and not merely *traits*: a social self, definable by "what" characteristics and typified by features associated with those of manual workers and people engaged in "making"; and a political self, inherently in possession of "who" characteristics. Needless to say, this projection of a society of whos and whats, each irrevocably separated from the other, has little in common with Arendt's later promotion of participatory democracy, unless democracy is restricted to the whos of public life.

Regardless of whether or not the context is that of democracy, however, the kind of disclosure that conceivably occurs cannot be known to those involved at the time of acting. Plunging into public space, that is, does not by itself inform the "plunger" what he or she has the potential to become. The quality (or indeed the very existence) of personhood is at that point as unknown as the outcome of the deed. Only if the outcome gains public acclaim by being recognized by others and then threads its way into a story is there any prospect of discovering the "who" of a person.[44]

Any deed that does not achieve public renown, therefore, not only obliterates itself as *action* but also conceals from its authors their identity. They cannot see themselves, nor can they be seen by others as anything but "what" persons; their "who" potential remains unrealized. There is an unmistakable "existentialist" element in the Arendtian presentation of the revelatory dimension of public action, which, not insignificantly, seems wholly consistent with her theory of knowing and acting. For, in this theory, actors, we noted, *cannot* control the outcome of their deeds; only retrospectively is there a chance for the *meaning* of an act to be discerned by those viewing it, talking about it, and judging it. Greatness and its concomitant "who" status are not, it appears, intrinsic or underived properties. Unlike the self-sustaining content of Arendt's "principles," they are contingent on processes of communication or mediation and, through them, on external appraisal and recognition.

Finally, in view of pronouncements made by Arendt on the "performance" character of public action, noted earlier, personhood may well be more of a *role* than the expression of some inner quality or essence

43 Arendt, "What is Freedom?," BPF, 154; *On Revolution*, 38–9.
44 Arendt, HC, 159, 171, 209.

seeking self-actualization – somewhat akin to the wearing of a mask in a play. The analogy Arendt herself draws between performances in politics and performances in the theatre lends support to such an interpretation. The actor "does not conduct himself according to an innate voice of reason but in accordance with what spectators would expect of him."[45] The dominant concern, therefore, is not "autonomy" but the "spectator," and *appearance* is crucial. Of course, this does not dispose of the problem of whether a given role is identifiable with the "who" or "what" of a person. This problem may stem from the contingent nature of greatness in politics (and history), but it may also be symptomatic of a profound ambivalence bedevilling Hannah Arendt's thinking about the nature of conscious *direction* in *self*-direction.

In the final analysis, therefore, while it is not in itself startling that glory or greatness is a matter of retrospective judgment, two critical questions remain unresolved. One is the difficulty of discerning at what point in time "greatness" can validly be established if, according to Arendt, "action" must never be viewed as a "completed process." The other is the lack of clarity about the source of people's self-understanding as autonomous agents in politics and history, since the distinction between whos and whats hardly helps to yield an answer. On the other hand, three things stand out incontestably: the first is that only the *transpersonal* within the personal yields potential self-revelation of "greatness"; the second that acting in politics *means* acting with others, who are equal in their personhood as citizens; and the third – though most important – that acting in this context must dispense with "banisters" of any kind apart from persons' imaginative self-projection of whether they can see themselves living with what they have chosen to do. For, in the end, it is this inherent contingency that is to qualify political pursuits as the supreme exemplar of action *per se*.

45 Arendt, *Lectures on Kant's Political Philosophy*, 55; see also HC, 167, and D'Entrèves, *The Political Philosophy of Hannah Arendt*, 18–19, according to whom Arendt simply was not able to resolve an acute tension "between a dramaturgical and a discursive conception of the public sphere." According to the first conception (he writes): "The public sphere is a dramatic setting for the performance of noble deeds and the utterance of memorable words, that is to say, for the display of the excellence of political actors. According to the second conception, the public sphere is a discursive space that arises whenever people act together in concert, establish relations of equality and solidarity, and engage in collective deliberation through the medium of speech and persuasion."

TRUTH, OPINION, AND PLURALITY

No other work of Arendt, to my mind, more strikingly reveals the extent to which she is prepared to uphold the sublimity of politics than her essay "Truth and Politics." Having elsewhere discussed its principal claim that politics towers even above truth,[46] I shall confine my remarks here to two seminal points of particular relevance to this chapter. One is that the confrontation between truth and politics runs parallel to her distinction between finality and infinity. The other, that it significantly prepares the ground for her attempted symbiosis of human plurality and human solidarity.

In this confrontation, truth is portrayed as external to politics and potentially hostile. Whereas truth is irrevocably final, fixed, and unequivocal, politics, the stuff of infinity, is endemically beset by uncertainty, and forever remains equivocal in its plurality. Also, the externality of truth to politics is as much a condition of the latter's autonomy as of the former's own validity. Neither, therefore, can preserve its own integrity if invaded by the other. And only then, Arendt concludes, can politics – delimited, yet unsurpassed – sustain its self-enacted distinctiveness and serve, through its existence, as the abode of principles that carry in themselves their own validity.[47]

Just as she refuses to place politics within the domain of established knowledge, Arendt locates it not within the orbit of truth but within the orbit of opinion, drawing here on Plato's distinction between knowledge and opinion. In a sense, however, her alleged borrowing from Plato is of secondary importance, if it is not indeed misleading, since Arendt wrongly suggests that Plato equates opinion with illusion.[48] More important, I think, is Arendt's avowal that opinion, unlike truth, is inherently challengeable and, thereby, anything but coercive. If truth compellingly demands cognizance as something beyond questioning, opinion can never make any such affirmation to indisputable finality. Hence, if truth precludes debate, opinion effectively invites it. Similarly, if self-evidence confers upon truths their coercive propensity, the lack of hard evidence supporting opinions makes them forever dependent on their persuasive

46 *Canadian Journal of Political and Social Theory*, 1 (1977), 29–57.

47 Arendt, "What is Authority," BPF, 138. This strikingly parallels Machiavelli's view that linking religion and politics corrupts both.

48 Arendt, "Truth and Politics," BPF, 233. In fact, Plato states that opinion can be true or false, and that it is not necessarily false or delusory, for we can have "correct beliefs" without knowledge (*Republic*, vi, 506).

force; from which it follows that opinion derives its strength not from intrinsic validity or unquestionable rightness, but from the extent to which it involves others, is believed by others, or is contested by them. Unlike truth, which is independent of numbers, the weight of opinion, notably in a democracy, cannot easily be detached from the question of numbers. Its mode of asserting itself publicly is therefore radically different from the mode in which truth asserts its own authority.[49]

If Arendt's opposition of truth and politics resembles Plato's distinction between knowledge and opinion, her contrasting the finality of truth with the infinity of opinion remarkably echoes Aristotle's setting apart (in the *Rhetoric*) things about which we deliberate from things which are beyond deliberation. Things about which we deliberate are like what he calls *enthymemes*, matters of skillful persuasion, while things beyond deliberation are like logical syllogisms, purely matters of analytical rigour. If the rightness of opinion is scarcely separable from processes of mediation and the counting of votes, the rightness of logical propositions has nothing to do with such processes. It is this distinction that Arendt is anxious to underline, and against the blurring of which she sounds her most trenchant warnings. Understandably she adamantly insists that opinion is the "hallmark of all strictly political thinking."[50]

When, however, Arendt maintains that opinion, though by nature plural and diverse, moves toward impartiality and unanimity as a result of discussion and deliberation, she goes well beyond Aristotle.[51] Far removed now from its resemblance to Millian multiplicity, opinion attains a degree of consensual unity, forcibly reminiscent of Rousseau's general will – a concept she professes to detest. To be sure, Arendt arrives at this (odd) position not *via* Rousseau but, as she claims, by applying Kant's idea of an enlarged mentality, "taking the viewpoint of others into account," and she calls it "representative thinking."[52] The more standpoints I have present in my mind while pondering upon an issue, the stronger will be my ability to represent them. This may indeed be so. However, would it necessarily make the opinion "more valid," as Arendt maintains? Moreover, what substantiates her conviction that whatever divergences of views exist are "bound to ascend to some impartial generality"?[53]

49 "Truth and Politics," BPF, 239–40; "The Crisis of Culture," BPF, 224.

50 Ibid., BPF, 241. Aristotle, *Rhetoric*, 1355a, 1356b, 1357a.

51 "Truth and Politics," BPF, 243.

52 "Truth and Politics," BPF, 242; "The Crisis in Culture," BPF, 219–22.

53 "Truth and Politics," BPF, 241–2. See also Ronald Beiner (ed.), *Hannah Arendt, Lectures on Kant's Political Philosophy* (Chicago: University of Chicago Press, 1982), 42, 7.

Arendt evidently assumes that in politics, notably in a discursive type of democracy, most conflicts are not real, fundamental, or permanent so that, given open and unrestrained debate, there is no reason why they should not lend themselves to effective resolution. Following Rousseau and advocates of "ideal speech situation," Arendt appears to believe that, freed from personal idiosyncracies or the particularism of special interests, opinions cannot but converge, and consensus cannot but materialize.[54] Any disagreement that remains after a thorough exchange of views simply cannot be real or other than purely technical. Provided that ideological parties and self-serving interest groups do not corrupt opinion, any differences that linger on cannot be more than differences over performative detail, that is to say, over matters resolvable by experts. One way or another, an opinion is bound to emerge that all can share and all can recognize as embodying the common good.

This optimistic thesis, however, runs counter not only to Plato's conception of representative thinking but also to contemporary political reality as we know it.[55] Plato, rightly I think, poses the problem (in the *Republic*, vi, 493) of combining representative thinking, in terms of what an assembly of people actually think or approve of, with what an impartial observer feels ought to be thought and done – a problem that to Plato seems insoluble. Arendt, by contrast, envisions representative thinking to attain a degree of generality that, in its indisputable validity, is indistinguishable from the universality of truth. The most troubling part of her interpretation of "processed" opinions, however, is that it conjures up a oneness, a collective "we," that threatens the legitimacy of dissent, let alone civil disobedience. For what is unquestionably valid as the common good must be valid for everyone; there can be no justifiable exceptionality. I am not suggesting that Arendt remotely thought of suppressing disagreement; all I am saying is that her projection of universalism into the "maturing" process of opinion seems rather discordant with her idea of plurality and her earlier attempt to *oppose* opinion to truth. And no less odd is the absence of any recognizable safeguards against the danger of undue pressure toward consensus in the transmutation of many voices into unison.

Quite apart from the notorious want of clarity concerning "representation" itself – its uncertain locus of reference as much as its varied meanings – Arendt therefore manages to obscure what Plato sought to clarify; namely, that opinion is what people do think, and not what they

54 "The Crisis in Culture," BPF, 220.

55 That people may profoundly differ regarding values and opinions in the *absence* of self-serving ends is a recurrent theme in my *Democratic Legitimacy*.

ought to think – or might think if exposed to pressures originating from
on high in the form of some Olympian authority of impartiality. After
all, with so much emphasis on unity and unanimity – if not universality –
we no longer know an opinion when we see one. Unless, therefore, we
view political divergences as no different from scholarly disputes which,
in principle, are deemed rationally resolvable, we cannot but reserve
judgment about Arendt's confident assumption that debate *must* produce consensus, provided it is open and wholly unrestrained. Notwithstanding those who assert that maximizing debate in politics deepens
cleavages rather than traverses them, there are others (like myself) who
have serious misgivings about raising expectations of unanimity in the
wake of "truly democratic dialogue" to quite such a pitch.

Curiously, there is a rather baffling asymmetry between Arendt's theory
of public action and her theory of public opinion. Whereas in the former,
because of the absence of a continuum between intentions and outcomes,
she stresses inherent contingency, in her analysis of public opinion she
postulates a necessary continuum between debate and ensuing agreement
in the course of enlarged thinking. Possibly, this postulate rests on
Arendt's implicit distinction between plurality and contentiousness which,
in turn, derives from her lack of sympathy for confrontational modes of .
politics, characterized in mainstream (liberal) democracies by *institutional*
oppositions. Together with the tactics of parties, interest groups, and competing governmental bureaucracies, these confrontational modes of politics, Arendt asserts, encourage not only deceitful machinations but also
rivalry as a virtual *commitment*. Hence, far from promoting the potential of
plurality *qua* cooperative diversity, adversarial democracy transforms individual plurality into segmental confrontationality, causing consensus to be
organizationally impeded. It follows that only the removal of institutionally
antagonistic commitments from civic deliberation, and their replacement
by segmentally uncommitted citizens, offers a chance for enlarged thinking and, thereby, the possibility of uncovering trans-segmental ground.

This may arguably indeed be so; but, just as arguably, it need not, for
even the absence of organized antagonism may *fail* to produce consensus. Moreover, it is by no means obvious why non-commitment should
be tantamount to impartiality as the condition of representative thinking. For, could it not simply mean indifference, when we in fact *cease* to
care one way or another? Yet, surely, to be impartial, we *have* to care
about such things as objectivity or fairness, as Arendt indirectly acknowledges in speaking of a commitment to truth.[56]

56 "Truth and Politics," BPF, 239; on impartiality being viewed as synonymous
with non-commitment, see also 242, 250, 262.

Unfortunately, it does not help matters that Arendt links commitment with "ideology," and either or both with deception, or deception, in turn, with *self-*deception. And what is particularly jolting in these linkages is her identifying self-deception with "lying to oneself," since, unlike lying to others, lying to oneself threatens the very existence of thought itself as much as of truth. It is "particularly jolting," because, even as a figure of speech, reflexive lying is quite different from phrases such as "debating with oneself," or "being angry with oneself"; for the latter usually express circumlocutions which, in moments of reflection, we discover in ourselves as forms of doubt or apprehension. Yet, clearly, neither of these involves wilful deceit; and just as non-commitment does not generate impartiality, so self-deception, by way of believing what happens to be untrue, does not involve a species of lying. Being the victim of illusions may be lamentable, but it is hardly reprehensible morally in the way lying plainly is.

To be sure, I may pretend to believe what in fact I do not hold to be true; but then I am not lying to myself, I am simply lying. Conversely, however, I cannot believe falsely because I mistake lies for truths, as many did in believing the American Administration's reports of the war in Vietnam.[57] But to deduce from "being lied to" the danger of "lying to oneself" is to stretch language rather unduly beyond its credible limits. For, whatever effects officially organized deception may have, systematic lying to oneself seems hardly one of them. This is not to deny that Arendt is perfectly correct in saying that government manipulation of the media poses a formidable threat to a political order, in that, over time, it is bound to erode civic trust.

Sagging trust, too, if backed by terror, can undeniably promote an atmosphere of distress throughout society as a whole. But this, once again, is not the same as saying that officially organized lying of necessity generates *self-*deception. Nor does it threaten thinking as such or the authenticity of believing, if I sincerely believe what turns out to be factually incorrect. For *believing*, as such, while it may be intense or vapid, cannot be true or false, unlike *beliefs* as propositions. Public opinion may rarely disclose the degree of impartiality Arendt appears to postulate, and yet still be a great deal more resilient than theorists of totalitarianism are wont to suggest. To find it imprudent, if not dangerous, to tell the truth publicly, is not tantamount to its having been lost. Not *telling* is not, evidently, the same as not *knowing*, just as delusion is not the same as deception.

57 "Lying in Politics," in *Crises of the Republic* (New York: Harcourt, Brace, Jovanovitch, 1972), 40.

THE ETHOS OF REPRESENTATIVE THINKING

Arendt is on surer ground in charging totalitarianism with obliterating the boundary between the private and the public. Her critique, on this score, goes beyond totalitarianism, however; indeed, it goes well beyond what libertarians or extreme right-wingers in liberal-democratic regimes would dare to maintain. For the latter would hardly take health, employment, education, or the environment altogether out of the orbit of public policy. Arendt, on the other hand, affirms that political action must have nothing to do with such social "instrumentalities," since these utterly fail to sustain "our personal identity in beginning something entirely new."[58] Rather, politics, she argues, must severely limit its range of activities, not only so as to yield scope for the disclosure of our personal identity, but also to enable politics itself to reveal its own unique distinctiveness. A politics that is swallowed by social issues forecloses, on this argument, the operation of authentic political principles. In seeking to provide "life's necessities," politics simply goes beyond the space in which it *can* act and, thus, in overextending itself, not only lowers its distinctive status but simultaneously raises false expectations. And, unable to meet these, as well as unwilling to admit it, politics perforce resorts to lying. Mendacity, therefore, is not the monopoly of totalitarian regimes; welfare-state democracies, with their vying parties and interest groups, find themselves equally forced to suppress truthfulness, in attempts to conceal their failure to honour promises made. In short, because of excessive policy claims and the inherent adversariness of mainstream democracies, public lying is a must.[59]

Without, as far as I am aware, making the distinction explicit, Arendt appears to set apart here, in a manner recalling Thomasius, the idea of truthfulness from that of truth. For, while viewing truth as potentially hostile to politics, she evidently regards truthfulness as essential to its proper working. Presumably, therefore, in her projected recovery of politics, and as part and parcel of her celebration of "new beginnings," truthfulness takes on an unmistakable importance in Arendt's much emphasized "how" of acting politically.

In view of this recovery postulate, politics, instead of being a mere instrumentality "serving wealth, trade, labour and welfare," is to purge

---

58 "Truth and Politics," BPF, 263. See also note 23 in ch. 4 (above) regarding Arendt's attributing the success of the American Revolution to its strictly *political* thrust, in the virtual absence of *social* aims.

59 "Truth and Politics," BPF, 263–4; also 235–6.

itself by adopting a new ethos, an ethos inseparable from a new *style* of act-ing. And it is thus that Arendt's central idea of "joint endeavour" is to find expression; namely, by humans, in their plurality, engaging as equals in the public realm, inspired by external principles that wholly transcend pri-vate inclinations and interests. Hence, whatever the new *content* of politics, it is clearly its new style that is to form the mediation of what she calls "rep-resentative thinking." This paramountcy of style, odd or not, is not really a bolt from the blue; for, in her use, it is very much in keeping with the ele-vation of "taste" as an essential component of practical judgment. Tower-ing high above "knowledge," it is meant to be integral to *action* proper.[60]

In saying that in politics practical judgment is commonly an exercise of sensibility rather than a display of factual knowledge or logical skill, Arendt, I believe, makes an important point. Echoing Thomasius as well as the older Kant, she in effect identifies political perceptions of the appropriateness of a given course of action with causal sources that chiefly involve a possession of good taste. Some commentators, not sur-prisingly, have expressed uneasiness over Arendt's appeal to good taste as a basis for practical judgments, arguing that an appeal to aesthetics deprives political action of its cognitive foundation, as it virtually ne-gates the role of rationality.[61] A number of critics also see Arendt's reli-ance on taste in her later writings as conflicting with her earlier views on practical thinking in which she rests the possibility of reaching consen-sus in politics on rationally deliberative processes.[62]

I am not denying that there are inconsistencies in Arendt's writings – few truly original thinkers are wholly consistent – but these charges

---

60 *H. Arendt's Lectures on Kant's Political Philosophy*, 10. See also Michael Denneny, "The Privilege of Ourselves: Hannah Arendt on Judgment," in Melvyn A. Hill (ed.), Hannah Arendt: *The Recovery of the Public World*, New York: St Martin's Press 1979, 245–74; and Leah Bradshaw, *Acting and Thinking: The Political Thought of Hannah Arendt* (Toronto: University of Toronto Press, 1989).

61 See, for example, R. Beiner's "Interpretive Essay" in *Arendt's Lectures on Kant's Political Philosophy*, 138–9; Jürgen Habermas, "Hannah Arendt's Communications Concept of Power," *Social Research* 44 (1977), 22–3; and George Kateb, "Aestheticism and Morality: Their Cooperation and Hostility," *Political Tehory*, 28 (2000), 6, 16.

62 See D'Entrèves's discussion of this point and his approving reference to Albrecht Wellmer's "Hannah Arendt on Judgment: The Unwritten Doctrine of Reason" (unpublished manuscript, 1985, 2–3) in his *The Political Philosophy of Hannah Arendt*, 130–8.

of inconsistency or unresolved tension seem to me unfounded. For, as far as I know, Arendt never changed her mind on the role of taste in practical judgment or on the limits and pitfalls of knowledge in deciding upon political action – whether or not her concept of "knowledge" suffers from being "antiquated."[63] And I certainly cannot recall that Arendt was at any time expressing awareness, let alone intellectual anguish, about the alleged hiatus between her cognitive theory of practical thinking and her aesthetic theory of practical judgment.

Hence, whether or not Arendt goes too far in excluding "life's necessities" from the orbit of political concern, she surely points in the right direction by calling for the cultivation of taste as the key to the emergence of a sense of appropriateness in the manner of acting in politics, and by insisting, therefore, that, in political action, the "how" is not easily separable from the "what." Nor is her merging of political conduct with a sense of honour to be derided, only because this dimension of public action is so commonly disregarded. What is less clear, however, as I indicated earlier, is the content of the activity in which representative thinking, good taste, and a sense of honour are to figure more prominently. She says a great deal about constitution building but little else; and what precisely day-to-day activity is to consist in remains rather obscure, if not, indeed, alarming. For would not constant "new beginnings" spell instability or, eventually, complete chaos?

Impressed as Arendt was with the American Revolution, did she mean to imply that the dramatic goings-on during and following its course should *characterize* the manner and purpose of acting together in politics? The point of posing this question seems reinforced by her so markedly focusing on what is exciting and by her drawing a number of theoretical inferences from the analogy of acting in politics and acting on the stage.[64] On the other hand, it is true to say that her "stage" conception of politics is largely confined to revolutionary action, in which many are onlookers rather than actors, whereas in "normal" politics Arendt parallels Rousseau's emphasis on civic participation, in which most people are themselves the actors.

63 As Habermas asserts in "Hannah Arendt's Communications Concept of Power," 22.

64 Especially in *On Revolution*, 269–72; "On Violence," and "Thoughts on Politics and Revolution," in Arendt, *Crises of the Republic* (New York: Harcourt, Brace, Jovanovich, 1972), 181, 232–3.

Admittedly, Arendt would be rather shocked by the parallel; for her idea of participatory politics diverges significantly from that of Rousseau in being both more exalting and more restrictive. More exalting, because it raises citizenship to universal membership and participation to a level of grandeur that even Rousseau would have found excessive, if not melodramatic. More restrictive, because in its content it excludes much that preoccupies Rousseau's concern with social inequality. But, whether she was melodramatic in her democratism or strangely narrow in her delimitation of politics, Arendt, as much as Rousseau, opted for "joint endeavour" and the pursuit of the common good within "representative thinking", as paramount principles of political agency – and did so without calculating costs, results, or sectional benefits.

The prospect of humans acting together in the creation of a common good in a climate of reciprocity, free from domination, upholding honour and good taste is surely an appealing one. Similarly, the idea of liberating politics from subservience to lobbying pressures of vying interest groups has its undoubted merit, especially if it is combined with attempts to curb the heavy hand of an anonymous, yet highly influential, government bureaucracy.

What is less beyond doubt – or more problematic – is the identity of the "whos" intended to participate in the envisioned republic. For it may well be asked how many would be attracted to a politics that soars to heights from which humanity's daily needs and tribulations were no longer within sight? Could such a politics offer much solace or gratification to any but the few, that is, only to those to whom loftiness of principles would suffice to induce them to insert themselves into the world of public action for the sole purpose of self-disclosure? Numbers apart, one really cannot help wondering if Arendt seriously underestimated, if not altogether misjudged, the extent to which humans, fearing finality, might even be more alarmed by the mystery of infinity. At any rate, it does seem puzzling why and how acts whose outcome and meaning lie in the distant unknown could enhance the chances of a broadly based type of active participatory democracy. Indeed, it almost looks as though Arendt's vision of politics conjures up a democracy that is a "-*cracy*" without a *demos*.

Does this mean that Arendt was at heart an elitist, and a utopian elitist at that? I rather doubt this, at any rate in the sense in which we commonly think of elitism or utopia. If there is something in the nature of an aristocratic streak in her political thinking, mixed with a dose of existentialism (in its literal sense of standing out of the ordinary), it is reminiscent of the kind of regime that Herder had in mind with the notion of aristo-democracy, shot through as it was with the populism of an earlier "revolutionary" era.[65] Leaving aside the issue of political labelling, it cannot be ruled out that there is a pronounced *supra*-political thrust in Arendt's redemptive notion of representative thinking which, like Kant's idea of an enlarged mentality, transcends the boundaries of Rousseau's republic in its thrust toward a common good. For with Arendt, as with Kant, this thrust seems to be in the direction of a *humanitas* as international fellowship, rather than in the direction of national unity. As such, it is profoundly didactic, as it is unsparingly exacting, presupposing a degree of "banister-free" commitment not easily to be achieved.

But then, Arendt, though hopeful, was only guardedly optimistic, and no more sanguine than Thomasius, Rousseau, or Kant. Regardless of her hopes or degree of optimism, however, the nature of her overall thinking, unfashionable though it was, nonetheless happened to have an exceptionally rousing effect. Certainly, in many of her younger contemporaries her writings and teaching provoked an unusually intense response and managed to inspire them with her own love of thinking as an activity of value and delight in itself. Perhaps it was precisely Arendt's particular way of putting things that had this effect, a way that succeeded in transcending the purely political in directions which, looking ahead, may indeed prove the most lasting.

ARENDT AND MODERNITY: CONCLUDING REMARKS

If it is asked, therefore, what Hannah Arendt will principally be noted for, I am not all sure that the obvious answer, "as a political philosopher," will be the correct one. Of course, it is premature to locate

---

65 Herder envisioned a participatory form of citizenship to emerge from a transition period of aristo-democracy, during which "men of the people" were to help their fellow-citizens attain a degree of civic freedom and maturity that would enable them to dispense with rulers of any kind, including Plato's "guardians," or, for that matter, "philosopher-kings." Furthermore, Herder's emphasis on civic *Zusammenwirken* strikingly foreshadows Arendt's notion of "acting together" in politics in place of monarchic and bureaucratic domination. All the same, what I am suggesting are intriguing parallels, not direct derivations. Although Arendt was not unfamiliar with Herder, I doubt whether she consciously followed him here. More likely, her thinking on citizenship had its roots in the writings of Aristotle, Montesquieu, Tocqueville, and Jefferson, as well as in the tradition of the American town meetings. For an account of aristo-democracy in Herder's thought, see my *Self-Direction and Political Legitimacy: Rousseau and Herder* (Oxford: Clarendon Press, 1988), 285–321.

Arendt's place in the history of ideas with absolute assurance, but my hunch is that it is chiefly for her imaginative critique of modernity that posterity will remember her.

That Arendt's insights into the conditions of our times contain important truths seems to me beyond dispute. Modernity may indeed have misjudged the priority of things, as it may well be in danger of being oblivious of the difference between the public domain and the private, between inserting oneself into the civic forum and inserting oneself into the market place of business, between good taste and bad taste in judging what is what and who is who, and between being deceived and seeing things as they are. In these respects Arendt was first and foremost a catalyst who relentlessly agonized over forces that, she felt, had sapped and snapped the continuity with a past which she sought to illuminate anew.

Arguably, in her sharp severance of the public world from the private world, she could be charged with creating solitudes whose boundaries are hardly as fixed as she might lead one to believe. Uncompromisingly keeping apart what neo-romantics and traditional natural right theorists tend to blur, she insisted on each realm standing by itself to preserve its singular distinctiveness and flavour. Neither could be derived from or reduced to the other. It is not clear, however, whether she also thought them irreconcilable, so that the life of public action and the life of private contemplation could never converge. What nevertheless seems beyond questioning is the originality of her theory of action and her theory of judgment. Both, to be sure, are controversial; at the same time, her emphasis on reflective thought in the former, and on taste as the guiding criterion of appropriateness in the latter, will give prodding cause for conceptual reappraisals in the exploration of both purposive striving and public endeavour for some time to come.

Likewise, there can be no doubt about her stand on the autonomy of political action. Possibly, however, because of her existentialist leanings, there is a certain ambivalence in her treatment of autonomy with respect to the causality of personhood, as well as in her approach to purpose and meaning. For in both instances agency seems problematically severed from an agent's intentions, and its meaning made to rest on the retrospective assessment by *others*. In taking this stance, Arendt was evidently seeking to reaffirm her distinction between making and acting, between working to a blueprint and creating something entirely new. Almost inescapably, however, she thereby courts the danger of obscuring the meaning of "meaning," and the difference between acting with a purpose in mind and acting with no direction.

Possibly, too, this stance was part and parcel of her call for dispensing with banisters to lean on, which, undoubtedly, was meant to intensify, and not to weaken autonomous *self*-direction, even if this implied plunging into the wholly unknown. More fundamentally, however, her stance was to act as a reminder of the endemic predicament of all genuine action, in that humans can never hope to be fully in control of their destiny, and can never be sure of their individual part in the shaping of history. Action, in this understanding, is an end in itself, together with the self-created process of thinking and judging. Reaching out into what is yet to be discovered, it is radically different from the process of knowing, in that the latter is bound up with what already exists. Unlike it, thinking and acting, in not being engrossed with the already established, stand on their own, regardless of outcomes, and thus have nothing in common with *usefulness*; whatever value they have is wholly intrinsic. "Knowledge," on the other hand, in involving preset objectives, is a mere instrumentality; potentially highly useful, but bereft of inner value.

Parallel with this distinction and its entailed repudiation of knowledge as an absolute or value in itself, there appears in Arendt's thought a pronounced unwillingness to absolutize standards of morality. This, on the face of it, creates an obvious gap between the "Kantianism" and the "Existentialism" in Arendt's overall philosophy. For she maintained that moral conduct was something that individuals have to decide for themselves, by asking themselves whether they are able to live with whatever they have chosen. Not surprisingly, this "relativism" has been found wanting, together with her elevation of taste over knowledge. Her response to these strictures has been to reaffirm her faith in practical judgment and the importance of thinking in and for itself. In short, as long as people need banisters to lean on, *right* action, or any *action*, is precluded and autonomous thinking is unthinkable.[66]

Clearly, on this view – a view that echoes Kant's – acting rightly, in an ethical sense, is not simply a matter of obeying external norms, as though they were instructions of a manual. Rather, the emphasis is on internal sanctions which, without going back any further, recalls not merely Rousseau, but, with its apotheosis of taste and inward form, the idol of the eighteenth century, the Third Earl of Shaftesbury. For, Arendt, when the chips are down, would sooner put her trust in

66 See note 36 above. Arendt kept reinterating this thesis in her works.

something akin to the inner power of aesthetic judgment than in the cognitive force of general precepts. Opting for reflective sensitivity in coping with plurality, rather than for logic in comprehending identity, she postulates the belief that whatever moral principle we cherish is tied to a prior pre-logical structuring of intelligibility and coherence.[67]

Perhaps it was in accordance with this belief that Arendt's quasi-Existentialist conception of meaning and her quasi-Kantian conception of practical judgment took shape in her own mind. Similarly, her quasi-Rousseauian manner of dichotomized thinking might be traceable to an approach that has its epistemic roots in a pre-logical grasp of core ideas whose underlying intellectual traditions no doubt call for deeper exploration than I can embark on here. I do wish, however, to

---

67 At the dawn of the eighteenth century, few works enjoyed a wider reading public than those of the third Earl of Shaftesbury. His *Characteristicks of Men, Manners, Opinions, Times* (1711) ran to no fewer than five editions within just over twenty years. "He profoundly influenced the best brains of our age," wrote Herder toward the end of the century (*Works*, Berlin: Weidmann, 1877–1913, XVII, 158). As for a view intriguingly foreshadowing Arendt's pre-logical categories, see Max Horkheimer, *Eclipse of Reason* (Oxford: Clarendon Press, 1947), 165–7. "The view that philosophical concepts must be pinned down, identified and used only when they exactly follow the dictates of the logic of identity is a symptom of the quest for certainty, the all-too-human impulse to trim intellectual needs down to pocket size," writes Horkheimer. Instead, he points out, concepts depend for their meaning on perceptual understandings that our inner experience and our use of language associates with them; for example, the metaphor "killing with kindness" is undestood as a *metaphor*, because we know from experience that the vocabulary of murderous weapons does not include kindness. Shaftesbury probably had the impact he had because he filled the emotive and aesthetic gap left by the predominantly Rationalist temper of mind that prevailed in early eighteenth-century Germany. Writers from Thomasius, Rousseau, and Kant to Goethe and Friedrich Schiller – whose *Aesthetic Education of Man* (1795) draws a close connection between aesthetic judgment and political sensitivity – certainly followed unmistakably in Shaftesbury's footsteps, as they also quite significantly anticipated Arendt's elevation of taste, which for her combined critical thinking with aesthetic feeling. Ernst Cassirer most adeptly captures this essential oneness in *Die Philosophie der Aufklärung* (Tübingen: Mohr, 1932), ch. 7; he also attributes it to Shaftesbury's seminal influence on eighteenth-century German aesthetics, in *The Platonic Renaissance in England*, trans. by James P. Pettersgrove (London, 1953), 186–99).

point to a number of moves in this direction which Arendt principally appears to share with Rousseau, despite her avowed aversion to his mode of thought.

For example, Arendt maintained, as did Rousseau, that debate among citizens, if freed from individual or sectional egoisms, could not but lead to agreement on what was good for everybody. Likewise, the ideas that freedom in society was *civic* freedom, and that political union had to be embedded in genuinely *public* opinion, were *sine qua nons* for both. Finally, there have been few writers more eager to recover the *polis* of antiquity, in response to a shared feeling that humanity was drifting in a sea without ports, that women and men were captives of a voyage they had neither intended nor were able to find meaning in.

Mixed with this bleak conviction, there nonetheless transpires a slender hope, common to both, that there might still be people with eyes to see, ears to hear, and minds to move, in whom the supra-personal, suffused with the personal, could have a chance to surface. And, if so, people may yet create conditions for the emergence of a more authentic, or less deceiving, world, in which a spirit of fellowship might take root. Buoyed up by such a modicum of faith, both strove to evoke a stirring of conscience, capable of disturbing the enfeebling complacency of those unable to perceive the value of anything beyond the gratification of material wants or the fancies of the senses, exhorting them toward more general or "representative" forms of thinking or, at a minimum, toward forms less beset with mere private gain.

Most impressively Rousseauian, too, is the premonitory note that Arendt managed to strike through the intensity of her warnings, the sweep of her language, and the Manichean complexion of her principal categories. In this way, she put in motion (again not unlike Rousseau) a profound questioning of existing self-understandings; not, however, without walking on a tightrope, in a perilous balancing act, at once tortuous and problematic. For Arendt wanted to do *both*: puncture the pride of the inflated and give succour to the meek. Likewise, on the one hand she wished to protect humans against bogus rhetoric in support of all-encompassing solutions by political means, as well as against delusions of grandeur, while, on the other, she had no desire to shut out prospects of attaining a maximally participatory democracy and genuine feats of greatness and glory. This precarious attempt, fraught with unpredictability, if not fragility, set the peculiar tone of Arendt's clarion call, at once shrill *and* muted, stridently radical *and* quietly traditional. Not surprisingly, her work did much to fuel misunderstandings and conflicting interpretations. Still, it was in all likelihood this odd mixture, together with its intellectual force and infectious fascination, that helped to confer upon her thought its unusually evocative property and arresting appeal – characteristics, once again, that vividly summon up Rousseau.

Although in her pre-logical, or perceptual, understanding of meaning, she favoured the sensibility of taste over the rationality of cognition, Arendt, as much as Rousseau, had no desire to abandon reason as the medium of reflection. Indeed, I believe it is precisely her ability for conceptual bridging, no less than her fondness for polarizations, that make Arendt, despite herself, a sort of spiritual contemporary of Rousseau. Hence, whether or not Kant was essentially a "deepened Rousseau" – as a respected Kant scholar has argued – it may not be entirely off the mark to describe Arendt as a supra-Rousseauian Kantian, albeit with a penchant for that variant of Existentialism most closely linked with the name of Karl Jaspers.[68]

Such pegs or benchmarks admittedly have only limited use and, possibly, even more limited validity. For, when all is said and done, what Hannah Arendt has bestowed on modernity, in being at once politically wordly and aesthetically transcendent, only Hannah Arendt could bestow. And, in the teeth of all her misgivings about modernity, her critique seems nonetheless sustained by a serene belief in a horizon of infinite openness, unmistakably beckoning the ever-latent prospect of human self-enactment.

68 See Lewis White Beck, ed., *Kant, Critique of Practical Reason and Other Writings on Moral Philosophy* (Chicago: University of Chicago Press, 1949), 6–7. See also Patrick Riley, *Kant's Political Philosophy* (Totowa, New Jersey. Rowman and Littlefield, 1983), 55, where Riley upholds Beck's thesis. Regarding Arendt's existentialism, see notes 2 and 53 above. There are unmistakable points of contact between Jaspers's conception of finality and infinity and Arendt's, although, unlike Arendt, Jaspers is closer to Kant in suggesting that the "barriers" between finality and infinity can be breached by humans' applying their power of reflective reasoning. At a deeper level, however, Arendt, whether she knew it or not, expressed typically religious modes of thinking, notably in the prophetic tradition. I have alluded to it in note 27 above, on the issue of "control" and "mastery" in the launching of action into "infinity," and a similar comment could be applied to her emphasis on *external* principles, on pre-logical criteria rather than "knowledge," on *humanitas* in "representative thinking," and on individual conscience as the ultimately paramount moral guide.

EPILOGUE

Highlights without Footnotes

OWING TO THE PARTICULAR CHARACTER OF THE BOOK, an overall conclusion or summary seems to me out of place. Instead, I intend to select a number of focal points and bring together overlapping issues of Part I and Part II.

Both principal thinkers who originally prompted the writing of this book, R.G. Collingwood and Hannah Arendt, strove to forge a sort of amalgam within political self-enactment between autonomy and interdependence, as well as between plurality and a common constituency. Above all, both wished to interpret "self-enactment" in terms of individuals acting together in pursuit of joint principles, and doing so freely, without the pressures of external commands. Accordingly, they searched for a foundational ethos on which to rest a politics of *self*-imposed ordinances that combined individual freedom with social mutuality, although neither was oblivious of the problems that bristle with the projected blendings.

In essence, their quest parallels a central concern of the themes and the voices included in this study: the creation of a consciousness of reciprocity within public life. At the same time, neither Collingwood nor Arendt took formal exception to the widespread belief that mainstream modern democracy has largely succeeded in merging principles of liberty with principles of mutuality, although both were aware of Kant's misgivings about the conceptual alliance between liberalism and democracy – a marriage, we found, that he regarded as a mismatch from the start.

They may possibly have felt that logically "blind" consistency might end up being depressingly futile, without yielding any tangible remedies. In fact they (notably Hannah Arendt) may have sensed that it might prove politically unworkable under regimes other than those invasively despotic and/or totalitarian. Possibly too, both could see that it was not necessarily, or even chiefly, a tension between two distinct conceptual traditions – such as that between liberalism and democracy – but rather one that arose from clashes between multiple understandings of "democracy" itself. Yet, whatever it was, precisely, that made Arendt and Collingwood consciously avoid focusing on the potentially fragile alliance between liberal and democratic principles, they evidently preferred to follow in the path of those to whom imaginative introspection and reflective circumspection offered a more valid way of matching liberty with mutuality than rigid adherence to logical consistency.

On one thing, however, neither would budge: there could be no truly *political* action unless, as a deed carried out in the public forum, it enshrined the universality of principle within the particularity of a given purpose. And, in this avowal, they strikingly echo the other voices of Part II, to whom something of a symbiosis between universality and particularity mattered just as much as that between self-enactment and civic reciprocity, or between public right and public reason.

HISTORICAL UNDERSTANDING

Thinkers who, like Thomasius, Rousseau, Kant, or Collingwood, looked for causes operative in human history, were at one in doubting that the methods applicable to such a quest were the same as those used to investigate biological or mechanical causes. Understanding reasons as causes demands instead (they held) a unique kind of *conceptually* mediated form of intelligibility, akin to that which Vico located (in his *New Science*) "within the modifications of our human mind." If anything (I suggested), this mode of understanding is closer to musical perception than to the characteristic mode of comprehension of the natural scientist or engineer. For it is a form of penetration into the heart of things comparable to sensing the innermost meaning intended by a composer in and through his or her music, so that the composer listening to its rendering feels completely understood.

This kind of intense reliving or re-enacting, which Wilhelm Dilthey and Max Weber made known as *Verstehen* – with regard to actions of the past – has, however, a potentially darker side to it. Why? Because it may imply apprehending reasons as causes not in a purely neutral or detached manner but rather with a degree of empathy that borders on sympathetic appropriation, if not justifying absolution. And this, in turn, raises the delicate question not only of whether such fervent minding, amounting to "indwelling," is achievable, but rather whether it is at all worth achieving. *Should* we, that is, even try? Should we want to fathom empathetically the reasons that prompted a Hitler or a Stalin to build extermination camps for the sole purpose of killing totally innocent women, men, and children? Should we thus wish to "understand" the well-nigh unfathomable?

And, if the answer to these troubling questions is in the negative, must we not conclude that there are limits to both our ability and our willingness to understand actions in history, whatever they are, and however motivated? Yet, if we do come to this conclusion, it is not necessarily tantamount to denying any didactic, or purely intrinsic, value to the study of history or ruling out the possibility of understanding reasons as causes. For either the study or the understanding, or both, could surely assist modes of more *nuanced* thinking, not only about the past but also about the present, and thus help to militate against undue historical and political naïveté or smart-alecky arrogance. And, whether or not such thinking would thereby deter us from becoming victims to facile slogans or to what I called blind consistency, it should tell us something about the contingency of historical causes. For, if nothing else, it might prevent us from mistaking historical consciousness for predictive knowledge, or from holding that whatever happened *had* to happen.

Clearly, mistaking causality for inevitability – or contingency for sheer fortuity – is apt to make a mockery of human choice. Indeed, by ruling out the possibility of alternative courses of action, such a misapprehension would altogether *distort* the meaning of historical consciousness and conflate historical causation with causation in chemistry, or rational necessity (as used by Hegel) with natural necessity. Kant viewed such conflations as products of overheated minds and referred to them as the invention of "predictive" history, designed to serve as a tool in the hands of politicians who prophesy that things will happen because they *want* them to happen. Of course, claiming predictive knowledge is a tricky business; for, even on the assumption that we learn from the mistakes of the past, it does not follow that whatever knowledge we thus gain is comparable to the instructions of a manual, or that, even if it were, everyone would want to heed the instructions. Regardless of any benefits that the study of history may yield, however, we could hardly understand it in terms of human reasons, were it entirely the work of unintended consequences or haphazard accident. Moreover, such randomness would deprive us of any sense of historical continuity. As Tocqueville put it, no longer being able to count on the past to throw its light on the future, we would be forced to cast about in utter darkness.

And yet, we want to believe that there *is* some continuity amidst all the discontinuity, some thread within the confused tangle. Usually we associate finding some such thread with the surfacing of purposive ends within patterns of thought that have temporarily been buried in people's consciousness. For example, it may happen that, after years of intimidation, terror, and repressions of all kinds, citizens regain their civic self-understanding because they are able to look back to a time characterized by freedom of expression, legality, and administrative integrity. In more general terms, we recognize purposive continuity in and through a collective memory, recalling a context of public life in which there is an intelligible link between people's shared purposes, their civic pursuit, and their eventual policy outcomes, even when we allow for the work of contingencies, whatever they are.

However – and that may complicate matters – there are, besides discontinuities and contextual accidents caused by human agency, occurrences whose coming about simply cannot be attributed to, or whose meaning cannot be derived from, *human* purposes or intentions. Thomasius, Vico, Rousseau, Kant, and Herder were all alive to such transcendent dimensions of historical causality, no matter how much they stressed the importance of human self-direction. Kant, indeed, we found, truly went out of his way in his emphasis on reason's ability to think supra-human causalities into the empirical world. And he did so, not to encourage passive acquiescence, but rather because he looked upon them as sources from which humans could draw confidence in their own power to shape events in history and take charge of their own destiny. Supra-human causalities, that is, were to inspire and embolden people to believe in the possibility of self-enactment, as well as to take credit, or accept blame, for making use of this possibility.

To be sure, postulating the role and importance of supra-human intervention in this way is likely to create ambiguity, so that the distinction between purposes *in* history and purposes *of* history not only loses clarity but also potentially thereby encourages worrisome abuses, notably in politics, by inducing rulers to claim to be merely the instruments of supra-human designs. On the other hand, the postulate of supra-human purposes need not – judging by the thinkers adduced earlier – negate modernity's faith in human self-direction or, for that matter, the mind's power of imaginative self-projection in its attempt to re-enact the past, breathe new life into it, and thus feel its pulse.

However humbling, therefore, the admission of supra-human causality may be to those professing total self-foundation in human reason, human creativity, and human will, it does not necessarily weaken modernity's determination to plumb the depths of the past and penetrate hidden layers of human thought and human action. And, whether or not

such a resolve succeeds also in effecting the degree of historical re-enactment that Collingwood envisioned, it surely does not detract from his
basic insight that, in the absence of purposive thinking beneath human
human agency – as a crucial assumption – we could neither understand,
nor not understand, human history, since we could make no sense of
"history" at all.

COMMITMENT AND IDEOLOGY IN POLITICS

Whenever we ask ourselves what to make of "commitment," viewed as
self-obligation, we might do worse (I suggested) than recall the way
Hobbes looked upon freedom; namely, as a creature with two faces: one
glancing backward to antecedent conditions, the other glancing ahead
toward ends to be accomplished. The first informs us about boundaries
of agency, its limits and range of opportunities, the second induces us to
pursue chosen goals and act upon them. Hobbes sought to make sure,
however, that we not mistake contexts for causes; that is, not assume antecedent conditions to *determine* the purposes on which we decide to act.
And he did so by making it quite explicit that it is our *internal* power (or
will) which, combined with reasoned judgment, forms the truly effective
source of any commitment to act.

The assumption of internal causation in this sense underlies not only
the notion of self-obligation as such but also (I believe) modernity's
conviction that humans possess an internal freedom to choose or shun
ends, in making things happen or preventing them. And it was principally this assumed capacity to choose between alternatives that, allied
with the enhanced consciousness of human self-direction, gave the impulse to the belief in a distinctly historical sensibility.

At the same time, having this consciousness and this sensibility need
not translate into commitments to act. What is it, then, I wondered, that
generates the causal force that enables us to bridge the gap between reasons as *purposes* and reasons as actual *commitments*? Or, to put it negatively, why are action-*promoting* reasons at times inadequate to operate as
action-*compelling* reasons? Are the former not convincing enough or are
they blocked by counter-reasons? Or, again, have we not "minded"
enough what we have known all along? Conversely, were we not quite
sure of some facts, or possibly altogether ignorant of others, particularly
those that might turn out to speak *against* acting? But, if in the end we
did decide to go ahead, what precisely was it that made the difference?

As the reader may recall, I admitted that I know of no generally satisfactory answer to these questions. However, I proposed the view that,

whatever we finally decided to do involved a switch in kind, and not merely in degree. That is to say, I suggested that it was not a case of suddenly knowing more, but rather one of knowing *differently*. Vague though this way of putting it may be, it seems nevertheless closest to the heart of the matter. At any rate, I expressed reservations about its being simply a question of cold calculation (by weighing pluses and minuses) or strict logical inferences, which inexorably bring about a transformation of credal reasons *for* acting into causal reasons *in* acting. For, plausible or not, neither calculation nor deduction seems a necessary, let alone sufficient, causality in spawning performative commitments.

I am not at all certain either (I confessed) that the switch from reasons as beliefs to reasons as commitments hinges critically on the degree of sincerity with which convictions are cherished or, for that matter, on how well they are factually grounded. In short, the switch from one to the other may be hard to pin down in all cases. Still, reasons as beliefs, in *politics*, especially within party-structured democratic variants, require a measure of prior meshing if they are to generate *joint* commitments. And, in this process, I suggested, ideological principles may arguably serve as appropriate mediating paths, as they may also, being publicly avowed, form binding commitments for their adherents, leaders and followers alike.

Yet, even if definite commitments to acting materialize in conformity with avowed purposive principles, such correspondence in no way establishes the validity of the commitments themselves. By the same token, there is no ground to suppose that the coincidence between purposive reasons and commitments based on them secures the validity of whatever *actions* ensue. For, while it may be granted that the notion of "commitment" implies principled forms of reasoning about action – notably *political* action – this implication does not in itself disclose anything about the appropriateness of whatever *reasons* are involved. On the other hand, the lack of coherence between reasons, commitments, and actions provides no incontrovertible proof of the absence of some putative unity between theory and practice (as I argue in ch. 2), let alone for the existence of forms of false consciousness, involving an endemic disconnectedness between thought, action, and reality in general.

Echoes of the Marxian link of such fissures with ideological thinking appear, somewhat incongruously, in Hannah Arendt's *Origins of Totalitarianism*. Although she correctly denies that lack of "unity" between reasons and commitments provides clinching evidence for false consciousness, or alternatively, that a doctrine's inner coherence provides proof of its truth, she nevertheless draws a doubtfully valid inference from the denial. For she charges that adherents of an ideology put so much emphasis on doctrinal consistency in order to establish it not only as a logically authentic belief system but also as an empirically authentic portrayal of reality. Deliberate deception, therefore, Arendt concludes, is an integral part of political ideologies, and, hence, only those who do not succumb to them are in a position to face up to the demands of reality.

Furthermore, arguing that ideologies are essentially employed as *weapons* in warlike strife, Arendt finds the question of truth and truthfulness totally irrelevant; after all, in war, as much as in love, all means are fair game. Viewing ideology accordingly as a weapon without which no battle can be waged or won, it seems perfectly reasonable for Arendt to infer that people committed to an ideology knowingly suppress the truth, if the cause they are cherishing overshadows conventional concerns with veracity. It is then also immaterial whether they believe in what they are propagating or, by the same token, if they greatly care about an ideology's factual grounding any more than about its doctrinal truth content. Clearly, its use as a weapon renders its cognitive status of no – or at best, only the most minimal – interest.

Undoubtedly, this may indeed be the case. On the other hand, it may equally be the case that citizens living in a country in which the official ideology is backed by militant forces, or even by governmental terror, may find it prudent to pretend to believe what they scarcely believe at all. Alternatively, they may have ceased caring about what is, or is not, true in what they are being told. Hardly believing anything anymore, they may no longer feel committed to whatever principles are involved, but simply acquiesce out of fear or opportunism. Oddly enough, however, totalitarian power holders, although they rely largely on fear rather than on persuasion, frequently go to great lengths to make their pronouncements *ring* true – a concession, perhaps, to modernity's faith in the power of reason and reasoned argument.

Not quite satisfied with Arendt's identification of ideological politics with the conduct of ruthless propaganda warfare, in which principles are viewed as merely tactical instruments, I question its underlying assumptions as well. In particular, I question her seeming conflation of deceiving and being deceived or her equating ideology as such with deliberate mendacity. To be sure, making promises that are not honoured, ignoring the limits of what can reasonably be accounted for, or undertaking commitments that are wholly one-sided, whether out of loyalty or opportunism, incurs the risk of dishonesty, of acting at the sacrifice of truthfulness. When, however, Arendt contends that because commitments are one-sided, non-commitments are therefore synonymous with truthfulness, openness, or impartiality, she surely goes too far. Granted, commitments usually militate against impartiality or total detachment; but so can non-commitments, by way of *ad hoc* pragmatism, as they can amount to sheer indifference when we simply no longer care one way or another.

Alternatively, if rather surprisingly, Arendt could be overestimating the causality of ideologies. I say "surprisingly" because, in light of what is known about the fortunes of militant ideological movements in the last two centuries, they have conspicuously failed as political trajectories; and this was most likely so because they had become trapped within the wheels of their own rhetorical excesses. Plainly, irresponsible rhetoric, regardless of its moralizing currency, is liable to forfeit purchasing power as a binding political commitment if, over time, it persistently fails to deliver what it avows to be enacting. Interestingly, Rousseau (we found) had more than an inkling of such self-entrapments; for, despite wanting to extend the limits of the politically attainable, he cautioned against indulging in a public rhetoric that cannot be matched by public deeds, lest it, like the use of sham "public reason," should empty "commitment" of politically authentic meaning, or, indeed, of *any* meaning, as a binding category of thought or speech.

The projected revision of ideology in politics therefore refrains from incorporating into it the idea of an epistemic-practical "unity," without seeking to deny that adherents of an ideology could genuinely believe in its soundness and genuinely wish to act upon it. Also, while the revision warns against making too close a connection between moral goals and political implementation, it by no means negates the importance of moral purpose in political commitments. Rather, the warning is meant to draw attention to the coercive dimension of political governance *per se*, lest unduly escalating the moral pitch might make ideologies politically inoperable unless they covertly imply the simultaneous inauguration of governmental terror. Alternatively, an overly close identification of political ideologies with strictly moral belief systems courts the risk of massive disenchantment with purposive ideas as such, in the event of rampant non-delivery of avowed goals.

The suggested reappraisal therefore questions the political wisdom of any such inextricable link and stresses instead the selective and multiple use of any one particular philosophical belief system, since the latter usually yields divergent *political* interpretations. Parties in mainstream democracies bear this out pretty well, as they also supply evidence for having learned to their cost that staking ideological end-claims involves political *consequences*.

So, whether or not political practitioners have ever heard of Weber's distinction between an ethic of faith and an ethic of responsibility, they have come to recognize that public rhetoric incurs serious dangers if it raises expectations it cannot possibly meet. Viewed from this practical perspective, then, no less than from the theoretical arguments advanced earlier, there is undeniably room for rethinking both the scope and the limits of ideological discourse.

If so, the suggested reappraisal may disclose that an ideological style of politics is potentially a good deal less forbidding, institutionally, than experience with totalitarian movements and despotic one-party regimes has hitherto led us to expect. Two supportive points, in particular, could be put forward in this regard. One is that the projected understanding might effectively encourage the *pluralization* of opinion groups which, acting as intermediary bodies, could serve as buffers between the governmental Leviathan and the individual citizens, and, thereby, guard *against* authoritarian, if not absolutist, regimes, rather than invite them. The other point is that the new understanding might forestall wholly unprincipled thinking in the form of an ideological vacuum which as likely could foster variants of anti-discursive and anti-democratic extremism, such as unchallengeable theocratic politics, if not outright totalitarianism, as it could variants of pragmatism.

If for no other reason, it seems misguided therefore to oppose ideological politics exclusively to pragmatism, as though they were the sole alternatives – where one is identified with "abstract rationalism," and the other with "concrete empiricism." Instead, I prefer to view an ideological style in its own right and, so viewed, present it as a mode of reasoned argument, designed to do chiefly two things: (i) mediate individual and joint purposes, and (ii) link general principles with particular policy objectives, as their explanation or justification.

Still, it might be objected that the pluralization of opinion or interest parties could promote political fragmentation rather than prevent the over-concentration of political power. By the same token, it might be argued that, ideological contestation in involving conflicts of principle, would *defy* political bridging, and thus virtually rule out compromise solutions. Objections of this kind cannot be ignored. Clearly, dogmatic assertions about the integrating potential of ideological politics are no less unwarranted than blanket associations with totalitarian regimes. All one can presumably say with any degree of assurance therefore is that promoting the articulation of divergent positions, by an ideological *modus operandi* of plurality, might minimize the marginalization of minority concerns and, thereupon, progressively augment an authentic sense of civic involvement and civic inclusiveness – neither of which, surely, would prove an insignificant bonus.

FROM HERE TO THERE: SELF-ENACTMENT

Self-direction, self-actualization, self-legislation, and self-mastery: these are undeniably lofty goals; but how are they to be pursued, let alone attained? This was the question confronting the thinkers of modernity who in one way or another cherished the idea of "autonomy." And most of them, on reflection, had to agree that before people, as individuals or nations, could become masters of their destiny, they would do well to first undergo an apprenticeship of sorts. In the remarks that follow I want to survey briefly how the writers included in Part II approached the apprenticeship toward self-enactment. All four, if variously, emphasized (conceptual) *mediation* rather than (physical) *determination* – paralleling in effect the distinction I made between (indirectly) "giving cause" and (directly) "causing."

After Thomasius, Vico, Rousseau, Herder, and Hegel, it became almost commonplace to view some form of historical conceptualization as an essential component of such mediation. Especially since the rise of European nationalism, a person's self-location and self-identification were thought virtually unfathomable without it. Not uncovering one's historical-cultural origins, or ignoring them, amounted, therefore, to jeopardizing one's authentic existence. Cosmopolitans were portrayed, accordingly, especially by Rousseau and Herder, as freefloating phantoms who, without any historical mooring of their own, preferred an abstract humankind to the historical reality of their ancestors. By turning their backs on their history, they were said to overlook a vital truth, namely, that universality demanded an anchorage within the historical soil of the concrete particular. Hence, bereft of such self-foundation, they were judged unfit to bring about their transformation from subjects to citizens, or from subject-peoples to self-governing nations.

Few, however, in this search for individual and political self-*Bildung*, went as far as Marx did in linking historical consciousness with the acquirement of revolutionary consciousness. Marx was undeniably right in holding that revolutionary change was unthinkable in the absence of historical consciousness, in that only the latter could embolden humans to believe that things *might* be different from the way they were. And he was right as well in viewing revolutionary consciousness as a commitment, in the sense in which Rousseau viewed civic self-enactment as a commitment within the new objectivity of civil society that had replaced the original objectivity of the state of nature. As Kant followed Rousseau, therefore, in regarding this new objectivity – in which one's own subjectivity had to blend with the subjectivity of others – as the requisite condition for the emergence of a consciousness of public right, so Marx saw it as the requisite condition for the emergence of a consciousness of revolutionary commitment.

Quite remarkably, therefore, Rousseau's profound insight that any wrong done to a person within the new objectivity of social life was a violation of principles of *public* conduct, and not merely a private injury, affected Marx's revolutionary thinking as much as it had affected Kant's legal thinking.

No doubt, Marx's thesis that a true consciousness of what was objectively valid implied its revolutionary enactment could not but enhance revolutionary commitments. However, such self-assurance is liable to backfire once vision and attainment follow divergent paths, creating a gaping hiatus between them. For Kant, such a discrepancy was a risk inherent in the use of self-fulfilling prophecies; at the same time he was no less aware than Marx was of its merits as an effective political strategy, referring to it as a clear instance of "predictive history," since it could be employed to promote people's confidence in self-enactment, in creating the institutional foundations they want.

But if Kant recognized the value of predictive history in building up people's self-confidence, he simultaneously realized that the outcome would take the form of augmented legality rather than the form of augmented morality. Why? Because, no less than Thomasius, he came to realize that, in order to cope with impulsiveness and counter people's egoistic and belligerent dispositions, "judicious coercion" cannot be dispensed with. But he had no illusions that legality, in combating strife and war – the "greatest evils that befall humanity" – would be enough to transform phenomenal humans (as they are) into noumenal ones (as they could and should be). All it might do is prevent them from annihilating each other in a hurry, or, at best, from losing all hope of one day establishing a kingdom of ends, in which they would cease to treat each other as mere instruments. Such development, however, Kant insisted, had to be the work of piecemeal constructivism. Revolutionary changes had to be avoided at all cost; not only were they inimical to legality but also, because of their high degree of contingency, incalculable in their result.

Thus roundly dismissing talk of revolutions being milestones in the forward march of humanity as the sales-pitch of political moralists, Kant totally exploded the thesis that they (or, for that matter, politics as such) could or should be viewed as instruments for the implementation of moral or religious virtues. Co-opting revolutions in this way would not merely court the danger of tyranny but would also induce people to put an almost Messianic faith in philosopher-kings to do for them what they should do by themselves. It would, in short, be no less than an open invitation to political paternalism and civic immaturity.

With the exception of Arendt, there were not many after Thomasius and Kant who were more outspoken in their hostility to the Platonic idea of philosopher-kings. Apart from sensing in this idea the danger of (insidious) paternalism, they associated it with the onset of an altogether deluded mentality. For both feared that, thus corrupted, people's minds would be far too distorted and inhibited to be able to advance public enlightenment and, with it, political self-enactment. Thomasius, in particular, never tired of exhorting people to battle the manipulative use of scare tactics – to which all kinds of prejudices lend themselves – in their striving toward *Selbstdenken*, the capacity of judging for themselves. Additionally, he also extolled a profound anti-authoritarianism, urging his fellow-humans to combat servility and submission to "authorities," lest they never learn to walk by themselves without ropes or "banisters" (as Arendt put it) to hold on to. Kant, to be sure, preached this as well, especially against religious tutelage; but, after having been threatened with dismissal, he never dared to be as boldly "subversive" as Thomasius before, or Arendt after, him.

At the same time, and by no means in discordance with the German Enlightenment, Thomasius was tormented by mounting uncertainty about human reason's ability to win the battle in its daily combat with human will. Also, with all his emphasis on *Selbstdenken*, Thomasius never lost sight of human interdependence or the need for mutuality and reciprocity in the service of the good. For he knew, and repeatedly stressed, that without the help of others the individual would be very little indeed; even thinking would be unthinkable, were if not "fired on" by the world in which each of us was embedded.

Placed into the liberal tradition, therefore, together with Kant, Thomasius's insistence on viewing self-enactment in this qualified way is of note. Apprehensive though he was of the strength of will in pursuit of the good, he would never have accepted Kant's strictures in terms of *self*-incurred immaturity. And this was so because Thomasius firmly believed, as did Rousseau after him, that much of the trouble with human volition was inseparable from defects within external conditions. Hence he flatly denied that people would willingly choose to remain immature, unless a variety of influences corrupted their will as well as their very thinking and reasoning. Clearly, Thomasius would not have waged persistent attacks against hereditary privileges, or promoted legal and educational reforms, had he not thought that institutions *could* make a difference to people's basic dispositions and attitudes. Nor would he have invested as much time and energy in writing for all able to read in the first German popular journal (which he founded), had he shared Kant's low estimation of his fellows.

It seems therefore sadly odd that Thomasius, who probably did more than any German thinker before him to encourage self-*Bildung* in an attempt to *create* a public, is now, even in his native country, so little known. Kant himself, although he realized his indebtedness to Thomasius's contribution to Enlightenment thought, appears to have been totally ignorant of his *social* philosophy, from which he could have learned quite as much as he claimed to have learned from Rousseau about ordinary folk. If anything, Thomasius was even more audacious than Rousseau in stressing, as Arendt was to do, that thinking was not the preserve of the educated few, and that women *as well as* men therefore had every right to be listened to, regardless of their walk of life, their wealth, or level of education. And while he admittedly advanced no specific constitutional changes, he did provide unmistakable foundations for these, upon which others could and did build.

BRIDGING PLURALITY:
CIVIC DECORUM *VERSUS* GENERAL WILL

There is an unmistakable parallel between Thomasius and Rousseau, in their concern with plurality. Yet, what just as unmistakably separates them is their political response to it – prefiguring somewhat the liberal-communitarian controversy of our own day.

Like Thomasius, Rousseau had no illusions about the diversity of human interests. "For every two men whose interests coincide," we found him saying, "there are a hundred thousand whose interests sharply conflict." Were this not so, both agreed, plurality, the central problem of politics, would either not have arisen at all or would have been resolved long ago; everything would go smoothly, and politics would be neither an art nor a science.

Similarly, not unlike Kant, Rousseau knew well that forming a political unity out of diversity was not simply a matter of appealing to affinitive likings. Although Rousseau denied Hobbes's thesis that humans were *by nature* combative, blaming *society* for it instead, he shared Thomasius's view that civil society was essentially typified by *dis*sensus rather than consensus. In contrast to a religious community which, almost definitionally, was consensual, a political society demanded ongoing processes of mediation if plurality was to be bridged. Finally, and not least significantly, both markedly transmuted the seventeenth-century understanding of "social contract" by making a state's sovereign existence and political freedom contingent on autonomously rooted standards of public reason and rightful mutuality, generated and upheld by its citizens. Yet, though viewing the basis of civil society almost identically, they did so with different eyes.

Of the two routes chosen, Rousseau's, if bolder and perhaps also nobler in its political aspirations, has so far proved unattainable, in mainstream democracies, at any rate. Rousseau appears to have chosen a route which, by postulating a single vision of the common good, paints him into a corner from which there is no easy or obvious escape. Not very convincingly arguing that if there are conflicting views regarding the common good they must be attributable to clashing private interests, he sought to rule out that people *could* disagree for reasons other than those deriving from "interests." This attempt, I maintained, seems rather disingenuous, because Rousseau himself conceded that religious beliefs could give rise to disagreements, and such beliefs, clearly, are not the same as private interests.

To be sure, when envisioning a degree of symbiosis between a communitarian civic ethic and a plurality of rights and freedoms for individual citizens, Rousseau, like Thomasius, did distinguish between source and structure – between civic bonds as such and their qualitative relatedness – as much as he did between people's actual conditions of life and the formal institutions governing it. At the same time, his overriding concern being to preserve the union, Rousseau was torn by doubt as to whether, once it was founded, public commitments to it could be left to rest on discursive agreement between a plurality of interests and beliefs. His faith in thus generating a united will was therefore at best a very hesitant faith.

Thomasius, not quite so engrossed with consensual oneness or a "general will" that, by definition, was always right, was prepared to cut the knot, as it were. One cannot, he felt, integrate pluralities in civil society, as though it were a religious order, without *imposing* unity; that is, by committing people to accept a putatively common good, authoritatively enunciated by a supreme will that claims to embody a single, indisputably valid, or permanently consecrated, all-transcendent truth. Less ambitious as a theorist, but more astute as a political jurist, Thomasius was by and large more comfortable with coming, institutionally, to terms with plurality; even as a person he was less touchy than Rousseau and, as a thinker, more tolerant. In essence, he looked for a mediating bridge between plurality and generality, resting on the joint pillars of prudential giving and reciprocal taking, and hence was prepared to settle for a civic mutuality that was contingent on appropriate administrative provisions for negotiated understandings – processes that Rousseau evidently found too chancy in their conditionality, and hence too uncertain to generate unity.

Also, unlike Rousseau, who never got around to writing his planned treatise on international relations, Thomasius was as much preoccupied with evolving international norms of civility as with the creation of a national decorum of power. In so doing, he was, like Kant after him, vitally concerned with means of avoiding war among nations, through bridging differences by way of reciprocal arrangements that, he knew, fell short of foolproof panaceas. For he realized that, while such understandings were highly contingent nationally, they were vexingly intricate internationally. His strategy here, therefore, remarkably foreshadows Kant's piecemeal constructivism – a route more patient, if less exciting, than Rousseau's.

But then, Rousseau's political philosophy, I suggested, was in its heart of hearts an either/or mode of thinking, alternating between intense radicalism of projection and intense resignation of implementation. Possibly, in view of this ambivalence he wavered between at least two opposite theories of political enactment: one, describable as emphatically "procedural," the other, perhaps best characterizable as "transcendent." In his first theory, governmental accountability is of the very essence; in his second theory, however, this is only doubtfully so, in that neither free discussion nor unfettered challengeability is self-evidently compatible with a general will, which antecedently contains its own intrinsic validation, regardless of opinions or numbers. For it looks as though a will thus sanctioned would possess a rightness to which citizens must defer, but in whose genesis they had no necessary part, at any rate on an ongoing basis. Whereas under conditions of procedural deliberation a general will only contingently *follows* acts of agreement, under those of its transcendent understanding, the general will effectively *precedes* these. In the former, people actively participate in articulating some common ground; in the latter they merely passively engage in accepting or confirming it. One course invites diversity and the possibility of legitimate dissent; the other deprecates diversity and virtually pre-empts dissent.

Thomasius, it is true, by no means questioned the need for the existence of shared core beliefs and well-defined civic commitments. At the same time, he most astutely perceived that, in practice, notably in politics – as a historically contingent phenomenon – formal definitions can only go so far. Most *astutely* also, because he thus poignantly anticipated Friedrich Nietzsche's memorable dictum (in *Toward a Genealogy of Morals*, 1887) that only what has no history (such as triangles) can be adequately defined. He knew, too, that wholly anarchic plurality had to be distinguished from civic pluralism; but this did not hinder him from insisting that the right to be different was as inalienable as the right to hold private property.

Accepting the need for agreement on the meaning of fundamental credal understandings, such as the keeping of promises, Thomasius nevertheless denied that such consensus perforce *entailed* accord on their political application. For he feared that conflating these two kinds of agreement could lead to a situation akin to that in which insistence on any one absolute truth (on what comprises the general will, the common good, or any other issue) would become indistinguishable from insistence on absolute power, and thereby entrain the abandonment of conditional authority. Similarly, Thomasius sought to avoid conflating common purposes, which humans may or may not have, with public objectives, which specifically characterize *political* activity. For he could see that *purposes* do not imply the existence of *policies* to enact them.

Thus, while advancing the idea of welfare as a universal common purpose, as a *political* objective he conceived of it in plural terms, allowing for the possibility that not everybody would interpret "welfare" in identical ways or conform to a single manner of its political pursuit. Thomasius's political thinking is here impressively analogous to his general philosophy of "reason." For, although he acknowledged that reason could speak in wholly unequivocal terms, and could then be its own explanation, he felt that at other times, or to different humans, it may speak in several voices; so that what appeared rationally valid to some could be less so to others. As in the case of reason, therefore, Thomasius pleaded for a measure of openness concerning the interpretation and implementation of common purposes, such as welfare, education, and other social values, as political objectives.

Broadly speaking, it is chiefly for adopting a more nuanced approach in this way that I regard Thomasius's political stance to be closer to mainstream democratic thinking. This is not to deny, however, that Rousseau's association of democracy with a uniquely moral will and the essential oneness of rulers and ruled may have greater appeal to nations with less certain roots in the liberal tradition of modernity. Evidently, they see no danger in this highly mysterious oneness or in the sanction of a general will that is *a priori* transcendent rather than procedurally emergent. Thomasius, possibly more deeply committed to liberal principles than Rousseau, could not suppress the fear (of which Rousseau was by no means unaware) that in putting prime emphasis on the oneness of rulers and ruled one was apt to obliterate the distance between those *exercising* power and those *authorizing* it and, thereby, to obscure who was accountable to whom. Clearly, the gap between Rousseau's two conception of governance is too wide to be got over without having to scuttle one or the other. Conditional authority can no more coexist with unconditional authority than spontaneous plurality with enforced unity. Liberal democracy may be an oxymoron or, at best, a useful illusion; but a transcendent political will that is beyond challenge, by virtue of its antecedent validity, ominously calls to mind characterizations of legitimacy known chiefly under despotic regimes.

Representative government undeniably raises problems of its own; but a oneness of governors and governed, while rendering representation otiose, nevertheless boggles the (liberal) mind, especially if it presupposes a hypothetically united will of the people, in which the people, in truth, may have had little or no share, but which they by definition have to accept as intrinsically "always right." Unfortunately, Arendt, despite her expressed dislike of Rousseau's unifying will, confers upon her notion of representative thinking characteristics of rightness and generality that suspiciously resemble those of the former. On the face of it, this *is* rather puzzling; so much so, in fact, that I shall return to it for a closer look in the next section.

As regards my preference for Thomasius's approach to plurality, it should not be construed to imply my non-awareness of the possibility that there are differences that simply *defy* mediation. On the whole, this could be so, since "bridging," we found, might be called for as an internal process – because individuals might themselves be torn by conflicting ends – almost as much as it might be needed as an external process, if and when they disagree about public goals or their political priority. And while public debate may assist (as Thomasius believed) in resolving the former as in mediating the latter, it is patently a moot point how much *governments* can do. For, once a political regime tries to encompass too many issues about which people strongly disagree, it courts the danger of overextending the boundaries of its effective scope. Far from reconciling divergences, governmental intervention may then make demands on tolerance, mutual understandings, or the striking of bargains which simply become too crushing. Ultimately, such interventional moves may indeed threaten citizenship itself.

In other words, bridging, too, has its limits. And this seems so, whatever construct we apply, be it Thomasius's "civic decorum," Rousseau's "extended selfhood," Kant's "enlarged mentality," or Arendt's "representative thinking." Each postulates a form of self-transcendence through prudential reciprocity, rational sentiment, good will, or empathy; but, in the final analysis, we have to be prepared to face an impasse, when the only available alternative known to a liberal is an institutionally safeguarded space for agreeing to differ – perhaps less *can* be more, whether or not it amounts to an escape route or to a testimony to the inadequacy of political skills.

Cold comfort though it may be, we may nevertheless draw solace from the fact that so far practically all major thinkers have met with an impasse as soon as they tried to move from vision to implementation in politics, as no one more painfully realized, or more honestly acknowledged, than our learned professor from Königsberg, Immanuel Kant.

"A NATION OF DEVILS": THE IMPASSE OF POLITICS

It seems that in no other writing did Kant portray the limits of the politically achievable in less uncertain terms than in his essay on universal history. Politics, he declares, is only as good as its practitioners; and since these for the most part are like the rest of humans as they *are* – and not as they might or should be – nothing straight can ever be crafted, at any rate without legal instruments of "universal constraint." Even a nation of devils, he argues, can then be made to realize that a *Rechtsstaat*, combining liberty with legality, is in everybody's best interest, without, admittedly, thereby also advancing morality or the voluntarism of "rightful decorum" into which Thomasius put his principal faith.

In addition to combining liberty with legality *within* states, Kant made the almost desperate attempt to bypass the seemingly inexorable impasse, by groping for a measure of plural coexistence *among* states. The operative term here is "measure" itself, since Kant searched for a merely peaceable live-and-let-live situation which, he felt, might perhaps be brought about by means of a strategy of gradual steps. In such piecemeal constructivism *beyond* the boundaries of strictly political entities, he hoped to find a way of making differences blend rather than inimically clash. And it was chiefly in this attempt that he remarkably foreshadowed Hannah Arendt's own idea of "representative thinking" as a possible route to the mutuality of human fellowship.

Undeniably, however, it is rather a moot point whether Kant would have been able to share Arendt's confidence in the extent to which she apparently believed it possible not only to overcome the impasse in politics but also to create suitable conditions of unrestrained public debate under which people (as they are) would freely agree to bring about whatever representative thinking (as she portrayed it) might call for. It is more likely that in this claimed confidence Kant would have suspected echoes of "political moralists" who, for entirely self-serving reasons, encouraged such illusory confidence. Dismissing much of it, together with any glib faith in moral progress, as wishful thinking, if not artful "humbug talk," he would have no truck with it. Why? Because in this kind of real or feigned optimism Kant saw at best a dangerously misguided thinking that could not but mask the fact that any steps taken politically in this direction are bound to involve the workings of infinite regress. In combination with deceitful attempts by political opportunists, human nature itself made sure of this impasse, by virtue of its innate servility and abject egoism. Even the most radical revolutions are incapable of overcoming these perversities.

More impressed, therefore, with Thomasius's idea of judicious coercion than with his voluntarist creed – and highly irritated by his erstwhile student J.G. Herder, who categorically denied that humans needed any overlords – Kant emphatically insisted on the need for political masters. Beyond the strictly private sphere, he declared, most people were like wild animals, requiring a tamer to control them for their own good. Thus, while he never ceased to adhere to the principle of self-enactment, "lawful coercion," which ensures reciprocal constraints, seemed to him a necessary part of "every just political constitution" in its gradual advance toward the ultimate goal of popular self-legislation.

For much the same reason, reforms had, in the first instance, to come "from the top downwards," preferably initiated, Kant felt, by enlightened autocrats such as Frederick II of Prussia, rather than "from the bottom upwards." And this was so, he maintained, regardless of the diverse perfectionist schemes that politicians or misguided philosopher-utopians claim to offer humanity. In reality, political reforms will go nowhere unless there is a master able to "break people's will" whenever they try to except themselves from the laws they have formally committed themselves to observe. The absolute requirement, therefore, is to find a master who could compel people, whether they like it or not, "to obey a *general* will" embodied in the laws of the land, under which "every man could be free." Regrettably, however, Kant agreed, this once again would provide no ultimate solution; for, even if such a master could be found, he also would be "an animal who needed a master."

Despite this obvious impasse Kant was, however, unwilling to capitulate. In addition to his gradual constructivism, by way of advancing legality within and beyond states, he put forward what I described as a cosmic-teleological strategy. Only, unlike the "Existentialist" Arendt, Kant still invoked history, nature, and Providence. Nevertheless, the difference seems more a matter of terminology than of substance, since it is hardly less odd to summon "truly authentic actors" to "plunge into infinity" than to urge people to put their trust in the purposiveness of nature or history. For the outcome of their actions is equally hidden from them.

Postulating such transcendent purposiveness was intended, however, to *augment* individual striving and personal initiative (we observed), just as Kant's recognition of the value of certain public goods was to augment trans-egoistic thinking by way of an "enlarged mentality," without which he could see no prospect of creating that universal respect which extends one's own freedom to others.

And it was above all his vision of an enlarged mentality, we noted, that Arendt professed to have been leaning on in putting forward her own notion of "representative thinking." I touched on this notion earlier, remarking that it suspiciously resembles Rousseau's general will, as the embodiment of unanimity. I want to elaborate here on my earlier comments because, despite appearances, Arendt's notion is in truth intended as an *alternative* to Rousseau's antecedently rightful *will*, and its virtual replacement by rightful *thinking*, as it also has, in its broader implications, more to do with effecting international mutuality than national unity.

Arendt's major premise is that political thought is by definition representative: the more standpoints I have present in my mind while I am pondering a point in dispute the stronger will be my capacity for representative (plural) thinking and the more valid therefore will be my (political) opinion. That the very process of representative thinking (thus understood) is implicitly disinterested, in excluding considerations of private interests or personal inclinations, constitutes Arendt's minor premise. From these premises Arendt infers (in "Truth and Politics") that, however clashing opinions are to start with, they are bound to "ascend to some impartial generality" by being discussed from all sides. In short, once people liberate themselves in open debate from their subjective egoisms and foibles, agreement cannot but follow – a view that remarkably mirrors Thomasius's belief in people's capacity to engage in reciprocal thinking, and one that Rousseau might have accepted. Kant, on the other hand, could at best only hypothetically have supported this stance, since in the world as it is he felt that, left to themselves, people would never willingly agree on anything.

Arendt's attribution of paternity to Kant seems therefore as odd as her reference to Aristotle in this connection is liable to mislead. For

Aristotle's concern is with representative *government*, for which Arendt has no use whatsoever. Also Arendt focuses on *opinions*, not interests; and opinions, she felt, cannot be represented. Representative thinking, therefore, is intended to *mediate* opinions, not to represent them.

In her treatise *On Revolution*, as in her essay "Truth and Politics," Arendt in fact expressly insists that representative government is to be sharply distinguished from representative thinking, since the latter has nothing to do with the counting of noses, the making of deals, the trimming of sails, and such like, merely in order to achieve majorities. Even when completely alone, she states in "Truth and Politics," I can make myself "the representative of everybody else" because "in this world of universal interdependence" (as she puts it) there is always a context of others; hence, the need for joint actions is not confined to formal processes of legislative assemblies. Echoing Thomasius, Arendt observes that, in the public realm, no individuals wholly by themselves are likely to make any headway by ignoring the existence of others. Consciously following Kant, she urges therefore (in "The Crisis of Culture") a mode of thinking in which selves, sensitive to the interdependence of plural differences, situate themselves "in the place of everybody else."

Nationally and internationally, Arendt's prime concern, therefore, is the need for transformed thinking, as much as the need for transformed willing, in an attempt to transcend Rousseau's emphasis on a monistic general will, as well as Kant's resigned acceptance of an insuperable impasse. No less intriguing in this concern is her attempted merging of cognitive and aesthetic elements, in place of exclusively following the path of purely empirical or logical understandings of coherence. Thus, when she approvingly quotes Aristotle in this context, Arendt is associating the phrase "what is good for themselves" not with Bentham's rational calculation in aggregating private interests, but rather with sensitively taking into account the opinions and values of others.

In singling out two recovery postulates in her work, I therefore rated her critique of modernity as the area in which she most excelled. For here Arendt's essentially perceptual approach, in which she values the intervention of taste as the pre-eminent criterion of appropriateness, scores most fruitfully, in that it goes beyond the political in planting the roots of human fellowship in the soil of culture, history, and something comparable to the mystery, if not sacredness, of *relatedness*, in and for itself. So doing, she is delving into the depths of an age that, with all its buttons for instant on-the-spot information, nevertheless mistakes not only making for acting, legality for morality, and organizational order for political order, but also, if not most worryingly, the realm of scientific-technological facts for the realm of human values. I say most worryingly, because it all too starkly discloses the giant chasm between the brilliant advances of scientific discovery and the almost imbecillic conditions in human affairs, notably in politics, which, instead of transcending barbarity, appears ever more fascinated by it.

This distressing discrepancy clearly was not lost on Arendt's perception of modernity, especially the contrast between its soaring self-confidence and its abasing self-disparagement. As we noted, Rousseau and Kant were no less conscious of this incongruity, remarking that the same science, while feeding our pride, was simultaneously shaking our faith in satisfying our increasing wants and in coping with the demands of everyday life. The intensity of this inner conflict, characterizing modernity as a whole, is all the more perplexing in view of its leading thinkers' having sought to promote the belief that the growth of historical and philosophical understanding might induce people to use their practical judgment to live and act more sensibly, by combining, as Arendt so assiduously tried to do, reflective thinking with sensitive feeling. For she felt convicted that it was precisely this combination for which the present age had an unprecedented need.

Arguably, it is above all in the international realm, therefore, that the merger of reflection and sensitivity contained in Arendt's idea of representative thinking could serve as a timely reminder of at least three sets of understandings. First, that in politics (including democracy) it is the *mediation* of opinions, interests, and belief systems rather than their *confrontation* which demands principal emphasis. Second, that preserving or promoting any particular constitutional or economic arrangement of public life is not a matter of mastery or military control. And third, though related, that striking first and talking later may be a failed strategy for seeking to proliferate an ethos of bridging differences, since mediation is unlikely to ensue from ignoring international norms and the unwritten law of the decorum of power.

Each of these understandings merely endorses lessons to be gleaned from history; notably, that military superiority is no warrant for political, let alone cultural, superiority, and that unharnessed force has a nasty tendency to rebound on those who have unleashed it. To be sure, such lessons are no more than truisms; yet what is obviously true, is, as a rule, no less true for all that.

In addition, what Kant made especially, if uncomfortably, clear, is that self-enactment calls in the first place for human selves with a horror of harming others. This message, too, which asks chiefly for the cultivation of a sense of reciprocity, is not new, but neither is it obsolete. For we might still gather from it that the possibilities of wrecking humanity are as great today – and as technologically real – as those of saving it, and that world-conquest (even in the service of democracy) could, in reality, amount to world-obliteration. Indeed, the greater the intensity of (democratic) self-righteousness, the more critical this gamble could turn out to be. Liberal democracies might be exceptionally vulnerable, since the eventuality of this threat could embarrassingly remind them that they are by no means as quintessentially liberal as their supporters believe or wish others to believe.

As super-powers they could, therefore, endanger not only their own existence but also the credibility of liberal democracy as such. And, all the more so, if they deliberately exaggerate the perils facing them in order to justify pre-emptive strikes, or use the fig leaf of democratic moralism to conceal self-serving savagery. Moral considerations aside, such moves are hazardous for mainly two reasons. The first is that flouting the principle of reciprocity clearly involves the risk of reprisals in kind, so that what you do to others, others can do to you. The second reason is that calculations of pay-offs, being notoriously chancy, are inclined to deceive people in respect of the true costs of what rarely are purely military undertakings.

Undeniably, such a scenario lends depressing support to warnings that Thrasymachus has already sounded; to wit, that once "anything goes," might alone makes right. And, in that event, the world becomes a prey to those possessing maximal (nuclear) power, as well as the most effective means for devising and disseminating catching (moralist) slogans. Still, the voices of Part II also variously disclose that good sense might somehow surface. If not, we are indeed "in a wretched situation," as James Madison declared no less emphatically than Rousseau, during the constitutional debate of 1788 in Virginia. For, then, "no checks, no form of government, can render us secure," since no union nationally or internationally is thus able to survive. But, "if there be sufficient virtue and intelligence in the community," the outcome will no longer depend solely on the virtue of our rulers but on the people's wisdom "exercised in their selection," so that it will rest "on the confidence in the people who are to choose them."

Once, therefore, conditions would emerge, sufficient to induce people to choose rulers able and willing to reduce at least *state*-organized brutality by enacting a reign of public reason – as Thomasius, Rousseau, and Kant portrayed it – they could help to sustain the belief that *humanitas*, as Arendt interpreted it, has not been entirely lost sight of. Especially, in view of the perils and the bare glimmers of hope, her idea of representative thinking might perhaps still succeed in warding off utter disaster. Were it to do so, we could surmise with a degree of assurance that it was what Hannah Arendt minimally wished so-called post-modernity to accomplish, given that humans have not ceased wanting to project themselves as co-authors of a world, in which *relatedness*, in its multi-faceted plurality, is the driving idea, and not "master-minding," in its emphasis on unity and identity, come what may.

Alas, it would need to be a world that advances talking, not taunting, large thinking, and not petty bullying, if it was to halt what to Arendt looked like a distressingly unimaginative progression of political bungling. But any such reversal, she made clear, would demand a sizably heightened sense of the "decorum of power" combined with a no less heightened sense of the reciprocal integrity within "public reason." Ultimately, as well as fundamentally, Arendt knew and made known, however, that there were no ready-made road maps to follow and no ready-made banisters to lean on; in short, that there were no universal signposts to guide tired humanity. Even an "enlarged mentality," she recognized, was not going to get far in politics unless it could draw on what to Collingwood was its *sine qua non*, the existence of general principles. And for Collingwood, as for Arendt, such principles rested not solely or predominantly upon logical inference but rather on something closer to pre-logical conceptions of practical judgment, mutuality, and the kind of purposiveness that embodies an experienced continuum between past and present and which, in its perennial thrust, stretches forth toward the infinite unknown.

Index